R. Paul Maiden,
Editor

Global Perspectives of Occupational Social Work

Global Perspectives of Occupational Social Work has been co-published simultaneously as *Employee Assistance Quarterly*, Volume 17, Numbers 1/2 2001.

*Pre-publication
REVIEWS,
COMMENTARIES,
EVALUATIONS . . .*

"**W**ELL WRITTEN. . . . Could serve as A TEXT FOR FIRST YEAR SOCIAL WORK STUDENTS in social policy as well as international social work. A valuable addition to social work libraries."

Dale A. Masi, DSW, LICSW, CEAP
*Professor, University of Maryland;
President, Masi Research Consultants,
Washington, DC*

More pre-publication
REVIEWS, COMMENTARIES, EVALUATIONS . . .

"**M**ORE THAN AN OVERVIEW. . . . ENABLES READERS to recognize, discover, and re-discover issues in different contexts and to question the pervasive paradigms of their own situation. Contains rich descriptions of how macro policies impact on service delivery and utilization at the workplace and in the public sector."

Dr. Riaan van Zyl, *Professor and Associate Dean for Research, Kent School of Social Work, University of Louisville, Kentucky*

"**A** VALUABLE CONTRIBUTION to the literature of occupational social work . . . identifies the commonalities and differences of practice across seven different countries. WILL STIMULATE BOTH PRACTITIONERS AND STUDENTS."

Brian McKendrick, PhD
Emeritus Professor of Social Work, former Head of the School of Social Work, University of the Witwaterstand, Johannesburg, South Africa

The Haworth Press, Inc.

Global Perspectives of Occupational Social Work

Global Perspectives of Occupational Social Work has been co-published simultaneously as *Employee Assistance Quarterly,* Volume 17, Numbers 1/2 2001.

The *Employee Assistance Quarterly* Monographic "Separates"

Below is a list of "separates," which in serials librarianship means a special issue simultaneously published as a special journal issue or double-issue *and* as a "separate" hardbound monograph. (This is a format which we also call a "DocuSerial.")

"Separates" are published because specialized libraries or professionals may wish to purchase a specific thematic issue by itself in a format which can be separately cataloged and shelved, as opposed to purchasing the journal on an on-going basis. Faculty members may also more easily consider a "separate" for classroom adoption.

"Separates" are carefully classified separately with the major book jobbers so that the journal tie-in can be noted on new book order slips to avoid duplicate purchasing.

You may wish to visit Haworth's website at . . .

http://www.HaworthPress.com

. . . to search our online catalog for complete tables of contents of these separates and related publications.

You may also call 1-800-HAWORTH (outside US/Canada: 607-722-5857), or Fax: 1-800-895-0582 (outside US/Canada: 607-771-0012), or e-mail at:

getinfo@haworthpressinc.com

Global Perspectives of Occupational Social Work, edited by R. Paul Maiden, PhD (Vol. 17, No. 1/2, 2001). *A broad survey of the development and current practices of occupational social work as practiced in seven countries around the world.*

Emerging Trends for EAPs in the 21st Century, edited by Nan Van Den Bergh, PhD, LCSW (Vol. 16, No. 1/2, 2000). *"AN EXCELLENT BOOK . . . . Relevant with respect to contemporary practice and current state of the art for EAPs. A sound disciplinary input for both program development and service delivery."* (William L. Mermis, PhD, Professor of Human Health, Arizona State University)

Employee Assistance Services in the New South Africa, edited by R. Paul Maiden, PhD (Vol. 14, No. 3, 1999). *Addresses the many issues affecting the development of EAP programs in the new South Africa.*

Women in the Workplace and Employee Assistance Programs: Perspectives, Innovations, and Techniques for Helping Professionals, edited by Marta Lundy, PhD, LCSW, and Beverly Younger, MSW, ACSW (Vol. 9, No. 3/4, 1994). *"A valuable resource and training guide to EAP practitioners and managers alike. Most importantly, it increases the sensitivity of women's issues as they relate to the workplace."* (R. Paul Maiden, PhD, Chair, Occupational Social Work, Jane Addams College of Social Work, University of Illinois at Chicago)

Employee Assistance Programs in South Africa, edited by R. Paul Maiden, MSW (Vol. 7, No. 3, 1992). *"The first comprehensive collection of perspectives on EAPs in an industrializing third-world country."* (Brian McKendrick, PhD, Professor and Head, School of Social Work, University of the Witwatersrand, Johannesburg)

Occupational Social Work Today, edited by Shulamith Lala Ashenberg Straussner, DSW, CEAP (Vol. 5, No. 1, 1990). *"A well-organized overview of social work practice in business . . . interesting and timely."* (Journal of Clinical Psychiatry)

Evaluation of Employee Assistance Programs, edited by Marvin D. Feit, PhD, and Michael J. Holosko, PhD (Vol. 3, No. 3/4, 1989). *"The definitive work in the field of program evaluations of EAPs. . . . A must for anyone considering planning, implementing, and most importantly, evaluating employee assistance programs."* (Dr. Gerald Erickson, Professor and Director, School of Social Work, University of Windsor)

Alcohol in Employment Settings: The Results of the WHO/ILO International Review, edited by D. Wayne Corneil, ScD (cand.) (Vol. 3, No. 2, 1988). *Valuable insights into attitudes about alcohol and the effects of its use with courses of action for educating and treating employees who need help with alcohol problems.*

EAPs and the Information Revolution: The Dark Side of Megatrends, edited by Keith McClellan and Richard E. Miller, PhD (Vol. 2, No. 2, 1987). *A serious examination of treatment methods that can be used to help working people cope with a rapidly changing economic society.*

Global Perspectives of Occupational Social Work

R. Paul Maiden, PhD
Editor

Global Perspectives of Occupational Social Work has been co-published simultaneously as *Employee Assistance Quarterly,* Volume 17, Numbers 1/2 2001.

The Haworth Press, Inc.
New York · London · Oxford

Global Perspectives of Occupational Social Work has been co-published simultaneously as *Employee Assistance Quarterly*™, Volume 17, Numbers 1/2 2001.

© 2001 by The Haworth Press, Inc. All rights reserved. No part of this work may be reproduced or utilized in any form or by any means, electronic or mechanical, including photocopying, microfilm and recording, or by any information storage and retrieval system, without permission in writing from the publisher. Printed in the United States of America.

The development, preparation, and publication of this work has been undertaken with great care. However, the publisher, employees, editors, and agents of The Haworth Press and all imprints of The Haworth Press, Inc., including The Haworth Medical Press® and Pharmaceutical Products Press®, are not responsible for any errors contained herein or for consequences that may ensue from use of materials or information contained in this work. Opinions expressed by the author(s) are not necessarily those of The Haworth Press, Inc.

The Haworth Press, Inc., 10 Alice Street, Binghamton, NY 13904-1580 USA

Cover design by Thomas J. Mayshock Jr.

Library of Congress Cataloging-in-Publication Data

Global perspectives of occupational social work / R. Paul Maiden, editor.
    p. cm.
    Includes bibliographical references and index.
    ISBN 0-7890-1423-8 (hard : alk. paper) – ISBN 0-7890-1424-6 (pbk. : alk. paper)
    1. Industrial welfare. 2. Industrial welfare–Case studies. I. Maiden, R. Paul.
HD7261 .G54 2001
331.25–dc21   200139487

Indexing, Abstracting & Website/Internet Coverage

This section provides you with a list of major indexing & abstracting services. That is to say, each service began covering this periodical during the year noted in the right column. Most Websites which are listed below have indicated that they will either post, disseminate, compile, archive, cite or alert their own Website users with research-based content from this work. (This list is as current as the copyright date of this publication.)

Abstracting, Website/Indexing Coverage	Year When Coverage Began
• BUBL Information Service: An Internet-based Information Service for the UK higher education community <URL:http://bubl.ac.uk/>	1995
• CNPIEC Reference Guide: Chinese National Directory of Foreign Periodicals	1995
• EAP Abstracts Plus	1994
• e-psyche, LLC <www.e-psyche.net>	2001
• Family & Society Studies Worldwide (online and CD/ROM) <www.nisc.com>	1996
• FINDEX <www.publist.com>	1999
• Human Resources Abstracts (HRA)	1985
• Index Guide to College Journals (core list compiled by integrating 48 indexes frequently used to support undergraduate programs in small to medium-sized libraries)	1999
• Index to Periodical Articles Related to Law	1985
• Medical Benefits	1985
• NIAAA Alcohol and Alcohol Problems Science Database (ETOH) <http://etoh.niaaa.nih.gov>	1991
• OCLC Public Affairs Information Service <www.pais.org>	1985

(continued)

- *Personnel Management Abstracts* 1988
- *Psychological Abstracts (PsycINFO)* 1986
- *Social Services Abstracts <www.csa.com>* 1985
- *Social Work Abstracts* 1988
- *Sociological Abstracts (SA) <www.csa.com>* 1985
- *Spanish Technical Information System on Drug Abuse Prevention "Sistema de Informacion Tecnica Sobre Prevention del Abuso de Drogas" (In Spanish) <http://www.idea-prevencion.com>* 1999
- *UP-TO-DATE Publications* 1996

Special Bibliographic Notes related to special journal issues (separates) and indexing/abstracting:

- indexing/abstracting services in this list will also cover material in any "separate" that is co-published simultaneously with Haworth's special thematic journal issue or DocuSerial. Indexing/abstracting usually covers material at the article/chapter level.
- monographic co-editions are intended for either non-subscribers or libraries which intend to purchase a second copy for their circulating collections.
- monographic co-editions are reported to all jobbers/wholesalers/approval plans. The source journal is listed as the "series" to assist the prevention of duplicate purchasing in the same manner utilized for books-in-series.
- to facilitate user/access services all indexing/abstracting services are encouraged to utilize the co-indexing entry note indicated at the bottom of the first page of each article/chapter/contribution.
- this is intended to assist a library user of any reference tool (whether print, electronic, online, or CD-ROM) to locate the monographic version if the library has purchased this version but not a subscription to the source journal.
- individual articles/chapters in any Haworth publication are also available through the Haworth Document Delivery Service (HDDS).

Global Perspectives of Occupational Social Work

CONTENTS

Preface: Towards an International Understanding of Occupational Social Work	xi
Acknowledgments	xiii
The Shadow Boxer: Occupational Social Work in Australia *Geoff Logan*	1
Occupational Social Work in Germany: A Continuously Developing Field of Practice *Holger Gehlenborg*	17
Occupational Social Work in India *H. Y. Siddiqui* *Neelam Sukhramani*	43
Occupational Social Work in Ireland *Maria A. G. Powell*	65
Occupational Social Work in Israel *Joseph Katan*	81
Occupational Social Work in South Africa *Angela du Plessis*	97
The Evolution and Practice of Occupational Social Work in the United States *R. Paul Maiden*	119
Index	163

ALL HAWORTH BOOKS AND JOURNALS
ARE PRINTED ON CERTIFIED
ACID-FREE PAPER

ABOUT THE EDITOR

R. Paul Maiden, PhD, is Associate Professor of Social Work in the College of Health and Public Affairs at the University of Central Florida in Orlando where he teaches Social Policy, Interventions with Substance Abusers and Strategies in Employee Assistance Programs. He is the MSW program coordinator, developed and coordinates the addictions certification program, and is a faculty member of the doctoral program in Public Affairs. Prior to this, he was Chair of the Occupational Social Work Program at the University of Illinois–Chicago for 13 years. In that capacity he developed and taught graduate curriculum in employee assistance programs, occupational social policy, substance abuse treatment and managed behavioral health care.

Dr. Maiden has extensive international experience, having directed a faculty exchange with the University of Witwatersrand in Johannesburg, where he was also a visiting scholar. He has led delegations of health and human service professionals to examine health and social welfare services in Southern African countries and has consulted with the U. S. Department of Commerce International Trade Administration in developing a health care trade mission to South Africa. He has been an active member of two U. S. EAP associations, the National Association of Social Workers, and the social worker section of the International Council on Alcohol and Addictions.

Dr. Maiden has published extensively in the field of occupational social work including employee assistance programs, substance abuse, workplace legislation, evaluation of work-based human services, AIDS in the workplace, alcohol abuse and domestic violence, welfare-to-work and managed behavioral health care. He is Editor and contributing author of *Employee Assistance Programs in the New South Africa* (1999), *Total Quality Management in Employee Assistance Programs* (1995), and *Employee Assistance Programs in South Africa* (1992). He is Associate Editor of *Employee Assistance Quarterly* and is on the editorial board of the *EAP Digest*. He has also presented at numerous national and international conferences. Dr. Maiden is also a Principal of Behavioral Health Concepts, Ltd., a domestic and international workplace consulting and training group based in Orlando, Florida.

Preface:
Towards an International Understanding of Occupational Social Work

The seed for this volume was planted when I presented a paper on developing an internationally integrated model for occupational social work at the annual conference of the International Council on Alcohol and Addictions (ICAA) in Lausanne, Switzerland in 1987.

Having entered the field of occupational social work (more specifically, employee assistance programs in the United States), the idea continued to germinate as I continued to compare existing U.S. practices with what I was beginning to learn about occupational social work practice across the globe.

Work organizations in many countries had a history of employing social workers that dated from their respective industrial revolutions. Some were known as welfare secretaries and other industrial social welfare officers. As you read through these articles you will begin to recognize the similarities and differences in the roles of these occupational social workers and the responsibilities of each in the social, political, and economic climates that shaped their workplaces.

Never were these contrasts so evident than when I first traveled to South Africa in 1990. There I met and worked with many occupational social workers who had been involved in a myriad of workplace issues during the apartheid era (see *Employee Assistance Programs in South Africa*, The Haworth Press, Inc., 1992). As my international travel increased and I came in contact with many other social work practitioners and academicians across the globe, I gained a much greater understanding and appreciation for the evolution, status and future of occupational social work in the international workplace. The countries represented here are by no means all-inclusive but are a sampling of how occupational social workers evolved and how they impact the workplace in seven different countries around the world.

R. Paul Maiden
University of Central Florida, Orlando

[Haworth co-indexing entry note]: "Preface: Towards an International Understanding of Occupational Social Work." Maiden, R. Paul. Co-published simultaneously in *Employee Assistance Quarterly* (The Haworth Press, Inc.) Vol. 17, No. 1/2, 2001, p. xiii; and: *Global Perspectives of Occupational Social Work* (ed: R. Paul Maiden) The Haworth Press, Inc., 2001, p. xi. Single or multiple copies of this article are available for a fee from The Haworth Document Delivery Service [1-800-342-9678, 9:00 a.m. - 5:00 p.m. (EST). E-mail address: getinfo@haworthpressinc.com].

© 2001 by The Haworth Press, Inc. All rights reserved.

Acknowledgments

An edited volume can be a difficult undertaking as the editor is dependent on each contributor to produce an article in accordance with the prospectus supplied. In this case, the task was made even more difficult because the contributing authors live in seven countries across the globe with almost as many different languages. For this reason I thank each of the contributing authors for their significant contribution in terms of time and content. I also thank them for tolerating the amount of time it took to bring this volume to fruition because of translation, linguistic nuances, editing and rewrites, along with my other writing projects, consultations and recent career transitions.

I would also like to acknowledge my good friend and colleague, Dr. Angela du Plessis, whose contributions in developing the initial prospectus helped me make this book a reality. I would also like to thank Keith McClellan, Editor of the *Employee Assistance Quarterly*, who endorsed the concept of this volume and provided continuous support, encouragement and feedback from first draft to final publication.

Finally and perhaps most importantly, I would like to acknowledge the invaluable contributions of my wife and business partner, Anschion E. Maiden, whose ongoing and tireless assistance with editing and preparing drafts of this manuscript most certainly assured that this volume did not become a terminal project.

The Shadow Boxer:
Occupational Social Work
in Australia

Geoff Logan

SUMMARY. This article describes the development and current practices of occupational social work in Australia. It explores the dissonance that has occurred in the social work profession arising from the conflicting views of the socioeconomic status of clients that social workers are most obligated to serve. The effect of a major shift towards privatization of the Australian social service system and the ability of occupational social workers to more readily adapt to this shift based on their experience outside of the public sector is also examined. The specific activities and contributions occupational social workers have made to assist workers in restructuring and downsizing is highlighted. Limitations of schools of social work to train occupational social workers are also explored. The article concludes with a discussion of the challenges faced by Australian occupational social workers in the future. *[Article copies available for a fee from The Haworth Document Delivery Service: 1-800-342-9678. E-mail address: <getinfo@haworthpressinc.com> Website: <http://www.HaworthPress.com> © 2001 by The Haworth Press, Inc. All rights reserved.]*

KEYWORDS. Occupational social work in Australia

Geoff Logan, MSW, is Lecturer at Curtin University School of Social Work in Perth, Western Australia and is a Human Services Consultant.

[Haworth co-indexing entry note]: "The Shadow Boxer: Occupational Social Work in Australia." Logan, Geoff. Co-published simultaneously in *Employee Assistance Quarterly* (The Haworth Press, Inc.) Vol. 17, No. 1/2, 2001, pp. 1-15; and: *Global Perspectives of Occupational Social Work* (ed: R. Paul Maiden) The Haworth Press, Inc., 2001, pp. 1-15. Single or multiple copies of this article are available for a fee from The Haworth Document Delivery Service [1-800-342-9678, 9:00 a.m. - 5:00 p.m. (EST). E-mail address: getinfo@haworthpressinc.com].

THE SOCIETAL AND HISTORICAL CONTEXT OF OCCUPATIONAL SOCIAL WORK IN AUSTRALIA

Over the past four decades in Australia the private practitioner has always worked alongside the public service social worker as a junior partner in the welfare field. This uneasy relationship is similar to the shadow boxer, always emulating the actions of the other without the two coming together at any time to share common skills and knowledge. To a large degree this indifference is due to historical features in the Australian welfare state and the way social workers generally perceive practice in the community. Although making up less than 10% of the 5,000 registered social workers in the country (Dodds, 1995), practitioners working in the occupational field provide the profession with challenging new approaches to service delivery in organizational structures.

Occupational social work in the Australian context may be defined as a specialization of social work practice in the workplace that promotes the individual's optimal adaptation to the current employment setting in preparation for changes to the work culture and social environment of the future. The occupational social worker employs a broad range of skills to accomplish these goals including policy analysis, strategic management planning, staff skills training as well as the traditional individual and therapeutic employee counseling.

Following the end of the Second World War and the subsequent introduction of the welfare state in Australia during the late 1940s, the Commonwealth Government Health and Social Security Department expanded to meet demands. In the wake of such universal benefits as Widow, Sickness and Unemployment Pensions, the need for welfare professionals to support the growing bureaucracies also increased. New Schools of Social Work emerged in the 1950s and 1960s to train the State welfare system workers for child care, foster care services, and home care.

At a time of increasing national growth, a perception emerged in the welfare field that an endless amount of Commonwealth Government support was available for welfare programs. To these social workers employed in the system, this philosophy fostered the view that appropriate targeting of inadequate social resources in the community could defeat the consequences of long-term poverty and social injustice. Social workers believed that the welfare state could meet this challenge and so poverty became the target of the profession for more than a quarter of a century.

While eliminating poverty and local injustices was the driving force of the profession in the 1960s, not all social workers agreed with this focus. Australian society was also changing. Women were reentering the workforce after the childbearing years following the Second World War and the increase in external migration added to the urban ills of our cities. Economic pressures gave rise to two-income families, suburbia, and private home ownership. Progressive thinking social workers believed the emerging new middle class would bring social problems of their own and the social work profession needed to confront these issues at the earliest possible opportunity.

Sadly, the impact of emerging forces had the opposite effect. Public service practitioners believed that emerging middle-class concerns would divert crucial funding away from the disadvantaged and that only after poverty was eliminated should the profession turn to these so-called secondary issues of welfare. For those who wished to explore the new territory, they could do so, providing they undertook the task without the aid of taxpayer money. As a result, the private social work practitioner emerged. Nevertheless, the suspicion of the public sector practitioner towards the newly emerging professional continued and widened as the occupational social workers carved out new areas of independent work in the changing Australian social work landscape. Unfortunately, the philosophical differences between the two groups have only increased over the years and even today there is a fear of dialogue between the two camps of social workers.

DOMAINS OF PRACTICE

During the 1970s occupational social workers were the fringe dwellers of the profession. Denied professional fees in the form of rebates from Hospital Benefit and Medical Funds, practitioners were forced into fee-for-service arrangements with clients to survive financially. Although the majority of professionals initially turned to middle-class clients who could pay for individual therapy, not all consumers met this criteria. Starting in the 1890s, Australia had a long history of labor-management conflict. Consequently, employees frequently sought solutions for work related problems outside the system. Both industrial and public sector unions were suspicious of management and warned employees not to trust employer sponsored programs that dealt with such issues as worker grievances, stressful workplaces, and personal issues affecting performance on the job, particularly when these problems were related to the use of alcohol and other drugs.

Unions believed that personal disclosures could at some time lead to an employee either being demoted or dismissed from employment. As a consequence, employees were encouraged to seek solutions from private practitioners for their problems. While counselors and therapists often provided temporary relief to workers in the form of problem focused and peer group support programs, the fear of disclosure discouraged long-term solutions.

However, in 1983 with the election of the Labor Party to power at the Commonwealth, a more conciliatory approach was introduced in industrial relations. The signing of a number of wage accords between the Australian

Council of Trade Unions, the Industrial Relations Commission, and the Federal Government paved the way for a less confrontational method of dealing with employer/employee disputes. Within this framework, owners and industrial managers were encouraged to develop internal occupational consultant departments. The role of the consultant team focused on providing a neutral ground for either managers or employees to raise issues of potential conflict before they became grievance issues.

Large public utilities such as Telecom (Telstra) Australia, Australia Post and the Defence Force frequently employed social workers as team leaders to be pre-dispute negotiators. Occupational social workers also contributed to the development of resource information for workers on industrial rights, the mediation of worker-to-worker disputes, and workplace agreements involving health and safety.

Despite these successes, the occupational social worker found the task of being part of the organization a difficult one. As an employee of an organization that expected the social worker to be both a mediator and facilitator between worker and management, many occupational social workers felt in conflict with the bureaucratic system. Management is generally undemocratic and the task of trying to promote fair and reasonable decisions from positions of limited power often produced resentment from both management and employees. Caught between the devil and the deep blue sea, by the end of the 1980s, social workers began leaving the industrial environment with a sense of disillusionment and resentment at having failed to significantly alter labor-management relationships in the private sector.

At the same time another powerful economical and political sentiment was beginning to exert its influence on the industrial scene. By the early 1990s, economic rationalism and the privatization of public assets debate started to see government organizations move towards a corporate style of management. This included the downsizing of staff numbers in those areas of work that could now be subcontracted out to private companies. Corporations bidding for key areas of public sector business indicated that certain so-called luxury services provided by the old system such as human resource management would not be continued under the new regime. Eventually, occupational consulting teams were included under this banner and many specialized training teams became victims of the cutbacks as public organizations awaited restructuring and privatization.

THE CONTINUUM OF OCCUPATIONAL SOCIAL WORK

While the 1990s saw a general retreat of the occupational social worker as an industrial employee, the outcome was not so bleak as it sounds. Practitioners survivied inside the corporate structure, although their roles changed over time. They began assisting organizations to develop policies for reorganizing staff. They consulted with staff to assess the economic viability of activities services for the coming years with a special emphasis on how services will be delivered and where staff needs to be deployed to improve efficiency. The role of the occupational social worker in this new environment is to provide clear guidelines and procedures for actions that assist workers with information to permit them to make rational judgements regarding their continued employment in a particular work setting.

For those practitioners working outside the structure, employment opportunities continue to be provided by previous employers in the form of outsourcing work. Organizational managers recognize the potential for labor relation disputes from employees who lose access to human resource services and see this as a way to overcome such resentment. As a consequence, private occupational social workers have formed partnerships with private companies to bid for counseling funds allocated by public utilities. In most cases, private consultants offer corporations guaranteed access to counseling for any employee facing personal problems and work adjustment problems. This is usually offered for a yearly per capita fee.

By the mid 1990s competition between private consultants for public contracts developed a healthy and invigorating form of social work practice. In order to secure business, practitioners have combined a fair and reasonable cost structure with a service that targets the particular requirements of each agency. To meet this need services are moving from traditional areas of counseling and therapy into other areas of service such as training in outplacement counseling and retirement counseling.

FACTORS IMPACTING PRACTICE DEVELOPMENT

By far, the most important impediment facing the Australian social work profession in coming to terms with this new direction in practice is its own ideological conflict. A recent article on the impact of economic rationalism on the social work profession (Webster, 1995) summed up the fears of the public service professional in the following statement:

> The attack on the disadvantaged has been unrelenting. A confidential "welfare cheat" hotline was trial tested in the Hunter Region by Social Security. This shortsighted approach encourages negative stereotyping of welfare recipients and is socially divisive. It will contribute to an increase in social alienation of those who already have to prove their degree of disadvantage in order to qualify for targeted benefits.

The fear of the disadvantaged becoming more dispossessed also has become an issue for those concerned with privatization. Social work practitioners in recent years have warned that minorities such as migrant workers, unskilled women in the workforce, unemployed youth and retrenched middle-aged men will suffer the most from these government policies. This concern was highlighted in the following statement:

> Privatization represents a threat to the lifestyles of these groups in society with whom and on behalf of whom social workers purport to work. The evidence thus far shows that it often produces outcomes that are dissonant with the principles of social justice. (Ernst, 1995)

To the occupational social worker, the concerns of the public practitioner are precisely the reason why all members of the profession need to be part of the privatization debate. Without being in a position to influence policy and restructure the workplace, the so-called middle-class worker of today will become the new working-class or dispossessed worker of the future. Occupational social workers in Australia believe they have been exposed to this new interface and are beginning to come to terms with the strategies required to shape the privatized workplace in the 21st Century. Only by coming to terms with this emerging social force will occupational social workers be able to redefine work for employees and in doing so, reduce the likelihood of workers ending up as welfare recipients.

CLINICAL ISSUES IN OCCUPATIONAL SOCIAL WORK

For the past four decades occupational social workers have been part of the Union movement on the Australian industrial landscape. Traditionally, their role was one of mediation between industry managers and employees over the application of industrial awards in the workplace. While these issues are still important, the focus of the practitioner's tasks in recent times has shifted more towards assisting in the introduction of workplace contracts for employees. The sheer complexity of contract award conditions now requires the occupational social worker to take on the role of an award advocate. Practitioners need to provide workers with clear interpretations of the implications of accepting or rejecting certain work conditions. Such demands have forced the award advocate to acquire specialists' skills in the areas of Industrial Relations and Industrial Law. More importantly, practitioners need to be able to communicate both the positive and negative sides of agreements for workers in a way that will enable employees to select the most appropriate condition for themselves, while allowing social workers to remain neutral advocates in the process.

In the case of evolving public utilities such as Hospitals, Children and Mental Health Institutions, occupational social workers in the past have worked at limiting how the medical model impacts on the holistic generic approach the profession takes towards patient rehabilitation.

However, with services being sold to private enterprise or subcontracted to commercial interests, practitioners have experienced a crisis of confidence in the role that they play in such agencies. In a recent edition of the Australian Association of Social Workers Newsletter, the following comments highlighted this dilemma:

> This forum provides the opportunity to understand the impact on these workers in a sector undergoing pressure due to a number of factors, including a government philosophically committed to privatization, the regionalization of health services, the loss of a distinct identity of mental health services through integration into the administrative structure of the health system, and rivalry between State and the Federal Government over the implementation of the 1992 Mental Health Strategy. (Coopes, 1995)

Under this new approach, practitioners are required to respond to market forces. The challenge for social work in health care in Australia is to find ways of responding to the demands of greater accountability while at the same time ensuring we are still meeting the needs of our clients (Edwards, 1995).

For occupational social workers outside the public system, who have been contracted to assist practitioners in reorienting their own institutional goals, emphasis has been placed on undertaking program reviews of social work services and formulating appropriate strategic plans for professional management. The aim is to provide clear policies and new protocols for social work practice, including the development of a case mix formula, and funding arrangements for specified institutions. In this way, admissions can only be guaranteed when funding is available. Such an approach assists social work practitioners to overcome the ethical dilemmas of having to make decisions regarding different categories of admission and discharge. This form of strategic planning permits institutional social workers to overcome their ambivalence about moving from public to private professional practice.

Since the early 1980s a number of fee-for-service EAP consulting organizations have set up practices in major Australian cities. These EAPs concentrate on such issues as career development, job performance assessment, alcohol and substance abuse evaluation and counseling, and the financial concerns of employees that influence their work performance. Although these problem areas remain the bread and butter focus of employee assistance programs, attention is now being focussed on the other end of the employment spectrum. In general, management consultants are finding that if the work environment does not sustain the changes undertaken by individual employees, the gains for the organization are wasted. Employee assistance program consultants are spending more and more time these days on corporate assessments for managers on how to make the workplace user friendly. One way of achieving this goal has been to encourage organizations to be more democratic in the decision-making process. By allowing specialist teams to be autonomous and set independent work goals and production targets, organizational social workers have been at the forefront as facilitators. They have been particularly effective at designing corporate structures for setting guidelines to umpire boundary disputes when mediation is required. "When employees feel that their organization is treating them fairly, then their reported levels of commitment will increase" (McDonald, 1995). Human service agencies in Australia are generally non-government organizations that are either religiously orientated or funded by State and Commonwealth Governments as nonprofit providers of community based welfare services. Heretofore, occupational social workers in these systems were concerned with the recruitment and training to work alongside professionals. They also have taken on tasks as support workers for the elderly and disadvantaged Aboriginals. Although these roles continue to be important to human service agencies, other welfare responsibilities are gradually being forced onto the private sector.

Agencies are taking on more of the day-to-day management responsibilities for dysfunctional clients or those with limited incomes assigned to legally sanctioned State and Commonwealth agencies. While non-profit organizations have been pressured into this role by the current welfare philosophy, this role has not always been beneficial for those community organizations. Client numbers have far outnumbered the resources provided, placing these agencies under enormous pressure to cope with less and less funding.

For occupational social workers employed or on contract to those agencies, the focus of practice now is to assist agencies to find ways of gaining a more equitable funding arrangement. The issue is highlighted by that fact that:

> There are people in government, particularly in current government, who are pushing privatization and also denying what currently is happening and not engaging in dialogue. The government is not recognizing how much the non-government agencies could even contribute to designing a good tendering process with the agencies. (Fariss, 1995)

Occupational social workers are tackling this concern by facilitating joint discussions between community agencies to act as a united pressure group on government agencies to review procedures on funding allocation. So far consultants have developed a number of principles relating to contractual arrangements, accountability structures and quality control approaches that provide the basis for community and State agencies to enter negotiations on more fair and reasonable terms.

Another form of clinical practice that has received growing attention in recent years is the Promotional Unit. This type of agency came into existence in response to social and welfare pressures in the community that require government agencies to respond immediately to those concerns. Often government bureaucracies by themselves are too slow to respond to public criticism. The way management deals with this dilemma is to set up target specific and highly flexible profession teams to tackle the social problem. Teenage violent crime and road accident task forces are good examples of these teams. They are usually made up of contracted consultants and seconded professionals from key positions in private and government agencies. Specialized units remain part of a legislative agency and report to the relevant Government Minister, although they are autonomous in their scope and field of operation.

Social worker consultants play a key role in the organizations that assist programs in self-care. Such units are often hotbeds of pressure with expectations that they achieve quick results. High workloads often result in continuous stress and burnout and long working hours in this task. To their credit, Australian social workers have introduced formal and informal debriefing procedures, supervisor training, mentor support programs, and sound policy guidelines, to deal with conflict and violent confrontations in the workplace. They have also provided a basis for managing the volatile nature of the Promotional Unit.

Finally, Specialist Dislocation Services are an emerging area of clinical work for Australian contractual practitioners. Like the Promotional Unit, dislocation services have been set up to deal with a specified concern, although in this case the solution is considered to be a long-term one. The Commonwealth Government's Job Link Program seeks to address unemployment for both young first timers and displaced older workers. Consultant practitioners seek to counteract the negative effects of the welfare mentality by turning retrenchment into a transition. The objective is to help the individual overcome feelings of powerlessness and depression by employing preventative strategies.

> One strategy is to focus on how people might undergo an effective change in career, should the necessity arise. Employees can be helped to identify previous transition solving skills, and to maintain them. Also of help is the use of staff appraisal for its intended purpose–for staff to assess their performance in a job, to identify the skill gaps and undertake further development as a precaution against future change. (McMichael, 1995)

Again, similar techniques include training on survival skills and how to manage change by participating in the reemployment process. For example, they sometimes involve employees as change agents in the grouping and rebuilding process. The more they are involved, the more they will own the results, and accept the new order (McMichael, 1995). To date, occupational social workers have demonstrated leadership in career transitioning and shown Commonwealth Departments like Social Security and Education, Employment and Training how to market their services to the unemployed in a constructive, creative manner.

EDUCATION AND TRAINING ISSUES

To some degree the educators in Schools of Social Work in Australia have ignored the gains made by the contract social work practitioner. Often recognition for occupational issues is piecemeal and left to individual lecturers and tutors to address. This ambivalent attitude by academics towards occupational social work is due to several factors. First, Schools of Social Work tend to be reactive rather than proactive towards new social movements. Few academics understand the impact economic rationalism and privatization are likely to have on the long-term practice of social work. Consequently, they tend to adopt a wait and see attitude before making fundamental changes to course offerings. Second, there are philosophical differences between social work professionals over whether or not we should be working with middle class clients rather than the disadvantaged. This also is reflected in the academic makeup of the majority of Schools of Social Work in Australia. Ideological differences run deep and debates usually result in widening the discourse between colleagues. Heads of Schools of Social Work usually are wary of creating further hostility between staff faculty who are already at odds over other theoretical differences. To keep the peace, occupational social work methodologies are tolerated informally in undergraduate courses providing they do not threaten the status quo of existing approaches to practice.

Inertia is the third point to consider. In Australia, existing practice patterns dictate a generic academic approach. Despite these cautions and the increasing distance between academic theory and practice, a concept of "practice wisdom" and generalist skills remains the educator's goal (Tierney, 1993). In addition, "the ascendancy of market liberalism has the capacity to impact directly on education by exacerbating ubiquitous pressures to produce graduates with dominant values who are compliant" (Bryson, 1994). Educators always have had to cope with pressures to produce acceptable courses and graduates.

Both of these views highlight an approach that has allowed social work academics to argue for continuing the generic approach to undergraduate training, thus sidelining other methodologies (including occupational social work) to post-graduate study. To a large degree, this is just an excuse to avoid examining the contributions made by occupational social workers in the field.

For those post-graduate students researching the occupational field, efforts are being made to link employee work practices with current broader theoretical positions. For example, they explore the use of employee assistance programs to focus on alcohol and drug use by employees in the workplace and look at how socialization and systems theories can be applied to the employment of compulsory contracts in rehabilitation. The aim is to bring specialized occupational skills and generic knowledge together in an integrated manner to maximize interventions in the work setting. "The major focus of social work intervention has been based on addressing the organization as a 'community at work' which forms the prime target and context of practice. This 'community at work' incorporates the political, organizational and individual contexts. The social work practitioner works within these spheres," to bring about an environmental change in the organization that will enable employees to address personal problems without fear of retribution from management (Sonin and Horne, 1996). In conclusion, "Schools of Social Work in Australia need to formally recognize the world of work as a specialization and develop educational programs, both undergraduate and post-graduate, that integrate social work practice with sound business principles and prepare practitioners to deal with unique policy and practice issues in the industrial arena" (Sonin and Horne, 1996).

ISSUES OF CURRENT PRACTICE

By far the most critical issue in current practice is the need for the generalist and occupational social worker to find common ground. In the Australian context both groups of practitioners are tackling many of the same social problems although from different perspectives. In the case of the employee assistance programs, for example, professionals from both sides of the fence recognize the advantage of how complementary views enhance treatment outcomes. The only problem is the way these views can be expressed collegially without threatening the position of one or the other. For those academicians willing to break the ice, several avenues exist for seeking joint participation.

The first of these relates to collaborative research. Both professional groups are interested in how privatization has affected present social problems. Again, a range of post-graduate research projects have focused on the dislocation and redeployment of workers in public organizations, such as restructuring to compete with industry, being sold to private companies in the commercial sector. Findings in the fields of telecommunications, telephone and express mail services have shown that non-technical and middle management staff are the most likely to lose their jobs or be forced to take redundancy packages during reorganization. These individuals tend to be poorly trained compared to the technically skilled staff, and find it very difficult to secure re-employment in alternative work environments. They are usually older workers whose training has been of an in-service nature and not transferable to the digital and computer economy.

In this field, contract practitioners are working on intensive, multilevel training programs to assist displaced midlevel managers to update their skills for redeployment in the workplace. Such an approach focuses on providing the unemployed worker with flexible and innovative skills that can maximize his or her potential to future employers. These practice frameworks "simultaneously operate across the micro/mezzo/macro levels of intervention." "Practitioners should also be working in the local community assisting in the development of regional employment responses and business/community partnerships which could be assisted by State and Federal Governments to foster employment opportunities" (McCormack, 1996).

A second approach is the use of fieldwork placements in undergraduate programs to demonstrate the usefulness of occupational social work as a legitimate social policy method and occupational alternative. Today, more and more social work students are expecting non-traditional placements including positions in politicians' offices and environmental agencies. Often these organizations do not have the funds to employ full-time social workers and use part-time contract practitioners to research and write position statements on emerging community issues. The fact that students work alongside contractors and are at the forefront of these developments, place them in excellent positions for informing public agency colleagues of new emerging social concerns requiring possible government policy and legislation.

The third area is the contract practitioners' existing relationship with management. Corporate managers usually perceive public social workers as do-gooders whose sole reason for wanting contact with employees is to push their social justice wheelbarrow and stir up workplace disputes. The attempt by contract practitioners to take a more balanced and mediating approach to these issues means that occupational social work has kept the door open for rational communication between themselves and corporate management. To some degree, contract practitioners already have started to translate social work approaches into corporate culture language to gain more acceptance and understanding. In part, the change in emphasis from social welfare and social justice issues to the more neutral terminology of human resource management has enabled corporate structures to embrace, for example, employee participation in the day-to-day working phase of production decision-making procedures. While this may be seen in terms of greater worker commitment and ownership in the workplace by management theory, occupational social workers can still interpret these events as empowerment and improvement in worker rights, even though a different language is employed.

To some social workers, such an approach may be perceived as a sellout to the capitalist system; however, for others this is the first step in formulating theoretical approaches that will enable social work to play a more constructive part in the privatization debate. Consultative practitioners in this country believe that if the profession can evolve approaches integrating both the public and privatization philosophies in post modern Australia, then social work can reestablish itself as a force in shaping the welfare state's response to future social policy and legislation initiatives in the field of employment.

FUTURE DIRECTIONS AND CHALLENGES

Clearly, the key challenge for the Australian social work profession in the 21st Century is for the generic and occupational social workers to establish a united front. Post-industrial society in Australia is facing the onslaught of unending and relentless attacks on our traditional way of life. For many in the community, this is a threat to the very core of their human existence. With little understanding and a general feeling that governments and politicians have let them down, many in society are turning to right-wing and extremist groups for solutions and moral support.

To those who have been in the social work profession for some time, this is not a new debate. Following the end of the Second World War, Australia opened its doors to large numbers of migrants from Europe and later from Asia. Similar voices were heard then, decrying the so-called breakdown of Anglo-Saxon society. At that time the embryonic social work profession was called upon to provide safe havens for these new migrant groups until they could integrate into the wider community. Social Work took up this challenge with enthusiasm and helped lay the foundation for Australia's largely successful multicultural society of today.

Although the demands of the current social problems facing the community are more complex and difficult to deal with, the current social work profession in reality has at its disposal a range of knowledge and skills not previously available to practitioners. To begin with, occupational social workers have been exposed to the repercussions of privatization and changes to society since the early 1990s. Contract workers know what impact unemployment and reemployment have had on individuals and families in the community. In recent years efforts have been made to adapt professional practices in social work to the workplace environment. As a result, contract workers are now forging equal employment opportunity infrastructures, recruitment and retention policies for minority and Aboriginal groups, child-care programs and union and employee consultative councils, suitable for engaging corporate management on their own turf in a way that permits social work to influence employment policies on the shop floor.

Another benefit the occupational social worker brings to current social debate is a long-time understanding that workers need to be treated as a total entirety. Practitioners in all service delivery systems know that if one aspect of an individual's social existence is neglected, then treatment frequently fails. A person's work environment is just as important as family life and these need to be treated as inseparable elements of service delivery. Private practitioners have led the field in this area by incorporating life survival approaches such as exit interviewing, family needs assessment, and stress management care into industry staff training programs. The outcome has been to educate management on a range of principles advocating the view that a productive worker is one whose social and work environments are in harmony with each other and this should be a key aim of good corporate practice.

Again, recent practice has demonstrated that to achieve such ends, social work practice needs to be flexible enough to make the link with other professional ideologies. Because of their exclusion for many decades from both inside and outside the profession, private practitioners were forced to experiment with new ideas to survive. This has meant exploring different combinations of counseling community work and training approaches to see what works or does not work. A recent article on this dilemma stated:

> At the training level, different styles of teaching/communicating are required, depending on the nature of the audience. Good interpersonal skills cannot alone provide the basis for successful training workshops/seminars. An understanding of adult learning principles and methods of instruction are required, and this in turn has to translate into a language which matches the nature and style of communication at particular layers within the organization. (Munn and Kennedy, 1994)

In Australia, occupational social workers have employed a range of new training techniques, from theater drama, simulated role playing, team building skills to bush survival courses to help develop new ways of tackling social problems in the workplace environment.

When one explores in-depth how various skills and knowledge can be applied to current workplace problems, a certain degree of optimism exists. To a large extent they represent the building blocks for challenging the issues of the 21st Century. Occupational social work is providing a beacon light for the profession to begin advocating a more positive and creative approach to solving work-linked problems. However, a sense of caution also needs to be expressed. Like every good foundation, brickwork needs to be held together with mortar and cement. The social cement, that gives strength to the profession's ability to address these issues, is the challenge for all social workers to unite and work together for the common good of practice. At this stage all of the elements are present, however no one as yet has been able to pull the mixture together.

Social workers on both sides of the issue need to be able to give and take on matters of ideology and social work practice. All practitioners must be able to see the advantages of the other and be prepared to integrate those ideas into their own practice. For without occupational social workers believing they have the respect of their fellow public practitioners and the willingness to come out of the shadow of the generic practitioner as an equal, the shadow boxing will continue the inequalities of the past. Only when the occupational and generic social worker come together as partners can the shadow boxer disappear and the profession genuinely address the concerns of future workplace practices in Australia.

REFERENCES

Bryson, L. (1994). Directions and developments in the Australian welfare state: A challenge for educators, *Australian Social Worker*, 47, 4, 3-10.

Coopes, C. (1995). Meeting needs in mental health services in West Australia, *The West Australian Social Worker*, April, 1.

Dodds, I. (1995). Approaching 4,000–with more to come, *AASW National Information Bulletin*, May, 1-2.

Edward, B. (1995). Keeping up with change–Social work practice in a hospital setting, *The West Australian Social Worker*, February, 1-7.

Ernst, J. (1995). Privatization and social work, *The West Australian Social Worker*, December, 1-7.

Fariss, N. (1995). Partnerships and process for achieving innovation: A perspective on providing services in the non-government section, *The West Australian Social Worker*, June, 1-5.

McCormack, J. (1996). Older workers: Roles for occupational social work, *Australian Social Worker*, 49, 1, 19-25.

McDonald, C. (1995). The challenge from within: Organizational commitment in nonprofit human service organizations, *Australian Social Worker*, 48, 1, 3-11.

McMichael, A. (1994). The retrenchment experience. The impact on social work, *Australian Social Worker*, 47, 2, 33-36.

Munn, P. & Kennedy, M. (1994). Consulting work: An option for social work towards the 21st Century, *Australian Social Worker*, 47, 1, 11-14.

Sonin, D. & Horne, D. (1996). Practitioners' experience in Telstra, *Australian Social Worker*, 49, 1, 31-36.

Tierney, L. (1993). Practice research and social work education, *Australian Social Worker*, 46, 2, 9-22.

Webster, T. (1995). Economic rationalism: The nature, influence and impact of the doctrine over the last decade in Australia, *Australian Social Worker*, December, 48, 4, 41-47.

Occupational Social Work in Germany: A Continuously Developing Field of Practice

Holger Gehlenborg

SUMMARY. This article describes the development and current practices of occupational social workers in Germany. It provides a history of the industrial health and social welfare system in Germany, including the placement of governesses in factories to help women adjust to entering the industrialized workforce as a result of World War I, and the transformation of these early workplace helpers to purveyors of Nazi ideology with the rise of the Third Reich and the subsequent efforts to restore their credibility. The author also traces the evolution of occupational social welfare functions over the past six decades to present day and suggests how this evolution is patterned after the social, political, economic and labor force changes that have marked Germany throughout this period. The predominance of occupational social workers as employees rather than contractors or consultants and employer preferences for internal programs are also explored as is the general absence of occupational social work services in the public not-for-profit sector. A successful alcohol intervention and treatment program developed for City of Stuttgart employees is one exception discussed. The author concludes the article by identifying efforts undertaken by the Professional Association of Occupational Social Workers to promote the recognition of occupational social workers and their value to a healthier and more productive workplace. *[Article copies available for a fee from The Haworth Document Delivery Service: 1-800-342-9678. E-mail address: <getinfo@haworthpressinc.com> Website: <http://www.HaworthPress.com> © 2001 by The Haworth Press, Inc. All rights reserved.]*

Holger Gehlenborg, MSW, is an Occupational Social Worker with the City of Stuttgart, Germany.

[Haworth co-indexing entry note]: "Occupational Social Work in Germany: A Continuously Developing Field of Practice." Gehlenborg, Holger. Co-published simultaneously in *Employee Assistance Quarterly* (The Haworth Press, Inc.) Vol. 17, No. 1/2, 2001, pp. 17-41; and: *Global Perspectives of Occupational Social Work* (ed: R. Paul Maiden) The Haworth Press, Inc., 2001, pp. 17-41. Single or multiple copies of this article are available for a fee from The Haworth Document Delivery Service [1-800-342-9678, 9:00 a.m. - 5:00 p.m. (EST). E-mail address: getinfo@haworthpressinc.com].

KEYWORDS. Occupational social work in Germany

THE SOCIETAL AND HISTORICAL CONTEXT OF OCCUPATIONAL SOCIAL WORK IN GERMANY

Occupational social work has an almost one-hundred-year tradition in Germany. Despite this fact, it has hardly succeeded in awakening the interests of the social or economic sciences in this field, in consolidating systematic research, or of becoming the subject of professional discussions in trade publications. Very few recent exceptions confirm the basic lack of interest in this field of social work practice. Scientific documentation on the development of occupational social work is, on the whole, fragmented. The few documents which are available portray developments of individual enterprises, which result in limited conclusions with regards to occupational social work trends. Publications on recent developments in the private and public sector are also rather limited (Googins et al., 1986). This article is therefore based only, in part, on scholarly literature due to the acute lack of historical or recent data with regards to the development and present situation of occupational social work in Germany. The greater part is subjective and based on conclusions obtained through personal experiences and in many discussions with colleagues.

Living conditions for workers in Germany worsened considerably towards the end of the 19th Century on account of increasing industrialization. The reasons for this were a crises-prone economy, the employment of women and children, low wages and long working hours. Industrial mass production leads to a rift between the association of work with family life. The establishment of industrial firms in urban areas increased the trend of rural to urban migration. The family as a unit became unimportant as a productive community and developed instead into a consumer society. The original purpose of having as many children as possible in order to guarantee social security and support in old age became a material burden in a factory worker's family. Low wages forced workers into living at subsistence levels, and daily risks such as diseases, disability, accidents or unemployment could not be kept in check.

It was only through the efforts of the German trade union movement, which started in 1868, and the subsequent strikes that decisive reforms in social security law were made. The Health Insurance scheme was introduced in 1883, the Accident Insurance in 1884, the Invalid and Old Age Pension Insurance in 1889, followed by the Unemployment Insurance for white collar workers in 1911 and the Unemployment Insurance for blue collar workers in 1927 (Lau-Villinger, 1994).

At first it was only on account of social and religious motivations that wives and daughters of some industrialists, who by means of food parcels and nursing care, assured the welfare of their company's employees. Home care centers for children were set up and health care forged ahead. The development of occupational social work was closely linked to the social, political and general economic conditions of the early 1900s. The Empire until 1914 with its patriarchal structure of society, the loss of the First World War and its devastating results on the economy, mass unemployment, weak unions, the introduction of democracy and increasing nationalistic trends, were the context of occupational social workers' first years in Germany.

At the turn of the century some socially minded entrepreneurs employed the first "Fabrikpflegerinnen" (factory nurses). These factory nurses were the precursors of the present day occupational social workers.

From 1900 to 1933 the factory nurses were assigned directly to management and were mainly qualified nurses, sometimes governesses, vocational schoolteachers and commercial clerks who were trained for their new job in a four-week course. The main objective was to support female workers in adapting to production conditions and decreasing production losses due to the double burden which women had to bear. One of the factory nurses' responsibilities was counseling on matters regarding housing, nourishment and child care. Additionally, she counseled on matters regarding alimony, guardianship and insurance.

During the national socialist rule from 1933 to 1945, the factory nurse's role in Germany was changed and she was used to promote Nazi ideology. Her title changed to "Volkspflege" (care of the people) at first, and then from 1935 to "soziale Betriebsarbeit" (social factory work). She was directly appointed as a member of managerial staff. Qualified nurses and governesses received additional training from the "Deutsche Arbeitsfront" (The German Worker's Front), a national socialist association of both employers and employees, in order to carry out their work as "soziale Betriebsarbeiterinnen" (social factory workers). The objective now was to help everyone to adapt to the national socialist principles by means of indoctrination, which included infiltrating family and educational principles with national socialist beliefs. Counseling was substituted by disciplinary and controlling functions in connection with education, work and health policies, as well as economic matters.

After the fall of the "Third Reich," material want, unemployment and housing shortages prevailed. The new stabilizing democratic state of affairs, under the supervision of the victorious powers, depended, amongst other things, on the rebuilding of the economy. The unions managed to wring out concessions step by step from the employers for enhanced employee benefits. They found huge support amongst the workers. They discounted occupational social work in 1957 as being "Sozialklimbim" (social nonsense), making it perfectly clear to the employers that they wanted a leading role in social affairs as well.

From 1945 to 1960 occupational social work was designated as "Betriebsfürsorge" (works welfare), and was, more often than not, assigned to management but also increasingly to the personnel department. The "Betriebsfürsorgerinnen" (works welfare workers) training took place in welfare schools and training colleges. An integral part of the course was an on-the-job training period in a company's welfare department. One of the main objectives now was to socially integrate employees by means of economic, family and individual stability which meant, in the rebuilding phase of postwar Germany, eliminating the employee's external problems caused by the war such as material needs, housing and family problems. Social work methods from the United States were adapted to give special cases individual assistance both to an employee and his family. Welfare work at that time was mainly geared to material deficits.

By the beginning of the 1960s the workers' material needs were guaranteed (on the whole) both by law and through collective wage agreements, in addition to wider social benefits. A politically critical student movement disagreed, sometimes radically, with the results of this prosperous and abundant society, women's movements gained influence and because of that, emancipated aspects in society and social work. The principle, "Hilfe zur Selbsthilfe" (help to self-help), was brought to the foreground of pedagogic methods and objectives.

On account of a change in its duties between 1960 and 1980 the new term "Betriebssozialarbeit" (occupational social work) gradually replaced that of "Betriebsfürsorge" (works welfare), which was now part of the personnel department. A special eight-term study course in social pedagogic or social work was introduced in 1971. By upgrading the studies, and with better pay, this sort of work became attractive to men as well. Occupational social workers' objective was now to increase productivity for the company by easing the burden on management, and assisting employees in surmounting personal problems. Individual counseling in psychosocial and financial problems was one of occupational social workers' priority objectives. Individual talks, house calls, sick visits, organizing internal self-help groups and group sessions were all part of the occupational social workers' repertoire.

Since 1980, social work employed by companies has been known as "Sozialberatung" (social counseling) or "Sozialdienst" (social service) and is mainly assigned to the personnel rather than the social department. The basic direction of service did not change much, but was often complemented by additional therapeutic qualifications. This field of work is gaining increasing interest among university graduates such as educators, psychologists and sociologists. One of the objectives of occupational social work is ensuring quality by motivating employees, in addition to giving them support in surmounting individual problems, and in motivating management to confront socially conflicting situations. Duties entailed counseling in cases of psychosocial conflicts at work and individual psychosocial distress situations. Moreover, management training courses are becoming increasingly important in improving social competencies. Theoretical communications and psychological counseling of employees and management, group discussions, informative meetings and management training courses have now become routine work.

THE SOCIAL FRAMEWORK OF GERMAN OCCUPATIONAL SOCIAL WORK

One of the pillars of democracy in Germany is modeled on "Sozialen Marktwirtschaft" (social market economy). This model of a capitalist economic order was the basic principle on which the economy was rebuilt after the Second World War. According to that principle, the State would be responsible for correcting all the socially undesirable effects of the "free market economy." It was especially important to guarantee free competition, e.g., against market dominating cartels, and to guarantee and adjust the incomes and pecuniary circumstances of groups who were not involved in the economic process. Matters which taxed the capacities of private initiatives such as social and health policies, educational and structural politics, were to be taken over by the State (Lau-Villinger, 1994).

At present, the German economy is undergoing a significant structural change (Meyers, 1990). Processes, which in some cases took years to develop, are now being fundamentally changed in enterprises and administrations. The introduction of "lean production" and "lean management" are two key elements in the restructuring process. The main objective is to reduce costs in order to remain internationally competitive.

The autonomous freedom of deciding collective wage agreements, which prevails within the economic framework between employers and unions, is meant to ensure the independence and direct responsibility of each side. Talks on collective wage agreements between employers and unions take place on a yearly basis in all the branches of the economy and are carried out in a given region. The first agreement for a given region is nearly always taken over by the entire branch across Germany. In these agreements, both increased rates and income structures for all employees of a certain branch in a given region are negotiated. These so-called "Flächentarifverträge" (collective wage agreements) do not align themselves to the economic situation of an individual company, and are therefore criticized for being too inflexible by the Employer's Association as well as, in part, by the "Betriebsrat" (works council). More and more so-called "Haustarifabschlüssen" (in-house wage agreements) between companies and unions are now occurring. Both unions and employers' associations have registered a decline in their memberships–so both parties are now striving to obtain flexibility in settling their wage agreements. The principle of collective wage agreements should not be given up altogether because its basic structure has proved effective and has assured a relative social stability in the German economy for decades.

The present difficult economic situation has strained relations between employers and unions. While conservative employers, in order to consolidate the economy, continually call for a deeper cut in social benefits and in some cases threaten to export jobs to countries with low wage costs, the unions are trying to keep the necessary new social rulings socially balanced.

It is clearly stated in the industrial relations law that all interests of staff in companies over a certain size (10 employees) must be represented by a works council. Works council members are excused from their main duties for all activities concerning the works council. The rules of the industrial relations law apply also, in principle, to the public sector where they are dealt with by special rulings. The interests of the public sector staff are represented by the "Personalvertretung" (personnel representatives).

THE SOCIAL WELFARE AND HEALTH CARE STRUCTURE

The government of Germany essentially guarantees the well-being of every citizen through a plan of basic state assistance (Stahlmann, 1994). This takes shape in the form of money or material assistance in an amount that enables the citizen to participate in social and cultural activities. It comprises money for the general run of the household, rent and heating, clothing and financial assistance for the purchase of furniture. Occasionally these amounts (e.g., in the case of a five household family) are higher than the working income of a single full-time job. All those who are not in a position to take care of themselves, either totally or in part (such as children, low-income groups, long-term unemployed, invalids or elderly persons), are entitled to this assistance. The cost of this basic social assistance falls on the shoulders of all taxpayers.

Unemployment insurance is another important element in the German social system. Financed 50% by the employer and 50% by the employee, unemployment insurance ensures that in the first years of unemployment, depending on family status and the number of children, 60% to 67% of the last net income is paid out. After a two-year period this percentage falls to 53% to 57% (Federal Assistance Law). As a rule the amount is more than the legal minimum existence wage of a single person. Programs to integrate the unemployed into a full working life and work employment schemes are also financed by this insurance.

Employees are obliged, depending on the amount of their income, to contribute to the government pension scheme and 50% of the contribution is paid by the employer. In this way employees are insured against any financial risks of work-related injuries or early disabilities. The old age pension is paid out of the pension scheme (Arbeitforderungsgesetz, 1992).

This fund also finances rehabilitation programs to maintain or reinstate the insured person's working ability. Self-employed persons may also contribute to this pension scheme. The national health insurance is not governed by the forces of the market economy.

Medical and rehabilitative care is statutory and is divided into three main streams. They are:

1. Basic governmental assistance for all citizens;
2. A statutory health insurance for employees;
3. Private insurance for self-employed and higher income groups.

The basic principle for medical treatment, which is of the utmost importance, is the freedom of therapy (i.e., the right to choose one's own doctor wherever one wishes).

Beneficiaries of governmental assistance are all citizens who do not have any income either on account of being unemployed, having no pension or because they are not family members of legally or privately insured persons. The costs of medical and rehabilitation treatments as well as medication are assumed by the state. Basic governmental care is handled by the statutory health insurance.

Employees are obliged by law to contribute to the national health insurance scheme, as long as their income is not above the current limit of DM6,000 per month. All medical needs for the employee and his family are financed from this scheme, whereby a minimal contribution for medication, remedies, hospitalization, etc., is necessary. The national health insurance is financed through contributions on a 50/50 basis by the employee and employer.

It is not compulsory for self-employed and higher income groups to be medically insured. They basically have the possibility to waiver all medical insurance and to finance any costs for medical treatment out of their own private pockets. They may insure themselves, if so desired, in private insurance schemes on a scale which they may determine themselves. For those who are fully insured the benefits are usually far more than those obtained from the governmental health insurance; however, they are much more expensive. Higher income groups receive a subsidy from their employers.

Judges, soldiers, civil servants in communal, state or federal offices are subject to special conditions. It is not compulsory for them to insure themselves like other employees. This is based on a historical legal ruling, which absolved civil servants from such payments. It is the government who bears the full costs of the pension scheme, and in the case of certain groups (such as soldiers and policemen) the health insurance as well. Other groups of civil servants have to privately finance between 30% and 50% of their medical insurance according to their family status.

As can be seen from this brief discussion, every German citizen is basically assured of a minimum subsistence level and health care guaranteed by the basic social and health schemes. Unemployment and old age pension schemes guarantee that in the case of unemployment and in old age, as a rule, a fairly decent standard of living may still be maintained.

The enormous costs of these social and health services, if one is to believe the statements of leading industrialists and some politicians, is hardly manageable. The high additional labor costs for unemployment, pension and health insurance are a problem for Germany's competitiveness on the world market. In the present economic and political discussions the reduction of costs is one of the main themes, which is why massive cuts, and structural changes in the social and health schemes are required. Political discussion should not, however, cover up the fact that with increasing job cuts, both in industry and in the service administrations, unemployment has increased tremendously with very noticeable social consequences, e.g., poverty, rising crime rate, and radicalization of minority groups.

POLITICAL RAMIFICATIONS

Present day social and health politics, as well as the high standards of public, social and health schemes, lead to the fact that occupational social work may now pull out of its classical social work duties and hand these over to the public social work offices. Their duties are neither determined by law nor by any wage agreements. In most companies voluntary social services have been drastically reduced or completely dissolved. Occupational social work must develop new areas of work independently of political factors, and take over tasks that are important for the social development of a company.

DOMAINS OF PRACTICE

Occupational social work is offered in Germany as an in-house service, mostly by large industrial and service companies as well as in the larger public sector administrations. Occupational social work has a 95-year tradition in the electronic, metal, metal related, chemical and mining industries. It was introduced in the last 30 years in the service industries such as large insurance companies, banks, and aerospace firms. However, with few exceptions, occupational social work has not been standard for very long in the public sector. It may be found mostly in large communal public offices and in federal ministries with their respective administrations, including the army. Hardly any occupational social work service has been introduced in federal state administrations, with the exception of the cities (e.g., Hamburg, Berlin, Bremen).

Occupational social work services are offered primarily by larger organizations employing at least 2,000 workers. Services are rarely found in small and mid-sized firms. It is estimated that there are approximately 1,000 social workers employed in workplace settings. More than 400 of them are members of the "Bundesfachverband Betriebliche Sozialarbeite" or Federal Professional Association of Occupational Social Work.

The Federal Republic of Germany's national general conditions of labor, such as labor protection and job security laws, do not consider the duties of occupational social workers as being instrumental in the implementation of such laws in a company. The services of safety engineers and occupational medicine have been defined in detail, but do not include psychological and social health domains. The new European laws, which are also to be implemented in Germany, gave added consideration to these aspects on the basis of the World Health Organization (WHO) Ottawa Charter on the promotion of health. A draft, however, for a new general labor protection law in which a standard health protection law for all companies was defined, but was ultimately rejected. For many reasons it has not been possible, up until now in Germany as opposed to other European countries, to solve complex occupational problems by legislature.

As a result, occupational social work has so far been an internal social service offered by the employer for the employees on a voluntary basis. There are no set rules either from employers, unions or other organizations with regards to occupational social work standards, duties or limitations. The tasks and quality of occupational social work are individually decided upon by each firm together with the "Betriebsrat" (works council).

On average, a qualified occupational social worker is responsible for 5,000 people. One of the largest employers of occupational social workers, Siemens AG, strove to reduce this to a 1:3,000 ratio. This number corresponds to the recommendations of the Federal Professional Association of Occupational Social Work in order to maintain the present standard of service.

While in some European countries occupational social work managed to establish itself as an external service, occupational programs have generally remained an in-house endeavor in Germany. This service has now been offered for about 15 years by freelance social workers, mainly to small and mid-sized companies. External occupational social work is not marketed as such, but rather as "company counseling." Even though the services rendered are, in part, the same as those given internally, specific products are developed for each individual customer as required, such as the improvement of health at work and intervention for substance abuse.

ROLES AND DUTIES OF OCCUPATIONAL SOCIAL WORKERS

Occupational social workers use personal, social and company resources. In order to be fair in a complex company internal problem solution, the range of services offered must span out much further than those of the classic individual counseling. Occupational social work services must be shaped to fit the needs of a company and its employees, playing a part not only in staff counseling but also in the development of personnel and organizational procedures. To do so it has to participate, over and above its task of counseling staff, in all matters handling personnel and organizational development and in a professional capacity on boards and working groups, especially those with personnel and social committees. Occupational social workers assume the role of a catalyst in the domains of work and health related communicative problems, and in initiating and moderating the developments of solution strategies.

The objective is basically to maintain and improve employee efficiency and productivity. In order to do so, occupational social workers initiate and promote procedures which serve to solve individual or group conflicts, broaden management's social and communicative abilities, stimulate the health and productivity of employees, and support work safety and company health protection schemes in addition to increasing the general contentment at work.

Occupational social work services are available to all employees regardless of their functions or status. Family members are also entitled to use the counseling service. A specific target group is supervisors and managers; however, whole organizational units may use occupational social work services.

The following list of duties explains the generally defined tasks of occupational social workers. These duties (few examples only) are modified and adapted according to each company's individual economic and social dynamics.

- *Employee Counseling.* There is hardly a theme in the psychosocial field that may not be used in a counseling session, regardless of an employee's position. Apart from personal, family related, social and psy-

chological problems, issues concerning jobs and work related matters are also dealt with. Problem areas range from conflicts at work; management matters and training; addiction problems; organizing internal and external assistance; dealing with issues of reintegration after treatment; financial problems and retirement planning.
- *Information, Instruction and Training.* There is a wide spectrum of possibilities such as communications workshops for managers and supervisors, education on the prevention of substance abuse, stress management seminars, and other educational programs geared to specific target groups. It is certainly very positive to note here that because it has to ascertain itself, in part, with regards to the above mentioned services, and fight against or cooperate with internal and external competition, such as a company's training or personnel departments, the integration process of occupational social work in a company is accelerated.
- *Organization Related Measures.* There are many possibilities for modern occupational social work, which come under this heading, such as setting up internal support services for former substance abusers; consultation to organizational units in specific matters, for example, in the personnel department with regards to the integration of an employee with a changed productivity profile; the participation on employer committees with regards to work related social and health problems, e.g., work safety committees; the initiation and execution of health care measures such as health circles and also the participation in organizational developments, e.g., team development under the aspects of cooperation, communication and working atmosphere. Some have also introduced the notion of total quality management as well.
- *Marketing.* Marketing occupational social work services has been neglected. Nevertheless, it is an especially important aspect of the job in economically difficult times and as a means of gaining exposure to manager and employees. Public relations work must be done internally, through an explanation of occupational social work duties and services, and by written comments on general and specific matters, e.g., in-house newsletters, staff meetings, and seminars for new employees. External public relations, such as professional lectures, press releases, cooperation with external services and promotions, serve not only in polishing up a company's image, but also to demonstrate that professional skills of the aspects of the occupational social worker are also important measures.

ORGANIZATIONAL AFFILIATIONS AND THEIR EFFECTS

Occupational social work today is usually affiliated with the personnel department of a company as a special unit, depending on the onus of its duties and the structure of a company, or alternatively with the social or medical departments. The loss of its high-ranking organizational classification in the early years as a member of managerial staff has inevitably lead to a loss of influence on the personnel and social policies of a company. One of the causes for this could be the fact that occupational social work concentrated far too long on the "private" problems of staff, giving individual therapeutic solutions in special cases, thus allowing the burden of structural company problems to fall on the employer. It was only through the expansion of working methods in the system that a new profile of occupational social work was developed. The development, for example, of company concepts in the 1980s for improving managerial skills with regards to substance abuse problems enabled occupational social workers to gain influence in shaping a company's personnel and social policies, as well as in the development of health protection schemes.

Since then occupational social workers have worked as competent partners on important committees both in companies and government agencies, setting up health and safety programs, communication structures or social policies. Other aspects of the effects caused by assigning occupational social workers to the personnel department are issues related to privacy, confidentiality and the resulting credibility given their role.

Confidentiality of social workers in Germany is stipulated by law in the German penal code book (§03). They are obliged to remain silent with regards to all data obtained on account of their position of trust. A social worker's commitment to confidentiality is equal to that of the medical profession.

It does not require them, however, to maintain confidentiality in the case of a criminal trial, or absolve them from reporting a criminal act. This legal rule applies to all social workers regardless of where they are employed. Other professional groups such as nurses, sociologists and educators do not have privileged communication prescribed by law.

Data protection is highly developed in Germany. This means basically that occupational social workers may only use and collect data with a client's consent. A written authorization is required with regards to computerized data. Information may not be given to a third party, e.g., the employer without the agreement of the person concerned. Data protection staff, both in companies and in government agencies, ensure that these rules are followed.

Legal regulations ensure very extensive protection of all personal data in occupational social work. Being organizationally assigned to the personnel department, occupational social workers have had to continuously fight against distrust. This is historically based on the time when data protection and confidentiality laws were not yet in use and occupational social workers were misused, in part, to the disadvantage of the employees, by the personnel department. The organizational affiliation to the personnel department, that is responsible for sanctions, disciplinary measures or discharges justified by economic reasons (mostly unproductive employees), causes some to identify occupational social work with the labor legislative aspects of the personnel department. This is a major handicap in developing trustworthiness and one of the reasons why it is necessary to put occupational social work on par with the safety departments, assigning them as an individual unit in management or in the administration within the organization.

PROGRAMS IN OCCUPATIONAL SOCIAL WORK

A trend that has gained momentum over the last few years in occupational social work is the development of programs for the prevention or reduction of work related problems. In this way programs promoting health and communication gained importance, e.g., nonsmoking campaigns, overcoming stress, group development and communications training, as well as addiction prevention programs.

The city of Stuttgart's municipal government's program for substance abuse prevention and support serves as an example for the development, introduction, execution and improvement of occupational social work programs. This program was honored in 1986 in the federal government's report on drugs, as being an exemplary model of occupational social work in the public sector.

THE REGION, THE CITY AND THE MUNICIPALITY

Stuttgart is a large city with approximately 550,000 inhabitants in the southwest of Germany. The city is an important trade and service center in the region, the state capital of Baden-Württemberg and seat of the federal state government. Well-known companies such as Mercedes-Benz, Porsche and Bosch have their headquarters here and there are many subsidiaries of other large German and international companies. The supporting care network for addicts within the city and its commuting area is very closely knit, spanning a wide range from self-help groups with differing values to addiction counseling centers, medical specialists, clinical detoxification centers and specialized clinics for addicts.

About 17,000 persons are employed in the city's municipality in various fields and professions. They are divided into about 50 public offices and self-owned government firms. The smallest office has 20 employees and the largest, one of the four governmental hospitals, employs 2,500 people. The 50 public offices are assigned to eight departments, e.g., culture, city planning or general administration, each with a Mayor at its head ruled at the very top by a Lord Mayor. Occupational social work is an integral part of the personnel department, which is centrally responsible for all basic matters appertaining to personnel. Two "Diplom-Pädagoginnen" and a "Diplom-Sozialpädagoge" are employed in the occupational social work division.

ALCOHOL USE IN GERMANY

The following statistics illustrate the social problem regarding alcohol consumption. For centuries, the Federal Republic of Germany occupied a top position per capita in the consumption of alcohol. Since the reunification of Germany, alcohol consumption has risen to its highest level of 12.5 liters of pure alcohol per head per year yielding an annual income in taxes for the government of about 7 billion DM. Conservative estimates suggest there are about 2.5 million alcoholics in need of treatment. Social costs as a direct result of alcohol consumption are estimated at a yearly 80 billion DM accounting for sickness, traffic accidents, loss of productivity, etc.

Alcoholism in the German Workforce

According to the statistics of the "Deutschen Hauptstelle gegen die Suchtgefahren" (German headquarters against addiction), 5% of a company's staff are alcoholics and a further 10% are at risk (Gehlenborg, 1994). In addition to that, the level of productivity is diminished and absenteeism is 16 times higher with alcoholics as compared to non-alcoholics. They call in sick 2.5 times more and are involved in 3.5 more accidents at work with absenteeism rising to 1.4 times more after accidents (Psychologic Heute, 1996). Apart from these facts, other elements have been recorded which may have negative effects both on output and the atmosphere at work: arriving late for work, unreliability in carrying out one's duties; work overload, overtime and psychological stress for the other employees; additional burdens for supervisors, the organization and personnel department; increased fluctuation in a department, and increased absenteeism by the non-addicted.

A survey carried out by the Stanford Research Institute (United States) in 1975 demonstrated that a loss of 25% of an addict's wage or salary should be estimated during the course of his illness. This means a loss of 12.5% of the total pay packet of an employer group with a 5% alcoholism rate (Das

Suchtbuch furdie Arbeitswelt, 1991). Even if the figures are only approximate, they still show a noteworthy economical volume.

Alcohol Use in Public Employment

Alcohol consumption at work with all its effects was tolerated for a very long time in nearly all departments of the civil service. It was only at the beginning of the 1970s that the personnel department began to seriously envisage means of improving the effects and legislative consequences of alcoholism, as well as the assistance to both the departments and persons concerned.

A key problem in the civil service at that time was the disproportionate handling of alcoholics. Blue collar workers were very often instantly dismissed when mistakes occurred, white collar workers on the whole were covered up for, and civil servants were only dealt with when it was inevitable. Despite the fact that these three different working groups were governed by very different industrial legislative conditions, the "Betriebsrat" (works council) still pressed for a change in this situation, their objective being to treat all members of staff equally.

"Arbeitskreis Alkohol" (The Alcohol Working Group)

At the beginning of the 1980s an informal working group was set up by the municipality's personnel department. Its members comprise occupational physicians, seasoned civil administrators and the works council. Although highly motivated, the group did not have any special competencies or positive experiences in dealing with problems of alcoholism at work, nor in the development of solutions to the problem. It was only later, when occupational social work insisted on being admitted into the group, that an innovative push was given.

A conference was organized in 1982 in cooperation with internal experts and external educational institutions on the theme "Alcohol at Work." The objective of the conference was to educate employers about alcoholism from different perspectives, and to motivate the municipal government into developing a program on addiction prevention. Social workers and psychologists presented information on the development and possible treatments for alcoholism. Representatives from Alcoholics Anonymous described its program of recovery and successes, while a representative from a German firm that established the first alcohol prevention program in 1975 presented findings on their experiences with a program.

At the initiative of occupational social work, high ranking executive staff and personnel, representatives were invited by the Mayor to attend this conference which lasted several days. The meeting was considered a success and the working group was reformed with new motivated experts and "Betriebsrat" (works council). They started providing counseling services shortly after the conference.

THE DEVELOPMENT OF THE ADDICTS SUPPORT PROGRAM

The objective of the conference was to obtain an internal binding legislation in dealing with high risk and alcoholic employees which would assure equal treatment for all, enabling an analogous application of the differing legal rules concerning civil servants, white collar and blue collar workers, and above all to offer help for both the department and person concerned.

With this sketchy objective, new ground was laid, as up until now there had been no model in Germany which dealt with the special legal peculiarities of the public sector. In a process lasting two years, existing drafts were examined, rejected, and a structure for the program developed step by step. During that period, occupational social work was responsible for supplying expert and therapeutic information, while personnel management and the works council were responsible for the examination and modification of the legal aspects, the realization and the acceptance by upper management. After a number of setbacks, the "Arbeitskreis Alkohol" (Alcohol Working Group) finally drafted a signature ready proposal in 1984, which after a considerable discussion at the executive levels of the city's administration and additional legal examinations, was signed both by the Lord Mayor and the personnel representative's chairman.

The core of the program consisted of a five-step intervention chain which would legally put pressure (in increasing degrees) on an employee who, according to industrial legislation, had violated his duties on account of alcohol consumption. Only when all intervening steps had been taken, offers of assistance rejected, and the violation of duties undeterred, could the employment be terminated.

Program Implementation

It was clear to the members of the "Arbeitskreis Alkohol" (Alcohol Working Group) that the success of the addiction support program depended mainly on the abilities and motivations of those applying it (i.e., the supervisors and management).

Finances were authorized and a concept for an educational offensive, geared at a certain target group, was developed as part of occupational social work's responsibility.

In order to begin the program the following training was provided:

1. A three-day course for high-level executives and personnel representatives led by experts in the field.

2. A three-day course for supervisory staff and middle level management, as well as personnel representatives.
3. A half- or full-day informative meeting within an individual government department for the head of that department, and other interested parties via occupational social work.
4. Two to three hours of information dissemination meetings for all other employees of a government department via occupational social work.
5. Lectures at board and public meetings and press publications on the subject.

The context of the different meetings was information on the origins of alcoholism and the course of the illness, co-alcoholism and ways of dealing with it by supervisors, works council and colleagues.

Continuing education programs were offered by both academic institutions and employer sponsored training. About 7,000 persons participated in these programs between 1984 and 1995.

Preventative measures were labeling foods containing alcohol in the canteen, prohibiting the sale of high alcoholic content drinks, reducing the assortments of wines and beer, as well as improving the assortment of non-alcoholic beverages on sale.

A significant factor was that occupational social work was fully supported by supervisors and management in applying the intervention steps discussed in the proposal. They motivated alcoholics to accept treatment and advised them on work and family related problems. They dealt with all formal requirements set by the social legislation for hospitalized treatment and organized post-therapeutic care. Occasionally occupational social work arranged for alcoholics to go to outpatient counseling centers, involving the patient's personal doctor in the treatment, and referring the patient needing detoxification to a hospital.

The Addiction Support Program's Modification Process

Over the course of time, some limitations of the addiction support program became evident. Occupational social work made a note of the limitations and offered proposals to the "Arbeitskreis Alkohol" (Alcohol Working Group) for formal adoption.

On occupational social work's initiative in 1992 and 1993, two evaluation conferences on the practice of addiction support for executive staff and personnel representatives from the city government were organized.

Participants at the conference confirmed that, on the whole, the program was of high quality, but that a few practical logistical problems had to be corrected. Preventative measures should be given stronger consideration, other forms of addictions should be included and a comprehensive reporting system developed.

During a one-year period of discussion, in a reactivated but renamed "Arbeitskreis Sucht" (Working Group Addictions) committee, a broad revision and an extended addiction support program was drafted. The new program was approved in the Summer of 1995 by the Lord Mayor and staff representative. The new agreement contained more preventative measures and a comprehensive reporting system complementing the modified intervention chain. The "Arbeitskreis Sucht" (Working Group Addictions) was officially introduced with specific duties, thus strengthening occupational social work's complex addiction related work.

The Outcomes

One of the more positive outcomes of the addiction support program is that supervisors found the structured confrontation techniques in dealing with staff members to be quite helpful. That is why the method is also used in other personnel problem areas. The most important element is that this assistance is an effective approach to dealing with other problems. Occupational social work was able to demonstrate its highly professional skills and competencies by participating in the development, implementation and operation of the addiction support program which, in relation to its internal acceptance, had very significant positive effects. Consequently, the management of the Arbeitskreis Sucht (Working Group Addictions) was assigned to occupational social work on a permanent basis.

The occupational social work program was also involved in issues related to other personnel matters such as the development of a women's program and the development of a concept for the improvement of work and health safety. It was also able to gain a regular voice on matters pertaining to leadership with regards to in-house development of educational programs and personnel development.

The quality of the addiction support program extended beyond the city's boundaries and became recognized abroad as well. It became a model for similar programs, not only in other public agencies, but also in private enterprises. Occupational social workers are often invited as guests and speakers in national and international congresses on the theme "Addiction at Work."

EDUCATION AND PROFESSIONAL CULTURE IN OCCUPATIONAL SOCIAL WORK

Each federal state in Germany has sovereignty over its cultural politics, which includes the educational system. This is why there are no unified federal training programs for occupational social work. Basically, social workers in Germany are educated at technical colleges and obtain a degree in

Social Work. As a rule one of the conditions for taking this course is having the "Abitur" (high school graduation). Other technical college degrees are Technology and Architecture. Colleges offering the Social Work degree are financed either by the federal states or by religious organizations. A degree from one of these colleges is classified directly second to a university degree.

Studies at these technical colleges are divided into a basic and a main course of study. They comprise six terms of theory and two terms in practical training. The curriculum for social work in all the federal states is relatively similar.

The aim of the Social Work degree is to teach the ability to professionally handle matters independently in the different fields of social work on the basis of scientific knowledge and methods. The degree should convey scientific knowledge and job related competencies, which would make it possible to describe, analyze and explain real life situations, to develop action plans and be able to reflect on and substantiate personal actions according to theory. The theme of the degree is orientated towards the human being, the primary concern of social work (Alkohol am Arbeitspatz, 1988).

Every technical college offers its students a choice of degree specialization out of a very extensive social work catalogue. The specialization is available only if a minimum of fifteen students have chosen them over an average period of several terms. The contents of the degree, principles, order and planning are all set over a given period by the individual colleges. After a set examination the graduate receives the federally recognized academic grade of "Diplom-Sozialpädagoge" (Graduate Social Pedagogue) or "Diplom-Sozialarbeiter" (Graduate Social Worker).

As the possibilities for work in the occupational social work field are limited, very few universities offer Social Work degrees with an occupational orientation. Emphasis is placed on dealing theoretically with matters regarding social and institutional aspects as well as general conditions, the history of occupational social work, the relevant legal fields in addition to its concepts, self-evidence, skills, crucial areas of work and methodical knowledge. Economic factors have lately gained in importance on account of growing demand.

There is an added necessity in the course to convey the fact that the company and place of work are important factors in influencing human growth and development. Historical and ideological barriers, which go back to the times of national socialism and the occupational social worker's role in it, added to an anti-capitalist residue from the seventies, tend to block an adequate confrontation with these factors.

The technical colleges' training is not sufficient to cover all the requirements needed for successful practice in occupational social work. A few personal qualifications in this field of work are also very important. These include a highly developed social sense, the ability to assert oneself and convince others, integrity, loyalty and the ability to adapt to different working groups and knowledge of hierarchies. Additionally, the ability to work under pressure, to deal with conflicts, and personal maturity is essential. Some companies make it a practice not to employ anybody in an occupational position who is under the age of 30 and/or has not had previous work experience.

THE PROFESSIONAL CULTURE

Despite a long tradition, occupational social work remains on the fringe of social work, and is still viewed suspiciously by colleagues in other branches, unions and work organizations. Its history is marked by an ongoing process of developing a professional profile, and continually defining and explaining public communal social work. This development process was and remains oriented to productivity and working conditions and with it the changes in the structure of communications, the quality of social relationships in companies and work organizations on the one hand, and the services spectrum of the public social sector on the other hand. What is noteworthy is the fact that despite the frequent difficult positions of occupational social workers in companies between the diverging interests of employees, unions and enterprises, the field of social work has been the subject of very little research. In fact, it appears that occupational social work is viewed with marginal importance in the social work literature and social science research.

Occupational social work is practiced in large companies and organizations with an employee-to-social-work ratio of approximately 5,000:1. It is only in the case of much larger enterprises that two or three occupational social workers are employed together. In order to assure professional and personal exchanges on a friendly basis, some regional groups in the more densely populated areas of Germany have joined together and, without any formal organizational structure or association, made it possible to have an exchange of information. Smaller professional meetings are sometimes arranged.

To date, professional associations of social work, unions and other organizations have not succeeded in organizing an association for occupational social workers, educators, counselors, etc. One of the reasons for this may lie in the fact that membership in classic professional associations depends mainly on qualifications such as training or degrees, which do not cover all the different professions involved in workplace practice.

In an answer to this dilemma, and after many preparatory years of work by a group of occupational social workers, the "Arbeitsgemeinschaft Betriebliche Sozialarbeit" (workers community of occupational social work) was founded. The initial members were from Southern Germany, but members from other areas of Germany soon followed.

The main task was to coordinate the many regional initiatives that already existed, to promote the acceptance of occupational social work as a traditional field of practice, and to promote the conceptual development of occupational social work. In assessing this field of practice it became clear that it was necessary:

1. to unify all occupational social workers in a solidarity movement over and above the limits of a place of work;
2. to overcome individualization and competition;
3. to make the professional activities more transparent, based on a company's specific corporate identity;
4. to take responsibility for the professional and political problems of the job; and
5. to have a strategic plan for the further development of occupational social work.

The initiators and leading team members were confronted during the course of their work with more and more challenges, which could not be overcome without a legally binding ruling for this developing association. It was on account of this, that after the necessary preparatory work the Federal Professional Association of Occupational Social Work (FPAOSW) was founded. FPAOSW considers itself to be an association whose prime objective is to develop the field of occupational social work. At the same time, and for the first time in Germany, the founding members of FPAOSW passed a motion on a "Conceptual Framework for the Professional Field of Occupational Social Work" (Bavarian "Rahmenstudiennordnung fur den Fachhochschulstudiengang Soziale Arbeit" of 21st September 1995).

With this proposal FPAOSW had made a first attempt to develop a set of standards of practice. The need for occupational social work was substantiated, opinions expressed on the occupational social worker's position in personnel management in work organizations, the fields of duties outlined, professional qualifications established, and working conditions postulated.

FPAOSW OBJECTIVES

One of the aims of this voluntary society is to support and promote science and research on occupational social work. In Germany, occupational social work has developed to the point where researchers and occupational practitioners must join forces, without prejudices, and come up with general conditions, methods, modes of procedure and aims in occupational social work, in addition to furthering the development of occupational curricula.

Another objective is the improvement of an educational choice for the specific requirements of occupational social work experts. That is why regional and trans-regional courses are being organized. The trans-regional yearly conferences have been organized by "bbs" since 1988. The theme in 1995 was "Costs Analysis and Marketing for Occupational Social Work." In 1996 ethics and total quality management were the two themes.

FPAOSW would like to close the gap in a presently unclear educational system, and develop themes that would be appropriate to the requirements of the different target groups.

One of the desired side effects of these educational programs is to improve communication among occupational social work professionals. In addition, it will be possible to develop consensus and unity in the practice of occupational social workers from one work organization to the other. Occupational social workers in Germany are eager to learn more about this field of practice in other countries. Professional articles are printed both from Germany and abroad in the "FPAOSW Forum" in-house magazine for members in addition to reports on regional activities and projects in occupational social work, opinions and information from the association. In this way "FPAOSW Forum" is a platform for all those who are interested in being conversant with this field of work and enables the general public who are interested in the subject to gain information on occupational social work.

Other FPAOSW objectives are the involvement on panels and in organizations, which are important for the development of this field. FPAOSW is active on political panels and is building up relations on operative levels with different social and health organizations. It also strives to maintain contacts with employers' associations.

In a modern-day Europe that is growing together politically, economically and socially, it is necessary to develop relationships beyond the national borders. In part, this resulted in the establishment of the European Network of Occupational Social Workers (ENOS) consisting of members from all European countries.

VALUES AND ETHICS
IN OCCUPATIONAL SOCIAL WORK

In most enterprises occupational social work services are performed by a single person or small team. The employer seldom gives concrete directives to occupational social workers. This enables an occupational social worker to have a free hand in defining his duties and setting his own criteria in this field, depending on his personal values and psychological or political points of view.

Autonomy, and the ability to make independent decisions, is one of the reasons for the low fluctuation rate in this field. In addition, there is the possibility of further education according to the individual requirements of the job. A special course with a certificate of therapist or supervisor for the therapeutic part of the job may be obtained, which results in an "added market value" in the social work field. Many other possibilities are available for anyone wishing to pursue further training in the organizational part of the job. The occupational social worker is able to take advantage of this wide range of courses, offered far more than in any other field of social work.

Another attraction of this field lies in the fact that occupational social work is generally more independent of hierarchy or official channels and therefore stands outside the usual structure. This requires an enormous amount of sensibility and thought in handling this freedom and in developing relationships with other working partners.

FUTURE PERSPECTIVES AND CHALLENGES

Occupational social work is in a process of continuous change, which is being determined by the economic forces of Germany on one hand and by the general social conditions on the other. Social welfare services have generated much discussion in Germany on account of the financial costs. A new direction is necessary and predominately economic models are gaining ground.

On account of the economic development, both occupational social work and social work in general are in a transitional period in which social services are being examined more than ever with regards to their usefulness in an enterprise. Occupational social work must face the challenges entailed and adjust accordingly. The following are several areas of future development.

Occupational social work must change its understanding of itself. It must see itself, amongst other things, as a manager of complex social processes. The management part of the service must be economically efficient, and must be demonstrated through critical cost analysis.

Occupational social work has to develop marketing strategies in which it can clearly show the profile of its services and prove it can be both internally and externally competitive. One should examine whether the term "social," as part of the company's internal name for the service, is applicable in the present times.

Occupational social work must examine its products with relevance to the company and make itself accessible to new target groups through new products. Feurer (1994) writes:

> Occupational social work contributes largely in companies and public sector organizations towards personnel and organizational development processes. One should especially point out here the new services, such as project management, team development and coaching are being of-

fered. It is in these growing areas of workplace development that occupational social work should market itself to both employers and customers. In large differentiated enterprises and government agencies occupational social work will not always encounter mutual respect and will often evoke rivalry and ostracism. It remains to be seen, whether occupational social work is able to successfully integrate itself with other departments and make use of its own competencies as was the case in company health promotion schemes. Occupational social work plays a role in widening the employees' negotiation scope, uses exemplary situations for improving communications and teamwork, which leads to a contribution in the structure and development of the organization.

Occupational social work must react with flexibility with regards to changes in the organizations of companies and public sector employers. It has become more frequent for work units to be placed elsewhere if not directly necessary for production. Occupational social work must prepare itself to offer its modified product as an external service and obtain the necessary commercial knowledge for this. It has to establish its own specific profile.

Occupational social work must develop professionally based general standards in dealing with science and research, and develop customers for this field on the basis of basic social work qualifications. It must ensure transparency both internally in a company as well as in competition with other companies.

Occupational social work must overcome its singularity and become more accepted from a professional point of view. It must actively engage its enormous potential in outlining social processes, and in finding a solution to the problems in its own field of work. It should not leave the continued development and conceptualization of this field of work for others to decide.

Should occupational social work and its organization succeed in overcoming these challenges and constructively develop solutions to the given problems, it stands a good chance of preparing itself adequately for an increasingly more difficult future. The courses of further education offered by the occupational social work association have been developed accordingly. It is up to the occupational social workers themselves to maintain and develop their profession, to be of value in the private and public sector and, above all, to the working people of Germany.

REFERENCES

Aichberger, Sozialgesetzbuch–Reichsversicherungsordnung, Munich 1995.
Alkohol am Arbeitsplatz, KGSt-Report 8/88, Publisher: Kommunale Gemeinschafttsstelle.
Arbeitsförderungsgesetz, in: Ergänzbare Sammlung Deutscher Gesetze, Neuwied 1992.

Bavarian "Rahmenstudienordnung für den Fachhochschulstudiengang Soziale Arbeit" of 21st September 1995, Munich 1995.

Bundesfachverband Betriebliche Sozialarbeit E.V. (1994) (publisher): Rahmenkonzeption für das Arbeitsfeld Betriebliche Sozialarbeit, Waiblingen.

Bundessozialhilfegesetz (1996) in: Arbeitshandbuch Sozialhilfe der Landeshauptstadt Stuttgart, Stuttgart.

Das Suchtbuch für die Arbeitswelt, Nr. 126 der Schriftenreihe der IG Metall, Frankfurt 1991.

Feurer, A. (1996) Menschen unterstützen Organisationen verändern, in: "Blätter der Wohlfahrtspflege."

Gehlenborg, H. (1994) Neues aus der Betrieblichen Sozialarbeit: Eine Rahmenkonzeption für das Arbeitsfeld, Sozialmagazin.

Googins, B., Reinser, E. and Milton, J. (1986) Industrial social work in Europe. *Employee Assistance Quarterly*, 13 (3), 5-8.

Hauptverband der gewerblichen Berufsgenossenschaften und Deutscher Verkehrsicherheitsrat (1990) (publisher): Alkohol im Betrieb, Bonn.

Kommunale Gemeinschaftsstelle (1988) Alkohol und Arbeitsplatz, KGSt-Bericht, Cologne.

Landeshauptstadt Stuttgart (1995) Dienstvereinbarung Suchtprävention und Suchtkrankenhilfe für die Mitarbeiterinnen und Mitarbeiter der Landeshauptstadt Stuttgart, Stuttgart.

Lau-Villinger, D. (1994) Betriebliche Sozialberatung als Führungsaufgabe, Frankfurt.

Meyers, G. (1990) Taschenlexikon, Mannheim.

"Psychologie Heute" (1996).

Schaarschuch, A. (1995) Einige Gedanken und Thesen zur Situation und Entwicklung der BAG BSA, in bbs-Forum, special edition.

Stahlmann, M. (1994) Lean Organization–Vom Schlankheitsideal zur Magersucht?, Forum Books.

Occupational Social Work in India

H. Y. Siddiqui
Neelam Sukhramani

SUMMARY. This article describes the development and current practices of occupational social workers in India. A review of the industrialization of India and subsequent child labor and worker protection laws that have been instituted is presented. The role and responsibilities of industrial social welfare officers introduced by statute in the 1940s to work settings such as mines, plantations and factories are also explored. The work and influence of the Sri Ram Centre for Industrial Relations in New Delhi and the Bombay Labor Institute in promoting and shaping the tasks of industrial social welfare are examined. Practice models, education and training and future challenges faced by India's occupational social workers are also discussed. *[Article copies available for a fee from The Haworth Document Delivery Service: 1-800-342-9678. E-mail address: <getinfo@haworthpressinc.com> Website: <http://www.HaworthPress.com> © 2001 by The Haworth Press, Inc. All rights reserved.]*

KEYWORDS. Occupational social work in India

THE SOCIETAL AND HISTORICAL CONTEXT OF OCCUPATIONAL SOCIAL WORK IN INDIA

Social work in the workplace has generated a lot of debate among social workers in India. Conceptually, the scope of such work is seen to include

---

H. Y. Siddiqui, PhD, is Professor and Head of the School of Social Work at Jamia Millia Islamia University in New Delhi, India. Neelam Sukhramani, PhD, is Lecturer in Social Work at Jamia Millia Islamia University in New Delhi, India.

[Haworth co-indexing entry note]: "Occupational Social Work in India." Siddiqui, H. Y., and Neelam Sukhramani. Co-published simultaneously in *Employee Assistance Quarterly* (The Haworth Press, Inc.) Vol. 17, No. 1/2, 2001, pp. 43-64; and: *Global Perspectives of Occupational Social Work* (ed: R. Paul Maiden) The Haworth Press, Inc., 2001, pp. 43-64. Single or multiple copies of this article are available for a fee from The Haworth Document Delivery Service [1-800-342-9678, 9:00 a.m. - 5:00 p.m. (EST). E-mail address: getinfo@haworthpressinc.com].

counseling, organization of support groups, concrete services, linking the individual to community services, training and staff development, and providing consulting to workers and management within the context of large-scale industrial or other commercial organizations. The activities a social worker is expected to perform in meeting workers' needs and in particular development needs and combining it with the broader organizational goals generate tension, which is inevitable. The employee welfare and development and corporate profits are two ends of a continuum and may often be difficult to reconcile within a philosophical perspective. It becomes all the more problematic in view of the professional commitment of the worker to the values of social justice. The social worker thus may have to make a conscious choice of being pro-management or pro-worker, though his/her activities may be the same. This has led to a debate among social work educators, in allowing industrial houses to become a major consumer of the products of social work departments.

In India, as well, the term occupational social work can be seen as being synonymous to industrial social work. The domains of industrial social work, however, primarily tend to be the units in the organized sector. While in recent years some non-governmental organizations (NGOs) have taken up issues of workers employed in unorganized sectors, such as the construction industry, carpet-manufacturing units, quarries and agriculture related workplaces, the involvement of trained social workers in these organizations is limited. With the gradual acceptance of this field as a legitimate area of social work practice in India, the involvement of trained social workers is expected to grow.

The continued lack of welfare amenities for agricultural and rural labor is substantial in light of the fact that this was included in the terms of reference of the Committee on Labor Welfare constituted in 1966. The committee recommended the provision of basic minimum welfare amenities such as drinking water facilities, provision of medical and health facilities (including family planning), protective equipment to ensure safety, provision of house sites free of cost and cheap houses on easy installments or houses on nominal rent, free educational facilities for the children of landless labor and rest shelters at their workplace. However, its inability to make any arrangements for ensuring the implementation of these programs, as it did in the case of the industrial sector, has resulted in the present state of affairs.

A similar trend seems to be discernible in the West wherein social work in business and industry is being conceived in the context of large-scale, organized sector, industrial organizations and not in other sectors, e.g., workers in the agriculture and unorganized sector such as cocktail waitresses, waiters, drivers and various other categories of workers in the service industry. In fact, it appears that, in the West, occupational or industrial social work is unknown to most business and industrial organizations, though wherever it is prevalent, it is conceptualized as an activity to meet the needs of workers or union members and the serving of broader organizational goals (Skidmore et al., 1988).

The emergence and acceptance of social work practice in a particular field largely depends on the availability of employers in the area. In India, initially social workers were generally employed in welfare programs of the state or in the private sector, which generally meant business organizations. Social work addressing issues related to work thus has emerged as an area of practice right from the time social work education started in 1936 in India. A large majority of the social workers graduating from schools of social work found employment in industrial units and other large-scale organizations. The prime objective of these social workers was to provide welfare facilities for the employees such as canteen, drinking water, rest rooms, day care facilities, etc. They were also expected to supervise the conditions of work of the employees such as wages, working hours, leaves, social security benefits, etc., and see that various legal requirements were complied with. Later the scope of social work professionals expanded to cover industrial relations and personnel management and more recently human resource management.

These social workers are designated as welfare officers, industrial relations officers/managers, or personnel/human resource managers. Some organizations also employ social workers exclusively to deal with individual employee problems such as absenteeism, drug addiction or alcoholism, etc. This, however, is not the predominant mode of social work practice in the Indian context, in the field of work related issues. "Thus within industrial organizations, a number of trained social workers are working but into departments as diverse as labor welfare, personnel, public relations, etc." (Viswanathan, 1963). These professionals perform a variety of functions. There is no consensus among social workers whether all of these are professional social work functions or some are simply managerial functions. This article will thus attempt to delve into the diversity of functions being performed by social workers in the industrial context.

The industrialization process with the development of the large-scale industries in India commenced from the middle half of the 19th Century (Srivastava, 1954; Bhatnagar, 1984). The industries that came up initially were textiles, coal mining, and railway construction. The pace of industrial progress until the First World War was regarded by many as being slow when compared to the size and population of the country (Srivastava, 1954). The conditions of labor in the early industries were extremely poor, hours of work were excessive, wages were low, working conditions were unhealthy, and the industrial labor drawn from the rural areas was totally unprepared to face the hostile unfamiliar urban milieu (Sinha and Sinha, 1986). Exploitation of child labor and absence of safety measures were common in the factories (Sharma,

1993). According to an ILO report, the hours of work in the textile industry went up to fourteen or fifteen in a day (ILO: New Delhi, 1957).

These conditions coupled with the gradual social awareness in urban industrial centers resulted in labor unrest. The period thereafter saw the passage of the First Factories Act in 1881, which primarily related to the question of child labor and minimum wages. On the face of it, this development may seem as fairly significant and probably instrumental in opening up a path for welfare measures, but the ethos of welfare was yet to get institutionalized in the society. The general status of a person, who had no property and no education, was considered inferior to that of the educated and propertied. The right to full-time paid work was unheard of. The feudal practice of employing successive generations for doing menial labor with no wages was widely practiced and the workers considered themselves lucky on finding full-time paid employment. The employer thought that they were rightful owners of the labor of the working class. The state generally confined itself to ensuring law and order and delivering justice to enforce the contractual obligations. However, even the law was generally interpreted to suit the propertied class. This is substantiated by the fact that although the Fatal Accident Act got passed in 1885 (which required the employer to pay compensation if it was proved in the court of law that the fatal accident was not due to the obvious neglect of the worker), its implementation entailed a number of difficulties to the worker who had suffered on account of the accident. The suit had to be filed in court which meant heavy expenses.

Further, ignorance, helplessness, lack of resources and the unfriendly attitude of some of the judges towards the working class reduced the Act to a paper exercise (Bhatnagar, 1984). Historians have argued that the British government in India had to legislate in favor of Indian workers to appease a section of British industrial interest who felt threatened by the cheap industrial labor particularly engaged in the textile industry.

Nonetheless, a positive outcome of this legislation was a growing consciousness amongst laborers that the existing work situation could undergo a change. Several efforts, consequently, were made to organize the laborers, and demand at various forums for their rights. This did result in the amendment of the factory act. The progress of labor welfare measures, however, was tardy till the end of the First World War. The First World War saw an increase in the number of industries in India and consequently an increase in the labor force. The check on the import of consumer goods during the First World War gave a stimulus to industrial growth (Srivastava, 1954). The industrial working population which stood at 316,816 in 1857 rose to 1,409,173 in 1923. The labor could no longer be neglected. Coupled with this, in the political field the introduction of the Montage Chelmsford Reforms and the incorporation of popular representatives in the central legislature and the governments in the provinces served to bring the various problems of the country to public attention. The other factor which contributed to a greater attention being given to labor welfare after the end of the First World War was a rising consciousness among workers through increased knowledge of general economic conditions and the trade union movement in other countries (ILO: New Delhi, 1957). The establishment of ILO in 1919 also gave an added impetus to labor welfare as it declared that poverty anywhere is a danger to prosperity everywhere. The importance of labor in the economic and social reconstruction of the world was in the process of being recognized (Punekar, 1992). The attendance of workers, employers and government representatives at the ILO meetings and the ratification by the Government of India of many of the International Labor Conventions gave a further impetus to labor legislation in India (Punekar, 1992). Simultaneously the struggle for national emancipation from colonial rule was also gaining momentum and this too seemed to be impacting adoption of labor welfare measures. "The struggle for national independence was influenced by socialist and communist influence generated by the Russian Revolution and came to be closely identified with the interests of the workers and peasants. Industrial workers were organized into trade unions. The organized industrial workers demanded improvement in their working conditions" (Sinha and Sinha, 1986). The birth of the first central trade union organization (All India Trade Union Congress) was recorded in 1920.

All these developments apart from being instrumental in the promulgation of labor legislation such as the Indian Mines Act, 1923, Workmen's Compensation Act, 1923, Maternity Benefit Acts (separate acts in each of the provinces), Indian Factories (Amendment Act, 1922), influenced the appointment of the Royal Commission on Labor in 1929. The Royal Commission on Labor was set up to enquire into and report on the then existing conditions of labor in industrial undertakings, plantations, etc., in British India. The commission made an in-depth survey of different aspects of health, efficiency, welfare, standard of living, and conditions of work, etc. (Sharma, 1993). Most of the suggestions made by the commission found approval with the government and were implemented. The commission can also be seen as the stimulus for the introduction of the labor welfare officers in industrial organizations.

The next significant development came after a decade and a half with the appointment of a Labor Investigation Committee under the chairmanship of D. V. Rege. This committee highlighted the importance of welfare measures for workers in improving their social and economic life. More importantly, it also emphasized the need for strengthening the enforcement machinery for the effective implementation of various laws (Sharma, 1993).

Incorporating the recommendations of the Royal Commission and Rege Committee, the government of Independent India enacted the Factories Act of 1948. What was significant in the Factories Act of 1948 from the standpoint of industrial social work was the introduction of trained social workers in the industrial organizations under the designation of a welfare officer.

THE ROLE OF A WELFARE OFFICER: A HISTORICAL PERSPECTIVE

The institution of "welfare officer," as has been stated above, owes its origin to the recommendation of the Royal Commission on Labor and the support that was given to this recommendation subsequently by the Labor Investigation Committee. The Commission recommended the appointment of labor officers to eliminate evil practices connected with jobbers. They had given considerable importance to the role of this officer and had said:

> He should be subordinate to no one except the general manager of the factory, and should be carefully selected. No employee should be engaged except by the labor officer personally, in consultation with departmental heads, and none should be dismissed without his consent, except by the manager himself, after hearing what the labor officer has to say. It should be the business of labor officer to ensure that no employee is discharged without adequate cause; if he is of the right type, the workers will rapidly learn to place confidence in him and to regard him as their friend. There are many other duties which such an officer can fulfil, particularly in respect of the welfare.

Section 49 (1) and (2) of the Factories Act lays down that:

1. In every factory wherein five hundred or more workers are ordinarily employed the occupier shall employ in the factory such number of welfare officers as may be prescribed.
2. The State Government may prescribe the duties, qualifications and conditions of service of officers employed under subsection (1).

According to section 18 (1) and (2) of the Plantations Labor Act 1951:

1. In every plantation wherein three hundred or more workers are ordinarily employed the employer shall employ such number of welfare officers as may be prescribed.

    The State Government may prescribe the duties, qualifications and conditions of service of officers employed under subsection (1).

In the 1952 Mines Act, this provision has been made under section 58 (q):

> requiring the employment in every mine wherein five hundred or more persons are ordinarily employed, of such number of welfare officers as may be specified and for prescribing the qualifications and the terms and conditions of, and the duties to be performed by, such welfare officers. (Government of India, 1969)

As regards the qualifications, duties, conditions of employment, etc., the respective Acts provide that the State Governments would frame necessary rules therefore. Accordingly, Model Rules were framed under these three central Acts.

DUTIES OF THE WELFARE OFFICER

The Model Rules framed under the Factories Act, 1948, to provide for the appointment of a welfare officer, had laid down a chart of duties for the welfare officers.

These duties were:

1. *Supervision of:*
    i. safety, health and welfare programs like housing, recreation, sanitation services as provided under law or otherwise,
    ii. working of joint committees,
    iii. grant of leave with wages as provided, and
    vi. redress of workers' grievances;

2. *Counseling to workers in:*
    i. personal and family problems,
    ii. adjusting to work environment, and
    iii. understanding rights and privileges;

3. *Advisory to management in:*
    i. formulating labor and welfare policies,
    ii. apprenticeship training programs,
    iii. meeting statutory obligation to workers,
    iv. developing fringe benefits, and
    v. workers' education and use of communication media;

4. *Liaison with workers:*
    i. to understand various limitations under which they work,
    ii. to appreciate the need of harmonious industrial relations in the plant,
    iii. to interpret company policies to, and
    iv. to persuade workers to come to a settlement in case of a dispute;

5. *Liaison with management:*
    i. to appreciate workers' viewpoint to various matters in the plant,
    ii. to intervene on behalf of workers in matter under consideration of the management,
    iii. to help different departmental heads to meet their obligations under the Act,
    iv. to maintain harmonious industrial relations in the plant, and
    v. to suggest measures for promoting general well-being of workers;

6. *Liaison with workers and management:*
    i. to maintain harmonious industrial relations in the plant,
    ii. for prompt redress of grievances and quick settlement of disputes, and
    iii. to improve productive efficiency of the enterprise;

7. *Liaison with outside agencies:*
    i. factory inspectors, medical officers, other inspectors for securing proper enforcement of various Acts as applicable to the plant, and
    ii. other agencies in the community with a view to help workers to make use of community services (Government of India, 1969).

The role of the welfare officer was thus intended as a person concerned about the implementation of labor laws, proper working conditions, harmonious labor relations, industrial peace, plan productivity and workers' well-being. He was thus expected to act as an advisor, counselor, and mediator and liaison man both to management and labor. In mining establishments, too, he was expected to perform similar functions. It is claimed that in practice, however, none of the welfare officers have either been permitted to perform the functions for which this officer was conceived or have not been able to perform these functions by themselves without any hindrance whatsoever from the workers' side or from the management. This institution has been for some time past the bone of contention, though for different reasons, for the employers as well as for the trade unions. The Committee on Labor Welfare appointed by the Government of India in 1966 thought it appropriate to solicit the opinion of various parties, including State Governments, Public Sector agencies, private employers' organizations, workers' organizations and eminent persons in the field of labor relations on the role and status of welfare officer. The question posed by the Committee was, whether the welfare officer should be statutorily protected and whether he should deal with personnel matters ordinarily, unless the establishment was too small to have a separate personnel officer.

VIEWS OF THE PARTIES

The State Governments by and large stated that the institution of welfare officers should be reoriented keeping in view the job, status, salary of the post, and powers which were essential for the utility of the officer. It was also suggested that welfare officers should be appointed by the Government and that employers should deposit their pay and allowances with the Government. Further, functions should be supervised by the State Labor Department to whom they would report and they should not be allowed to represent employers in disputes. Personnel and welfare functions should be clearly defined and assigned to different officers. In order to be effective the welfare officer should enjoy the confidence of both the employers and the workers. He should not ordinarily be given personnel work. His main job should be to work as a liaison between the workers and the employer. Employers should be prevailed upon to change their outlook in regard to the functions of the welfare officer, as otherwise there was little hope that the situation could be improved by any legislation (Government of India, 1969).

The public undertakings felt that welfare officers should be part and parcel of the Personnel Department. Besides being conducive to their advancement this will also lead to better results. Statutory protection is not necessary for the officer to function effectively if he knows how to do his job tactfully. To be effective a welfare officer should necessarily enjoy the confidence of his employer and equally so of the workers. Statutory protection was not desirable and he should not handle the personnel matters. Some of the public sector undertakings, however, emphasized the fact that it was difficult to draw a line between personnel functions and matters pertaining to welfare of workers. To be functionally effective the welfare officer should also deal with personnel matters. Some also said that statutory protection should be made available to the welfare officer; otherwise, he would become a tool in the hands of management which would go against the interest of the workers. In small establishments the welfare officers should be given statutory protection in regard to their emoluments, status and conditions of service so that they may be able to discharge their functions effectively and at the same time command confidence both of employers and workers (Government of India, 1969).

The Central Employers' Organizations said that compulsory appointment of welfare officers by law should be done away with. They should not be given any statutory protection, as their effectiveness would depend upon their ability and the confidence that they create in the employer and the workers. A welfare officer should not be statutorily protected because such protection would encourage a tendency to adopt the role of an outside authority. It was also suggested that there should be one officer to look after the welfare and personnel functions as these functions in an organization were indivisible, more so in case of smaller units.

The workers' organizations, in particular, maintained that unless there was a radical change in the duties, responsibilities and status of the welfare officer, he was not serving any useful purpose. It was necessary that he should be statutorily protected, should not perform the duties of a personnel officer and should not be under the control of factory management. It was also suggested that smaller units, which had limited numbers of employees, should be grouped together and one welfare officer should be appointed to look after the welfare amenities in such units. There should be a Central or State cadre of welfare officers, which should be responsible to the Government (Government of India, 1969).

RECOMMENDATIONS AND VIEWS OF THE SRI RAM CENTRE FOR INDUSTRIAL RELATIONS

Sri Ram Centre for Industrial Relations, New Delhi, on behalf of the committee, went into great detail on the genesis, role functions and training of the welfare officer. Some of the recommendations which the Centre arrived at after taking into consideration all the pros and cons of the utility, need, role and status and the terms and conditions of the welfare officer were as follows:

i. The appointment of a labor welfare officer should continue to be a statutory requirement in factories, mines and plantations.
ii. For employment in factories or mines a labor welfare officer should have a Master's degree or equivalent diploma from a "recognized" school of social work/labor institute/Department of Labor and Social Welfare and should have a working knowledge of the language of the region in which employment is sought.
iii. Labor welfare officer training courses run by several States and Labor Commissioners' Examinations to qualify for the job of labor welfare officer should be scrapped.
iv. The "neutral" or "buffer" role currently assigned to the labor welfare officer should be modified. Sections 49 and 58 of the Factories Act and the Mines Act respectively, and the rules framed thereunder should be amended to require the labor welfare officer to function as a part of and on behalf of the management. He should be entitled only to such protection as was available to other management functionaries in the enterprise. His employment should be a subject matter of bargaining and individual contract. As such any provisions relating to his status and salary should be abolished (Government of India, 1969).

The few available studies on the subject supported the general view that labor welfare officers were not able to discharge functions assigned to them. Most of these officers were not given the role and status envisaged for them by the State. In many companies, they were essentially the supervisors of various welfare programs for workers. In other cases, they were also associated with recruitment, wage and salary administration, grievances handling, conducting enquiries, etc. The cases where they played an effective role in the formulation of personnel policies were very few. There were several reasons for the deviation of the practice from the norms set by the statutes. First, many employers felt that the statutory basis of the labor welfare officer was an infringement of their rights. The feeling was all the more acute as employers were not even free to either assign duties to the labor welfare officer or to treat him like other officers. In the final analysis, an officer cannot be more effective than permitted. Management's cooperation was a sine-qua-non for the effective functioning of the labor welfare officer. The committee therefore felt that whereas the statutory obligation to employ labor welfare officers should continue to exist, the companies should be given freedom to mould officers according to their own needs, provided the basic requirements regarding welfare functions continue to be met in the enterprise. There is no denying the fact that in the context of the total industrial picture in the country, labor welfare symbolizes personnel management field.

STUDY BY THE BOMBAY LABOR INSTITUTE

The Bombay Labor Institute of the Government of Maharashtra also conducted a study of "Labor Welfare" and "Welfare Officer" in Indian Industry, in 1966. The study stated that various viewpoints exist regarding the role of "Welfare Officer" in Indian Industry.

"Some look upon him as 'Staff Advisor,' while others think of him as a 'Buffer Zone' between labor and management. The 'Third Force' theory was also popular among certain sections, while some professionals emphasized his 'Nonaligned' role. Schools of Social Work, which conduct the professional training program for this cadre, however, favored his role as a 'Social Worker in Industry.' In its view, in practice, the role of Welfare Officer at least in part resembles that of a staff specialist having no independent power and authority in the line of organization. He does not make the policy, but all the same he can contribute to it, and this may not add to his popularity but it surely adds to his value. As an advisor he has the responsibility of giving conscious advice, whether it is palatable or not, while as a functionary in the organization he has to implement some of the management's decision" (Government of India, 1969).

The professional social work training institutes felt that the welfare officer plays the role of a social worker in the industry. They were of the view that the labor officer must be seen as a social institution of a professional character, designed to deal with problems of relationship in industry. It was, in essence, problem solving within industry. It is clear from the qualifications and requirements of these officers that they are intended to inculcate the social work attitude and discipline. What is required in the present circumstances is a clear understanding of social work in industry and the place of the welfare officer in the context of duties laid down under the relevant rules. It is felt that in the role of welfare officer, there is a strange admixture of social work orientation and business orientation. The personnel officer is employed by a private firm with the understanding that his orientation would be a business one rather than a social one, and the welfare officer, originally intended to have a social work orientation, will function as a personnel officer. There is a conflict of objectives in orientation itself, i.e., between welfare work as an enabling function and personnel welfare work as a disciplinary function. According to an American expert, "We in the United States would never think of trying to combine them (welfare and personnel works) in one and the same person, because the job to be done in either case, is so big a job that one person simply cannot do both; certainly one person cannot do justice to both, besides, neither of the personnel management or industrial relations functions is labor welfare to his social work way of thinking" (Government of India, 1969).

According to a paper submitted by Professor Kudchedkar in a conference of Schools of Social Work in India, held in Varanasi in 1964, "Even among enlightened employers and progressive industrialists, the institution of industrial jurisprudence sometimes is the negation of the labor welfare philosophy and social work practice" (Government of India, 1969).

VIEWS OF THE WELFARE OFFICERS' ASSOCIATION AND OTHER PARTIES

In their written replies submitted to the Committee as well as in the oral evidence tendered before it, some of the associations of welfare officers demanded that they should be made part and parcel of the personnel departments of establishments in which they serve. There was a feeling that if the welfare officer was not given personnel duties, he would be isolated as there was no cadre structure to offer any avenue for promotion to the welfare officer.

The Committee noted that there are three things if they are to work happily and efficiently, namely, the economic satisfaction of a reasonable livelihood, the social satisfaction of working together as members of a group, and the individual satisfaction of doing a job well. The concept of personnel management, though of comparatively recent growth, is the child of scientific management and the awakened sense of social responsibility evidenced in the countries of the West at the end of the 19th Century. The term "Personnel Management," which originated in America, can be taken as synonymous with such functions as labor welfare or labor-management, personnel or staff management, industrial relations or human relations in industry. The actual title is of little significance if the job done is the same (Government of India, 1969).

The functions of the welfare officer have already been dovetailed with the Personnel Department. There are a large number of welfare-cum-personnel officers who are further divided into two categories, "those looking after welfare functions and some personnel functions and the other looking mainly after personnel functions including functions relating to disciplinary action against the workers, etc. These officers are interchangeable. This not only gives strength and status to the welfare officer but also ensures for him a better prospect in the course of time and, at the same time, enables the employers to fulfil the purpose of law, that is, to appoint an officer to look after the implementation of welfare facilities and other allied welfare problems" (Government of India, 1969).

The Committee thus recommended for the appointment of a welfare officer in factories, mines and plantations, to ensure that the management appointed a person exclusively to look after welfare needs of their workers and also to help them in discharging their statutory obligations for implementation of statutory welfare measures. The Committee felt that with the growing realization of the need, place and role of welfare amenities, not only in the maintenance of industrial relations but also in the enhancement of the productive capacity of a worker, by the employers themselves, it was not necessary to appoint a welfare officer solely for the purposes of looking after welfare activities. Such officer, it felt, can be part and parcel of the Personnel Department of the management. However, in order to ensure that the welfare amenities, statutory or otherwise, were provided and organized properly, the Committee recommended that the management should designate one of the existing officers of their Personnel Department as welfare officer to fulfil the purpose of the law. The Committee further recommended that the management should ensure that only such officers of the Personnel Department were designated to look after the welfare activities who were properly qualified to hold these posts and have an aptitude for welfare work (Government of India, 1969).

It was gradually realized that the labor welfare officers found it difficult to perform direct practice functions within the industry. It was felt that their services need to be supplemented with those of full-time social workers. While few organizations supported the latter concept, a large number still adhered to what had been imposed statutorily. The nature of social work practice within a particular organization was thus determined by the nature of its management philosophy.

NATURE OF OCCUPATIONAL/ INDUSTRIAL SOCIAL WORK PRACTICE

There are primarily two models of service delivery visible in the practice of industrial social work in India: institutional and community based. While the former entails work within the confines of the industrial organization the latter locates the social worker in colonies inhabited by the industrial work force. An underlying phenomenon visible in both the models is the absence of a collaborating effort between different organizations. Each organization establishes its own set-up for providing welfare services for its employees. This is significant since many organizations are unable to set up separate departments for social work on account of the cost entailed in establishing a separate set-up.

With a view to describe the nature of industrial social work practice in India it may be relevant to describe the work by the social workers within the context of these models, the nature of issues and problems addressed, the unit of work (employee/family/community) and the relative application of the various methods of social work practice.

MODEL A: INSTITUTIONAL

Within the institutional model, a distinction can be made to understand the nature of work undertaken by the welfare officer, who is a trained social worker but primarily deals with labor welfare functions, the work of human resource development personnel and that of a social worker who is recruited for the purpose of social service delivery functions within the organization. The nature of these roles is briefly outlined here.

Statutory Welfare Functions

The labor welfare officer has a long list of welfare functions which the law expects him (very seldom her, as the area has been overly male dominated as is the case with the entire factory management) to perform. The officer has to address and assist the factory management in the fulfillment of their obligations under the Factories Act of 1948, which includes provisions relating to health, safety and welfare, working hours and conditions of work, leave and related matters and other amenities such as the benevolent scheme payments, pension, gratuity payment and superannuation funds, etc. Certain non-statutory welfare duties regarding the provision of food (canteen), sanitation, housing, education of children, social and recreational facilities, employee counseling for individual personal problems also fall within his purview. He is also expected to look after certain committees for production, safety first, welfare and cooperative societies and supervise their work. Further, he is supposed to initiate measures to raise the living standards of workers and in general promote their well-being (Mhetras, 1990).

Non-Statutory Welfare Functions

Professional full-time social workers designated as social workers to provide social work services in industry are, generally, also located in welfare centers established for the employees within their premises. Such welfare centers are used for medical checkups for the employees, educational benefits for their children and certain other fringe benefits. The social workers are expected to deal with employees who have been referred to them for having problems such as chronic absenteeism and other behavioral problems. Some problems most often encountered are addictions, chronic physiological ailments, familial problems and psychological ailments. Other problems may include job satisfaction, demotion and down-grading, disappointment and frustration over lack of advancement in the company, and disturbance or breakdown in relations with fellow employees and/or with the supervisor. Self-referrals are limited but not totally absent.

The intervention strategy primarily used by the social workers is counseling. The problem of alcohol addiction being fairly high, social workers have at times started therapy groups within the company. Referrals are used to ensure long-term treatment and follow-up by other welfare organizations outside the workplace. Apart from addressing the present organizational needs, social workers have in some cases started preventive strategies. In Mahindra and Mahindra (Automotive Division), Bombay, for example, absenteeism as well as other work-related problems were on the rise on account of diabetes. The situation was getting worse due to the poor information base, neglect of the disease in the initial stages, lack of regular treatment and follow-up, etc. The social worker developed a three-phased program to deal with the problem. In the first phase an exhibition was organized in the workers' canteen, exhibiting the various aspects of diabetes such as the nature of the disease, the causes, who could be more prone to it, and complications of disease if left unattended. The exhibition also provided an opportunity for employees to register themselves for undergoing the diabetes detection test. The second phase involved the detection tests, which were coordinated by the social worker. Adequate medical facilities at the welfare center were provided as a follow-up to individuals having tested positive for diabetes in the third phase.

Human Resource Development Functions

Within the institutional setting human resource development is yet another area of social work practice as well. It is of more recent origin. The need to help the employee to improve his overall skills to increase his productivity and chances for his own career advancement led to the establishment of training and development departments in the large-scale organizations, in particular. Training and development programs are thus becoming a priority area in the new approach to human resource planning. Group counseling as an activity as part of staff development programs is also gaining ground. Social workers are being employed to carry out the process of assessment of training needs, and thereafter to develop, conduct and evaluate the training programs. The human resource development personnel are located either in the Personnel Department or have a separate identity of their own. The status of human resource development functions is higher than welfare and on par with personnel and industrial relations.

MODEL B: COMMUNITY BASED

Industrialization has led to a large-scale migration of families from the rural areas to the urban areas, as pointed out earlier. These families generally settled down in as close an area as possible to their workplace. Initially, these were unauthorized slums. Gradually these very colonies got authorized and thus most often resulted in a majority of the employees of one company staying together. Some organizations have developed their own colonies for their employees. Thus, to begin with when the concept of social work in the industry was catching up, some social workers were located in the colonies of the employees. The objective was to look into the overall development of the family instead of the individual employee in isolation. Recreational-cum-educational programs for the community as a whole were also organized by the social worker. But the concept of employee colonies has become redundant in recent times, particularly in large cities, on account of growing pressures on urban land. Where employee colonies are still in existence, the social workers in some cases have a community base.

In some cases the social worker is employed as a community worker, in communities which the organization may have adopted as part of their social commitment. This kind of community work is done under the scheme of social responsibility of the industry. The industrial and business houses are encouraged to undertake programs in the backward areas. They are given some tax relief to carry out these programs. These communities are generally different from the workers' colonies. Generally it may be a slum or a nearby rural area. The worker may undertake a variety of activities including education, health, women's development programs, housing, awareness generation around population problems, AIDS, drug abuse or alcoholism, etc.

ORGANIZATIONAL LOCALITY AND ITS IMPLICATIONS

The social worker and the welfare officer are generally part of the Personnel Department. The social worker may report to the welfare officer or the personnel officer. In some organizations where there is more than one officer dealing independently with Personnel, Industrial Relations and Labor Welfare, the personnel manager is generally placed higher than the other two. This trend results in the relegation of welfare functions to a junior officer (Kudchedkar, 1990).

Thus, organizational structure indicates the low priority placed on welfare functions and still lower on social work functions. This naturally affects the investment of resources for the same. Secondly, lack of autonomy also distorts the role of the social worker and the welfare officer. The decisions about their professional roles are often made by people who may not be fully versed in social work philosophy and its objectives.

On the other hand, whenever social workers are employed as human resource managers, they are on par with the personnel manager even though they may be part of a separate department.

EDUCATION AND TRAINING FOR OCCUPATIONAL SOCIAL WORK

Social work education in India started in the second quarter of the present century as pointed out earlier. From the inception the courses were organized to cater to the needs of different fields of practice. This led to development of field specialization courses in social work education. One of the fields for which the professional workers were prepared was labor welfare. Since the field provided a maximum number of well-paying jobs, a large number of students opted for labor welfare as a specialization. The experience of these professionals soon indicated that they were catering to the managerial needs of the organization rather than dealing with workers' issues and problems. This led to a major controversy in social work education. Later with the emergence of a developmental perspective in social work and the consequent demand for a generic course, field specialization was questioned. In particular, labor welfare was considered as falling outside the scope of social work practice by a section of social work educators. In practice, two trends are discernible. Some schools have developed separate courses in industrial relations and personnel management/human resource management, while others are still offering specialization in some fields including industrial relations and personnel management.

It is relevant to point out that wherever separate courses have been developed, there is a drastic reduction in the core social work content. The thrust of the exclusive courses on human resource management is to prepare professionals for managerial roles rather than human service. The fact that the schools of social work offer a specialization in personnel management and industrial relations and not in industrial social work is reflective of the low priority of welfare functions in industry. Very few social work schools offer fieldwork placements in the social work departments/counseling centers of industries. Research in this field is also fairly limited.

ISSUES IN CURRENT PRACTICE AND FUTURE DIRECTIONS OF OCCUPATIONAL SOCIAL WORK

Even after half a century of acceptance of the suitability of trained social workers to deal with the work related issues within the industry, the debate continues: "Is there a place for social work in industry?" The sentiments expressed in an article in the sixties are reiterated even now.

Viswanathan in his paper "Social Work in Industry" in 1963 had debated the issue: "It seems there are at least two opposing ideological standpoints, which are prevalent. On the one hand, there are some social work educators and practitioners who maintain that industrial social work is a farce. The value orientation of social work is that the resources of society must be used to bring about maximum opportunities for the individual, whereas that of industry is primarily profit, and hence the values of social work and industry are incompatible. On the other hand, there are those who feel that there need not be any inherent contradictions or conflicts in the goals of industry and social work; in fact, some of the best social services have been organized by industry. The alliance of social work and industry might represent humanitarianism at its best. Social work and industry are both institutions of society. They derive support from each other. The emerging concept of social work in industry refers to the reciprocity of objectives" (Viswanathan, 1963).

In 1993 Sharma noted, "The threat to the profession of a social worker in an industry lies in the fact that he/she operates in a secondary setting, having welfare oriented functions which are not associated with the profit making goal of the industry. Moreover, a social worker is concerned with intangible and non-quantifiable services unlike other functions in the organization . . ." (Sharma, 1993). However, the employers seem to be in no doubt about the suitability of social work professionals as the continuing demand for trained social work personnel indicates.

One of the major issues, however, remains the balancing of the welfare functions with that of the managerial functions. The reasons for this are partly structural and partly individual in nature. In some industries the managers have a large discretion to allocate resources to the welfare activities, particularly where they follow a human relations approach to industrial relations. In such a case according a low status to welfare is an individual failing. However, in industries that still follow a traditional nonprofessional approach to human resource management, the lack of resource becomes structural in nature. The social workers employed in helping roles outside the cadre of management professionals, however, are given a lower status in the organizations. The career advancement opportunities for such professionals are also limited and are far inferior to those in the management cadre. The social workers thus are unwilling to accept helping roles within the industrial organizations.

The more important issue for social work practice in industry will arise on account of the process of globalization of the economy. These developments will have a vital impact on the policies and practices of the large-scale organizations. The very approaches being followed to deal with work related issues will undergo major changes. The very context of human resource management will change. This may perhaps introduce more individual related activities as opposed to the primary focus on industrial relations related issues. The community focus is already on the way out as far as the employee related activities are concerned. Yet the possibility of social work in industry developing a different character in the future and more broadly the possibility of occupational social work developing into a separate area of specialization is rather remote.

Occupational social work as an area of social work practice is expected to address issues related to workers. But so far it has largely catered to workers in large-scale organizations only. The National Committee on Labor Welfare has made some specific recommendations for extending welfare facilities in the small-scale and cottage industries. Over the years some of these recommendations have been implemented by the Government but social workers have by and large not found any role viz-à-viz these schemes. The Committee has also paid some attention to agricultural and other workers in the rural areas, but besides fixing of minimum wage levels not much has been done. Enforcing the minimum wage legislative provisions in rural areas is still a major problem affecting millions of workers. Only some non-governmental organizations (NGOs) are active in this area, but trained social workers have not found this as a potential field of employment.

CONCLUSIONS

Social work interventions in dealing with issues in a practice area inevitably reflect the predominant social policy model in a society. In the United States in particular and in developed nations in general, the social work interventions have focussed on the psychosocial correlates of individual behavior in different contexts. Hence, occupational social work explained problems of absenteeism, alcoholism and other forms of deviance as largely individual problems. The consequent modes of intervention assumed a therapeutic role.

In the context of developed nations, the existence of an institutionalized model of welfare, coupled with greater freedom to employers to hire and fire, a weak labor movement and a bureaucracy and judiciary which believed in enforcing the law of the land, created a work environment where production, work ethics and costs of production predominated. The definition of industrial social work therefore explicitly included "the serving of broader organizational goals of the setting" (Government of India, 1980). The problems of workers thus were defined as problems of individual maladjustment to be dealt with by therapeutic interventions by the helping professions. The organizations were willing to invest in helping the workers if this reduced the cost of absenteeism and related costs of health and other related services. Social workers were not involved in managerial roles.

Industrial social work in India right from its inception got institutionalized as part of the management system, due to historical reasons. The majority of social workers began their careers as middle-level executive employees. The professional identity of these workers is directed more by their job description than their professional education. Their power grew as they exhibited skills in managing large-scale organizations employing thousands of workers. Their managerial roles helped them acquire a very prominent place in the organizational management. Specialized management education in India developed in late 60s and early 70s. It has recently acquired greater prominence with the opening up of the economy. However, the management courses focussed on training personnel in the area of marketing, finance and production and to a lesser extent in managing personnel. There is a general feeling, since no studies have been conducted, that social workers are more effective in personnel management, as they possess better professional skills in human relations.

The work environment in India thus was and is tailor-made for social work professionals. Management needs a professional who could serve its interest yet possesses the skills to develop linkages with workers and union leaders. Further, he is also expected to deal with the bureaucracy to satisfy legal requirements. The growing militancy of workers' unions and state patronage of workers made the management dependent on the skills of the social work managers. The social workers thus dealt with policy matters and dealt with shop floor problems, too. They made important contributions in developing welfare policies but found little time to look into individual problems. The organizational priorities including those of unions pushed individual problems such as alcoholism and absenteeism to the bottom of the social service programs. It is equally interesting to note that mental health issues, work strain, divorce or family and marriage related problems are fairly infrequent in the Indian context at the worker level. Further, there are indigenous mechanisms in the form of family support groups, neighborhood groups and community pressure groups, which generally take care of these issues. The workers generally do not feel the need for professional helpers. The income stability, job security and improvement of general standards of living still dominate the workplace agenda, in the case of industrial workers. Thus, it seems, industrial social work in India will continue to be management oriented. The management orientation of industrial social work has given it the prime status among the social work professionals in the market. The current thrust on training and human resource development in the large-scale organizations has further strengthened the social workers' role. Designing training programs and improving the social functioning competence of employees and their productivity related skills within the work setting has opened up new challenges for social work professionals.

The demand for industrial managerial social workers is thus likely to grow unabated in India. The predominance of management orientation may at times act as a negative factor in developing welfare services for the workers. The social workers employed in helping roles outside the cadre of management professionals are given a lower status in the organizations. The career advancement opportunities for such professionals are also limited and are far inferior to those in the management cadre. The social workers thus are unwilling to accept helping roles within the industrial organizations.

However, it is interesting to note that in the United States in the late 70s a conference of industrial social work practitioners noted, that the future is promising for the growth and expansion of industrial social work practice. Social work is uniquely suited to the industrial setting, given the profession's commitment to a "social functioning," as opposed to the illness approach common to other helping professions. It was noted that "social work as a profession holds a dual commitment to social service and social change, which best meet the multifaceted interests of trade unions and employer sponsorship" (Akabas et al., 1979).

Around the same time in India a national committee appointed to review social work education in the country noted, "It is important to note that an inquiry into the causes of poverty and the evolution of measures for its elimination was the responsibility of social work. Unfortunately (both in India as well as elsewhere) this emphasis was lost sight of in the early stages of the growth of the profession. It took up the cause of assisting people in their adjustment to an industrial, urban and metropolis dominated social milieu rather than identifying the causes of poverty and working for its removal" (Government of India, 1980).

The Committee also pointed out that though the schools of social work have started to conceptually accept that the profession's main concern would have to be social change for the removal of poverty, in practice they have not achieved much. The concern for mass poverty still is a major theme in debates on the scope of social work practice in India. Schools, however, differ in their response to the need for such changes in their curricula. However, now that social policy perspectives are undergoing a major change, though its direction is not very clear, social work practice may undergo a change as well. If the management in industry acquires the power to hire and fire, the labor movement will be weakened. Such changes are likely to influence the practice of social work in industry.

REFERENCES

Akabas, S.H., Kurzman, P.A. & Kolben, N.S. (eds.). (1979). *Labor and Industrial Settings.* New York: Columbia University School of Social Work, Hunter College School of Social Work, Council on Social Work Education, National Association of Social Workers, p. 5.

Government of India (1969). *Report of the Committee on Labor Welfare.* New Delhi.

Government of India (1980). *Review of Social Work Education in India Retrospect and Prospect.* New Delhi: University Grants Commission.

International Labor Office (1957). *Labor Legislation in India.* New Delhi: ILO.

Kudchedkar, L.S. (1990). *Emerging Trends in Personnel Management.* Bombay: Tata Institute of Social Sciences.

Mhetras, V.G. (1966). *Labor Welfare and the Welfare Officer in Indian Industry.* Bombay: Bombay Labor Institute.

Punekar, S.D. et al. (1992). *Labor Welfare Trade Unions and Industrial Relations.* Bombay: Himalaya Publishing House.

Sharma, A.M. (1993). *Aspects of Labor Welfare and Social Security.* Bombay: Himalaya Publishing House.

Sinha, G.P. & Sinha, P.R.N. (1986). *Industrial Relations and Labor Legislation.* New Delhi: Oxford and IBM Publishing Co. Pty. Ltd.

Skidmore, R.A., Thackeray, M.G. & Farley, O.W. (1988). *Introduction to Social Work.* New Jersey: Prentice Hall.

Srivastava, K.N. (1954). *Industrial Peace and Labor in India.* Allahabad: Kitab Mahal. Also see, Bhatnagar, D. (1984). *Labor Welfare and Social Security Legislation in India.* New Delhi: Deep and Deep Publications.

Viswanathan, N. (1963). Social Work in Industry in *Indian Journal of Social Work,* 24 (2), p. 63.

Occupational Social Work in Ireland

Maria A. G. Powell

SUMMARY. This article describes the development and current practices of occupational social work in Ireland. The author traces the origins of social work practice in the Irish workplace, the impact of the human relations movement on early industrial social work and the reemergence of occupational social welfare services. An analysis of Irish occupational welfare programs and recently emerging employee assistance programs is also presented. The article concludes with a discussion of the future of occupational social work in Ireland and the impetus European Community Directives are expected to have on improving and developing the health and welfare of employees in Ireland. *[Article copies available for a fee from The Haworth Document Delivery Service: 1-800-342-9678. E-mail address: <getinfo@haworthpressinc.com> Website: <http://www.HaworthPress.com> © 2001 by The Haworth Press, Inc. All rights reserved.]*

KEYWORDS. Occupational social work in Ireland

THE SOCIETAL AND HISTORICAL CONTEXT OF OCCUPATIONAL SOCIAL WORK IN IRELAND

Occupational social work (OSW) services in Ireland need to be considered in the social and political environment in which they operate. The island has a total population of approximately five million people. Of these, 1.5 million

---

Maria A. G. Powell, MSoc.Sc., is an Occupational Social Worker and is completing her doctoral degree at the University of Dublin, Ireland.

[Haworth co-indexing entry note]: "Occupational Social Work in Ireland." Powell, Maria A. G. Co-published simultaneously in *Employee Assistance Quarterly* (The Haworth Press, Inc.) Vol. 17, No. 1/2, 2001, pp. 65-79; and: *Global Perspectives of Occupational Social Work* (ed: R. Paul Maiden) The Haworth Press, Inc., 2001, pp. 65-79. Single or multiple copies of this article are available for a fee from The Haworth Document Delivery Service [1-800-342-9678, 9:00 a.m. - 5:00 p.m. (EST). E-mail address: getinfo@haworthpressinc.com].

live in Northern Ireland which is part of the United Kingdom, while 3.5 million live in the Republic of Ireland. This article will focus on the latter population which is mainly concentrated in cities such as Dublin (population 1.5 million), Cork (population 150,000), and Galway (population 100,000). Occupational social work services have largely evolved in these urban areas with densest employment. They operate within a social system which provides a comprehensive health care service which entitles persons to public hospital services irrespective of income, and a social welfare system which requires employers and employees to contribute towards insurance cover for certain types of benefits such as unemployment benefits, disability benefits, and pension provisions. In addition to the statutory social insurance benefit scheme for the employed and self-employed, there is a supplementary social assistance scheme which provides income maintenance in the form of assistance allowances for the non-insured and their families. Although the economy of the Republic of Ireland has been buoyant in recent years (rate of inflation less than 3% since 1993, current rate of inflation 1.5%), there is still a high rate of unemployment (11.9% of the workforce). Along with many developed western European societies, the social problems associated with high unemployment combined with the consequences of marital breakdown on the family unit, drug addiction in the young, and child sexual abuse present ongoing pressing issues in Irish society. They pose major challenges for social policy decision-makers, in terms of ensuring availability of adequate levels of health and the social services provision needed to address them.

In the context of this social and political environment, OSW has grown and developed from the early part of the 20th Century. This article provides a review of the origins of OSW in Ireland of the present models of service delivery, and some of the clinical issues practitioners are likely to encounter. Finally, the future directions of practice are discussed as well as the major challenges occupational social workers are likely to encounter as we enter the 21st Century.

ORIGINS OF OCCUPATIONAL SOCIAL WORK IN IRELAND

The concept of Industrial Social Work, as it was initially coined, originated in the early 1900s during the Welfare Movement. The ideology behind this movement which came to be known as welfare capitalism refers to a system of benefits and services voluntarily provided by employers in an effort to socialize an unskilled and badly needed workforce at a time of rapid industrialization (Brandes, 1970). Similarly, in Ireland "the welfare phase refers to a series of voluntary initiatives undertaken in certain companies to improve the conditions of factory workers, particularly in relation to pay, working hours and health and safety provisions" (Gunnigle and Flood, 1990). Some progressive employers influenced by humanitarian ideals and religious beliefs undertook to improve working conditions and to create a more humane working environment for employees. One component of this initiative was the employment of welfare officers, although this was generally restricted to a few large employers in major cities (Gunnigle and Flood, 1990). Miss Violet Sargent was probably the first to be employed in Ireland in this capacity by Messrs. W. & R. Jacobs, the Dublin biscuit manufacturers in 1912, according to her nephew. She was trained by St. John's Ambulance Brigade in London, a voluntary first aid organization, and the Alexandra College Guild in Dublin, which provided a certificate course of instruction in Civic and Social Work. Miss Sargent, whose job was classified as "Assistant Social Secretary," directed her work toward "making women better employees and helping them to do their jobs better." The welfare of men was also provided for, as "young men were often trained to make suites of furniture before they got married." The factory also provided recreational and educational facilities such as swimming and gymnastics, as well as reading, writing and arithmetic classes. While participation in classes was voluntary, a week's extra holiday a year provided an incentive.

Welfare practice in industry, however, was not always perceived as mere philanthropy. While there is little information on the early function of welfare services in Irish industry, in British industry welfare work was often criticized for its paternalistic nature, despite the well-intentioned provisions of such benevolent schemes as treatment facilities for the sick and assistance with grants, loans, transport and accommodation, in addition to counseling for employees, provided by welfare officers. The welfare officer was described as a "benevolent spider," whose tentacles reached into every part of the organization (Martin, 1967). The very concept of welfare was deemed to be fundamentally "an attitude of mind" on the part of management, which in turn influenced the method by which management activities were undertaken (Hopkins, 1955). It was suggested that industrial social workers sometimes had difficulty in managing their roles, because they became too actively the "conscience of management," urging reforms which were not acceptable to workers (Anthony and Crichton, 1969a). Similar criticisms are to be found in the American literature. In a review of social work practice in business and industry in the United States between 1875 and 1930, welfare was rationalized first and foremost as humanitarianism, but with two further goals. These were:

a. the creation of an improved, loyal working force who kept in line with management values and ideals; and
b. the maintenance of a contented workforce who would have no desire to unionize, but rather would trust management to look out for its best interests (Popple, 1981).

John Henry Patterson, owner of the National Cash Register Company and one of the early exponents of welfare work in American industry succinctly characterized employers' attitude to the development of welfare programs in industry, when he stated, "It pays!" (Patterson, 1902).

The demise of welfare programs in Irish industry has been associated with a diffusion of the role of welfare officers. In the 1930s their work was incorporated into the new profession of personnel management which had begun to develop at that time. An analysis of the historical development of personnel management in Ireland suggests that the impact of the welfare approach was linked from the outset with a caring approach to employees. Dealing with issues such as health, working conditions and personal problems continues to be very much in evidence in modern personnel management practice in areas such as counseling and the provision of sickness benefits and staff loans (Gunnigle and Flood, 1990). In Britain, too, welfare programs appeared to gradually fall victim to the ambitions of personnel managers (Anthony and Crichton, 1969b). Similarly, in the United States the classic case study of Joseph Bancroft and Sons textile factory in Delaware by Nelson and Campbell (1972) illustrated how welfare services became institutionalized into the new field of personnel management, as services formerly provided by welfare workers came to be seen as the minimum standards of decent working conditions and not merely as gratuities by employers.

Thus, while welfare work may have justifiably been subjected to criticism for its paternalistic attitude, in Ireland, as elsewhere, it established the necessity of identifying and satisfying the needs of employees. It also precipitated efforts by some employers to develop certain standards in respect of employees' working conditions including even the quality of their housing. It has been argued that the enlightened attitude shown towards the welfare of employees at Jacobs biscuit factory in Dublin at the turn of the century, and their appointment of possibly the first paid social worker, marked a pioneering point in the development of social work in this country (Darling, 1972).

THE IMPACT OF THE HUMAN RELATIONS MOVEMENT

The Human Relations approach to management which focused on problems created by work organizations in the large factories of a new industrial era was the next major approach to affect the development of OSW in Ireland. This philosophy proposed that productivity was enhanced by focusing on workers and their needs, the satisfaction of which were essential for the overall effectiveness of the organization. The Hawthorne experiments into employee productivity, conducted at the Western Electric Company in Chicago between 1927 and 1932, showed that the social context of work and group cohesiveness within the workplace far exceeded any monetary incentives or fringe benefits in increasing productivity (Mayo, 1934). These studies demonstrated that the informal structure within the organization operated to affect the behavior and motivation of workers (Roethlisberger and Dickson, 1939). Studies by Herzberg (1966, 1976) drew attention to the enormous advantages that satisfying the human needs of workers can have on their motivation to work and on organizational effectiveness. This approach was manifested in Ireland, to some extent, by the 1955 Factories Act, which legislated appropriate physical conditions and preventive measures regarding occupational disease in certain types of factories (Shillman, 1956).

THE REEMERGENCE OF INDUSTRIAL SOCIAL WELFARE IN IRELAND

Elements of both Welfare Capitalism and the Human Relations approach to management can be seen in the kind of occupational welfare services, which were later developed in some Irish organizations. Large industrial organizations such as the National Electricity Supply Board and the national telecommunications network Telecom Eireann, were among the first to reestablish welfare services in the workplace in the early 1970s, and today these companies are still one of the largest employers of welfare officers. During the same period several welfare officers were selected from within the Government Civil Service Departments, and trained to provide a welfare service for staff. Today the Irish Civil Service employs twenty-one welfare officers to provide a range of employee assistance services for employees.

Occupational social work services were developed during this period in other large industrial organizations in Dublin. Hilda Madden, who was appointed in Guinness' Brewery in 1969, suggests that they provided mainly casework services for employees and their families and for retired employees or their widows at times of crises such as a sudden death in the family, an accident in the workplace, unexpected layoff or alcohol related problems. The social worker would, in addition, act as a consultant to management in connection with both individual cases and groups of personnel, and sometimes recommend and process action to alleviate problems. The social worker would not allow herself to be cast, however, into the role of police person inquiring into absenteeism or management problems (Madden, 1982). Thus, even at this early stage of development, it is evident that social workers were trying to define their independence from industrial relations issues.

In the last ten years, OSW programs have been established in public service and state controlled (quasi-governmental) organizations such as Dublin Corporation, the County Council, the Central Bank and one of the country's eight regional health boards. In 1992, a head social worker and five professional social workers were appointed to the Department of Defense, to develop their personnel support service for staff throughout the country's military organizations. Advice on housing problems, legal aid, financial issues or referral for health services and bereavement or child and family counseling is provided to personnel (Ennis, 1992). Some recognition of the professionalism of social workers in designing and developing services is suggested by these appointments. Eurocontrol (the body responsible for the safety of air navigation in ten European Community countries based in Brussels) also recently employed an Irish social worker, with a Belgian colleague of the same training, "to set up an OSW service for the employees of the agency and their families" (Fitzgerald, 1992).

The latest development in the field of OSW has been the emergence of Employee Assistance Programs (EAPs). These have been described by the National Institute of EAPs as health promotion programs in the workplace (Quinlan, 1990). The impetus for health promotion activity in the workplace was stimulated in Ireland by the Report of the Government-convened Barrington Commission of Enquiry into Safety, Health and Welfare at Work (1983). Following its publication, the enactment of the Safety, Health and Welfare at Work Act 1989 responded to Barrington's main criticisms of existing legislation by:

a. unifying much of the existing legislation, i.e., the 1955 Factories Act and the Safety in Industry Act 1980,
b. extending the range of application of previous legislation to all members of the workforce, instead of confining it to factory workers and builders, and
c. providing a framework for promoting action by all employers (not just those in the manufacturing and construction industry) to promote as well as to protect the physical and psychosocial well-being of workers.

The Confederation of Irish Industry had for more than a decade supported the redeployment of a proportion of public health expenditure to areas of preventive medicine and the concept of initiatives such as EAPs and health screening in the workplace (Power, 1990). But the 1989 legislation for the first time extended occupational safety and health protection to all employees, and in conjunction with the European Community Directive on the introduction of measures to encourage improvements in the safety and health of workers, by addressing the well-being of workers in a comprehensive way rather than focusing on specific safety hazards, it has imposed new obligations on employers to implement these well-intentioned provisions. A National Health and Safety Authority was established within the Department of Labor in 1989 to promote and enforce, if necessary, the implementations of the provisions of this Act.

In this section the roots of OSW have been traced back to the Welfare Capitalism at the turn of the century, through the Human Relations movement which developed in the post-war years, and the more recent development of Employee Assistance Programs (EAPs) as a health promotion activity in the workplace. Thus the foundations of a multidisciplinary approach to the provision of occupational welfare services in the workplace were established. As the following review of present models of service delivery shows, a diversity of educational and professional backgrounds are represented by practitioners in this field of practice today.

MODELS OF SERVICE DELIVERY

There are two main systems of service delivery operating in the Irish workplace. These are OSW services and welfare/employee assistance programs (EAPs). These are not mutually exclusive and overlap occurs in some organizations. The training and practice of both of these service models are considered separately here.

Employee Assistance Programs

Employee Assistance Programs (EAPs) evolved as a concept in the United States in the 1960s and 1970s. They were initially designed by management in some large industrial organizations to help reduce the cost of absenteeism and poor work performance resulting from alcohol related problems (Googins, 1975; Sonnenstuhl and O'Donnell, 1980). Program elements frequently documented as essential for the successful implementation of such services are summarized as follows:

a. a written personnel policy approved by management and union representatives,
b. a clear policy structure and practice principles, including confidentiality guidelines,
c. sponsored treatment through a network of approved specialist referral resources in the community, and
d. ideally, the provision of education on health and wellness, substance abuse prevention, family problems, stress management and improvement of work performance (Heyman, 1971; Roman, 1980; Dickman, 1985a).

These programs have developed rapidly in the United States since the 1970s, probably due to their presumed potential to reduce absenteeism, improve employee morale and promote productivity (Chadwick 1982; Everly et al., 1985; Shain et al., 1986).

In Ireland EAP initiatives have been supported by the Confederation of Irish Industry over the past decade (Power, 1990).

The extent to which EAPs have developed here is unclear. Quinlan (1992) has pointed out that some of the traditional welfare services inaugurated in large industrial organizations and the public service in the 1970s have been restructured and welfare officers regraded with the more appropriate Employee Assistance Officer title and role. Proceedings from the EAP Institute's annual conference in 1992 suggest that several disciplines including personnel and human relations managers, occupational health nurses or addiction counselors are also involved in the delivery of EAP services, which have broadened from a focus on occupational alcoholism to an approach which responds to a wider range of personal problems in the workplace (Quinlan, 1992). Thus, EAP practitioners are of diverse backgrounds and of varying academic qualifications. This has also been found in the development of the EAP field in the United States (Kurzman, 1992). As yet there is no specific path of study or training in this country which leads to a nationally recognized qualification as an EAP officer. Although some social workers are employed in the field of Employee Assistance practice, this is very much the exception. As mentioned already, the appointment of social workers in the Irish military services to complement the already existent personnel support service is a unique situation.

In order to rectify the deficit in professional training for employee assistance practice, several institutions have inaugurated training courses of varying academic content in recent years. These include the development of certificate courses for practitioners by the Institute of Personnel Management in Ireland in 1988. This training provides a basic working knowledge of all aspects of chemical dependency, stress related problems and/or other personal issues such as emotional and psychological difficulties, marital, legal and financial problems (Dunne, 1991). In 1994, University College Cork introduced a part-time undergraduate diploma course in employee welfare for practitioners in the field. Its introduction is described as a response to the need for formal training of practitioners engaged in Employee Assistance/Welfare work, and the recognition that this field of practice is developing at a significant rate (Staunton, 1994). The oldest and largest University in Dublin, Trinity College, within the last five years has introduced a one-year full-time Diploma course in addiction counseling and a general Diploma in counseling available to non-graduates who already are practitioners in the field of counseling. The University Industry Centre at University College Dublin has incorporated some course content on Employee Assistance Programs in their two-year, part-time multidisciplinary Diploma course, designed to meet the academic competency requirements of the Safety, Health and Welfare at Work Act, 1989. Thus the emergence of EAPs in the workplace has provided new opportunities for the training of practitioners and others in the helping professions, and for the development of professionally based teaching programs in this new arena of practice.

Occupational Social Work Programs

Social workers, who are employed in the area of OSW, have all completed a three-year nationally recognized University course of study in the Social Sciences, leading to a Bachelor of Social Science degree. Such courses are available in three Universities (University College Dublin, Trinity College Dublin, and University College Cork). To practice social work, a further one-year full-time postgraduate training course in social work theory and practice, including supervision, is required, which leads to the Diploma in Applied Social Studies, a recognized professional qualification in social work, or a Masters qualification on successful completion of a dissertation. A specific postgraduate qualification in OSW is not as yet available in Ireland. It would appear by virtue of their generic training in the behavioral sciences that professional social workers with graduate degrees possess a theoretical background that enables them to effectively assess and address the source and consequences of personal and work related problems which beset employees, and to advocate for changes in the work environment. As Vigilante (1982) points out, taking the work situation into account in assessments and interventions enables the social worker to become engaged in the combination of conditions that affect individual behavior. Similarly, Donovan (1987) expressed concern about the implementation of practice models that ignore poor working conditions and stressful work environments as determinants of individual problems. The assumption from this is that by using systems theory (Goldstein, 1973) as a conceptual frame of reference in assessing problems in the workplace, social workers are capable of providing a comprehensive approach to service development. By incorporating the work environment as a significant factor in assessments and interventions, this approach to practice has some parallels with the concept of workplace health promotion. This health strategy aims to promote health and well-being in the workplace, in addition to avoiding health hazards and treating those who have developed illnesses. In a review of health promotion activities in seven European countries including Ireland, published by the European Foundation for the Improvement of Living and Working Conditions in 1989, one of the criticisms made of many workplace health and safety initiatives was that too much emphasis was being placed on reforming the behavior of the worker, and not enough on altering the workplace environment (Wynne, 1990).

A recent account from an Irish social worker suggests that occupational social workers may have a broader vision of their role than responding to people's problems. By virtue of their professional values, what they expect of themselves in terms of standards of care for employees may be more than what is demanded by their employer. On the other hand, the resources at one's disposal, the organizational climate within which one works and whether one is the first incumbent to the post, all have a bearing on the scope of services provided (Higgins, 1992).

The kind of problems which occupational social workers seek to address as distinct from EAP practitioners is difficult to discern. Little or no research has been done in Ireland, to differentiate the policy and practice of different types of programs, and meaningful comparisons between practice activities can only be made when a common criteria of measurement is used. While it is hypothesized that EAPs are now emphasizing a proactive holistic approach to addressing employee well-being, as opposed to focusing on specific problems such as alcoholism (Dickman, 1985b), the role and scope of practice is constantly debated in the literature. The assumption that deteriorating work performance frequently results from behavioral problems in the individual is likely to dictate practice orientations, which are "reinforced by the commonly accepted measures of EAP success, such as increasing employees' productivity by decreasing absenteeism, tardiness and sick days and improving cost benefit ratios" (Googins and Davidson, 1993).

While there may be some overlap, in Ireland the concept of EAPs seems to be more closely associated with the concept of welfare than social work. In 1993 the Irish Association of Welfare/Employee Assistance Counselors was founded, in order to stimulate training and access supervision in the field and to develop a code of ethics in counseling. This group now has a membership of approximately one hundred and fifty persons (McCabe, J. Founding President, personal communication). In practice it would appear that social workers are much less associated with Employee Assistance Programs and most are members of the European Network of OSW. By not aligning themselves too closely with any particular treatment model, they may find, as has been hypothesized from observations of OSW practice in Switzerland, Germany, France, and Holland, that "they are more free to identify emerging human needs and respond appropriately" (Googins et al., 1986). In addition, the systems approach of incorporating the work environment into the assessments and interventions would seem to be more compatible with the concept of promoting the health and welfare of employees in a comprehensive way than the presumed individual personal problem focus of employee assistance practice.

It has been suggested elsewhere that social workers' comprehensive approach to service development gives them an advantage in the employee assistance field (Kurzman, 1993; Tanner, 1991). It still remains a challenge, however, for social workers in Ireland to define what they do, to demonstrate that their comprehensive training is relevant, and to illustrate that the services they provide are worthwhile. The literature also highlights the need for social workers to develop accountable and effective administrative practices due to contracting resources, unless other professions who lack counseling skills are to manage and evaluate our programs in industry for us (Prochaska, 1987).

In summary, there is insufficient empirical research in this area to make a definitive distinction between the practice of EAPs and OSW services. As Rutman aptly states, "program labels often do not provide a clear understanding of the activities that are actually implemented" (Rutman, 1977). In Ireland employee assistance is a continuously developing field of practice, and practitioners are in the process of developing their professional identity. It may be assumed from the OSW literature that social workers use a systems approach to assessments and interventions, which includes the evaluation of the work environment as a potential determinant of employees' individual problems. The feasibility of implementing this approach to practice remains unclear in the context of Irish services.

FUTURE DIRECTIONS OF OCCUPATIONAL SOCIAL WORK IN IRELAND

The field of occupational social work in Ireland is clearly set to expand considerably in future years. The enactment of the 1989 Safety, Health and Welfare at Work Act and European Community Directives have provided a legislative framework within which services aimed at improving and developing the health and welfare of employees will be structured. This has placed responsibility on all employers to address the safety, health and welfare of employees in a comprehensive way. Therefore more services are likely to develop in a variety of workplace settings, including many small businesses previously immune to such considerations, instead of only in large corporations as in the past. One immediate responsibility placed on employers is to have prepared "Safety Statements," which outline the provisions made by the employer to secure the safety, health and welfare of employees. This requirement was defined by the National Authority for Health and Safety, established by the Department of Labor to enforce the provisions of the 1989 Act. However, this Authority has stated that it would be loath to implement enforcement procedures until a full awareness of the legislation has been created (Wood, 1990). A study of health promotion activities in seven European countries including Ireland (conducted by the European Foundation for the Improvement of Living and Working Conditions), concluded that an information base outlining principles of good practice in the area would help to raise the awareness needed to develop innovative health promotion actions in the workplace (Wynne, 1990). A lack of knowledge among management staff of the potential benefits of such initiatives was specifically mentioned as a formidable barrier to the promotion of workplace action for health and well-being in the Irish context.

The concept of EAPs or OSW services is just one, albeit small, component of health promotion activities in the workplace. In Ireland, little empirical data is available which explains how programs are designed, what their goals are, what kind of staffing and resources are required to meet these goals, or what measures will be used by management or practitioners to indicate the most effective mode of service delivery. Thus, a fundamental step in the future development of OSW practice in Ireland is the collection of a data base which establishes in clear, objective and measurable terms what different types of programs actually do at present, and what their long-term objectives are. More difficult to assess, but equally important for future planning, would be an analysis of the effectiveness of each type of program. In addition, analysis of individual program hypotheses, i.e., the basis upon which employers seek to address certain kinds of problems, needs to be examined, as management's rationale for program implementation is likely to dictate to a large extent the scope of services. Just as welfare services developed at the turn of the century were not wholly philanthropic, neither is their implementation likely to be based on purely health grounds. Their promotion needs to be justified, especially as employers fund them. Based on this kind of information, a logical approach to identifying ways in which occupational welfare services for employees may be developed and improved can be instituted. Despite the fact that legislation is in place which encourages the implementation of practices in the workplace to ensure the safety, health and welfare of employees, the ways and means by which the latter can be developed are left open to interpretation far more than health and safety issues.

In Ireland, the future development of EAPs and OSW services is likely to involve educational structures at various levels, including the undergraduate University curriculum of Social Science students and the postgraduate training of social workers. The need for expertise in the field of EAP practice has been well-demonstrated by the inception of formal training in a variety of courses by different institutions as already detailed. OSW will undoubtedly become a specialist option in postgraduate training at University level. This is likely to develop in response to the expected growth in the field of occupational welfare and the opportunities for employment in this area. Given this eventuality, decision-makers at management level should be aware of the skills, knowledge and values most applicable and compatible with the provision of social services in the workplace. While social workers would appear to have the professional advantage at this stage, specialization in the policy and practice of OSW at postgraduate level may be an important factor in advancing a much needed empirical based practice in the future development of this field. Such a program is likely to incorporate many facets of education developed by proponents of EAPs in recent years to deal with their new responsibilities, as well as the more traditional broader based skills of the Social Science graduate.

GOVERNMENT/EUROPEAN PUBLICATIONS

Directive 89/391/EEC "On the Introduction of Measures to Encourage Improvements in the Safety and Health of Workers at Work." EC Offices, Moleworth Street, Dublin.
Report of the Commission of Inquiry on Safety, Health and Welfare at Work. Chairman–Mr. Justice Barrington, 1993. Government Publications Sale Office, Sun Alliance House, Molesworth Street, Dublin.
Safety, Health and Welfare at Work Act, 1989. Government Publications Sale Office, Moleworth Street, Dublin.
Workplace Action for Health: A Selective Review and a Framework for Analysis. European Foundation for the Improvement of Living and Working Condition, Working Paper No. EF/WP/89/30EN, p. 3.

REFERENCES

Anthony, P. and Crichton, A. (1969). *Industrial relations and the personnel specialists.* Batsford, London. (a) p. 162, (b) p. 149.
Brandes, S.D. (1970). *American welfare capitalism: 1800-1940.* University of Chicago Press.
Chadwick, J.J. (1982). Cost effective health promotion at the workplace. In *Managing Health Promotion in the Workplace.* R.S. Parkinson (ed.). Sage, California.
Darling, V. (1972). Development of social work in the republic of Ireland. *Social Studies*, 1 (1), 24-37.
Dickman, J.F. (1985). Ingredients of an effective EAP. In *Counseling the troubled person in industry: A guide to the organization, implementation and evaluation of employee assistance programs.* J.F. Dickman, W.G. Emener, and W.S. Hutchinson (eds.). Charles C. Thomas, Springfield. (a) pp. 40-52, (b) pp. 7-11.
Donovan, R. (1987). Stress in the workplace: A framework for research and practice. *Social Casework*, May, 259-266.
Dunne, C. (Nov. 1991). Employee Assistance Certificate. *Course description.* 1PM1.
Ennis, M. (1992). Occupational social work in the forces. *Irish Social Worker*, 1 (2).
Everly, G.S. and Feldman, R.H.C. (1985). *Occupational health promotion: Health behaviour in the workplace*, Wiley, New York.
Fitzgerald, M.T. (1991). Marie Therese Fitzgerald for Brussels Post. *Irish Social Worker*, 10 (3), 16.
Goldstein, H. (1973). *Social work practice: A unitary approach.* University of South Carolina Press, Columbia, SC.
Googins, B. (1975). Employee assistance programs. *Social Work*, Nov., 464-469.
Googins, B. and Davidson, B.N. (1993). The organization as client: Broadening the concept of employee assistance programs. *Social Work*, 38 (4), July, 477-484.
Googins, B., Reisner, E.L. and Milton, J. (1986). Industrial social work in Europe. *Employee Assistance Quarterly*, 1 (3), Spring, 1-22.
Gunnigle, P. and Flood, P. (1990). *Personnel management in Ireland: Practice, trends and developments.* Gill and MacMillan, Dublin, 27-39.
Herzberg, F. (1966). *Work and nature of man.* World Publishing Co., New York.

Herzberg, F. (1976). The managerial choice. To be efficient and to be human. Dow Jones-Irwin, Homewood, IL.
Heyman, M. (1971). Employer sponsored programmes for problem drinkers. *Social Casework*, Nov., 547-552.
Higgins, M. (1992). Surviving occupational social work. *Irish Social Worker*, 11 (2).
Hopkins, P.R. (1955). *Handbook of industrial welfare*. Pitman, London.
Kurzman, P. (1992). Employee assistance program staffing: Past, present and future. *Employee Assistance Quarterly*, 8 (2), 79-88.
Kurzman, P. (1993). Employee assistance programs: Toward a comprehensive service model. In *Work and well-being: The occupational social work advantage*. P. Kurzman and S. Akabas (eds.). NASW Press, Washington, 26-45.
Madden, H. (1982). The Irish scene. *Irish Social Worker*, 1 (3), Oct.-Dec.
Martin, A.O. (1967). *Welfare at work*. Publ. Batsford, London, 245-281.
Mayo, E. (1934). *The human problems of an industrial civilization*. Macmillan Co., New York.
Nelson, D. and Campbell, S. (1972). Taylorism versus welfare work in American industry: H.L. Gantt and the Bancrofts. *Business History Review*, 46, 1-16.
Patterson, J.H. (1902). Altruism and sympathy in works administration. Eng. Mag. XX, January, 579-580.
Popple, P.R. (1981). Social work practice in business and industry: 1875-1930. *Social Service Review*, June, 256-269.
Power, C. (1990). Health promotion: A business perspective. In Conference proceedings on "Managing poor performance: The EAP response," by the National EAP Institute. University Industry Centre, University College Dublin, Nov. 16.
Prochaska, J.M. (1987). Middle management in human services. *Social Casework*, Nov., 567-570.
Quinlan, M. (1990). Conference Proceedings: "Managing poor performance: The EAP response," by the National EAP Institute. Dublin, Nov. 16.
Quinlan, M. (1992). Proceedings: 7th Annual Conference on Employee Assistance Programmes. "Changing the Work Environment," by the EAP Institute. Dublin, Sept. 17.
Roethlisberger, F.J. and Dickson, W.J. (1939). *Management and the worker*. Howard University Press, Cambridge, MA.
Roman, P.M. (1980). Medicalization and social control in the workplace: Prospects for the 1980s. *Journal of Applied Behavioral Science*, 16 (3), 408-421.
Rutman, L. (1977). *Evaluation research methods: A basic guide*. Sage Publications, London, Ch. 3.
Shain, M., Suurvali, H. and Boutilier, M. (1986). *Healthier workers: Health promotion and employee assistance programs*. Lexington Books, Massachusetts.
Shillman, B. (1956). The factory legislation of Ireland. *(Vol. 1 Factories Act 1955)*, John Falconer, *The Irish Law Times and Solcs. Jour.* 2, Crow St. Dublin.
Sonnenstuhl, W.J. and O'Donnell, J.E. (1980). Employee assistance programs: The whys and hows of planning them. *Personnel Administrator*, 25 (11), 35-39.
Staunton, D. (1994). *Course description–Diploma in employee welfare 1994/1996*. University College Cork.

Tanner, R. (1991). Social work: The profession of choice for EAPs. *Employee Assistance Quarterly*, 6 (3), 71-84.

Vigilante, F.W. (1982). Use of work in the assessment and intervention process. *Social Casework*, May, 296-300.

Wood, S. (1990). *Innovative workplace actions for health: An overview of the situation in seven European countries. Consolidated Report.* Wynne, Work Research Centre, Dublin, May, p. 27.

Wynne, R. (1990). *Innovative workplace actions for health: An overview of the situation in seven European countries.* Wynne, Work Research Centre, Dublin, May, pp. 89-90.

Occupational Social Work in Israel

Joseph Katan

SUMMARY. This article traces the development and current practice of occupational social work in Israel. Governmental structures, the health care system and the delivery of social services through the public and private sectors are identified. The prevalence of social workers employed in each of the sectors is also reviewed. The roles, functions, and perceptions of occupational social workers in the Israeli workplace are analyzed. Professional preparation and training of occupational social workers are discussed. The article concludes with the author's future projections for the continued development and impact of occupational social work in Israel. *[Article copies available for a fee from The Haworth Document Delivery Service: 1-800-342-9678. E-mail address: <getinfo@haworthpressinc.com> Website: <http://www.HaworthPress.com> © 2001 by The Haworth Press, Inc. All rights reserved.]*

KEYWORDS. Occupational social work in Israel

THE SOCIETAL AND HISTORICAL CONTEXT OF OCCUPATIONAL SOCIAL WORK IN ISRAEL

Since the establishment of the State of Israel in 1948, two main features have characterized Israel's sociopolitical structure: political centralization,

---

Joseph Katan, PhD, is Professor of Social Work at the Bob Shapell School of Social Work, Tel Aviv University, Israel.

[Haworth co-indexing entry note]: "Occupational Social Work in Israel." Katan, Joseph. Co-published simultaneously in *Employee Assistance Quarterly* (The Haworth Press, Inc.) Vol. 17, No. 1/2, 2001, pp. 81-96; and: *Global Perspectives of Occupational Social Work* (ed: R. Paul Maiden) The Haworth Press, Inc., 2001, pp. 81-96. Single or multiple copies of this article are available for a fee from The Haworth Document Delivery Service [1-800-342-9678, 9:00 a.m. - 5:00 p.m. (EST). E-mail address: getinfo@haworthpressinc.com].

and dominance of major political parties and organizations. Political centralization is reflected in the government's view of its goals and functions in the areas of economy and human services, where caring for the primary social needs of various groups and improving their well-being are perceived as obligations of the state. This view is supported by the vast majority of Israeli citizens, who consider the government responsible for safeguarding and ameliorating their physical and economic well-being.

The broad support for government involvement in the social services arena has been only partially affected by changes in the coalition government regimes since 1948. However, the forces pressing for active government involvement in human services have been counterbalanced by non-government organizations that have played a major role in the delivery of social services to specific groups in the population. These organizations have expanded in recent years, and attained a more powerful position in provision of human services.

Thus, the Israeli welfare system is characterized by a "mixed economy" which involves different types of organizations. The main functions and activities of the government and non-government organizations and the extent of their involvement in provision of human services are briefly reviewed below.

THE CENTRAL GOVERNMENT

At least eight government organizations provide direct and indirect services to various populations. The activities of three bodies–the National Insurance Institute (NII), the Ministry of Labor and Social Affairs, and the Ministry of Health–are particularly relevant to workers and will be described below.

The NII operates within the framework of the Ministry of Labor and Social Affairs, with a special legislative status that gives it considerable autonomy. The NII protects various groups, including workers, through two types of income maintenance benefits:

1. *Universal contributory benefits*
   These include old-age allowances (for men at the age of 65 and women at the age of 60), survivors' allowances (for widows and orphans), general disability insurance, work injury insurance, unemployment benefits, maternity benefits, child allowances, and long-term care insurance.
2. *Noncontributory benefits*
   These include alimony payments for women, income support benefits for people living below the poverty line, and benefits for victims of enemy actions.

The Ministry of Labor and Social Affairs plays a key role in financing and regulating the delivery of a wide range of personal social services to various groups such as families, children and youth, the aged, and the disabled. Nevertheless, the main responsibility for delivery of most of these services is assumed by the municipal welfare departments and voluntary service organizations. The ministry enacts social and labor legislation and disseminates guidelines to organizations providing personal social services. The ministry also operates in the areas of labor relations, labor exchange, and vocational training.

Since the National Health Insurance Law took effect on January 1, 1995, the Ministry of Health has played a prominent role in financing and regulating the delivery of medical services to the public. In fact, every Israeli citizen is entitled by law to a basket of comprehensive medical services. Four major sick funds, all of which have the legal status of nonprofit organizations, are responsible for providing these services.

Other ministries involved in financing, regulating and, in certain cases, supplying social services include the Ministry of Immigrant Absorption, the Ministry of Housing, and the Ministry of Education.

THE LOCAL GOVERNMENTS

Every local authority is required by law to establish a department of social services. While these departments vary in scope, diversity, and quality of activities, they generally provide the following services:

- consultation and treatment for individuals and families;
- linkage and referral of clients to other agencies;
- child welfare services;
- services for the elderly;
- rehabilitation services for the handicapped, deaf, and blind;
- community organization activities.

Since the municipalities receive most of their funding from the Ministry of Labor and Social Affairs, the activities of the local departments are monitored and supervised by the Ministry. Despite strong government involvement, many local departments have attained a certain degree of autonomy in recent years, which has enabled them to develop new projects that respond to specific needs.

PUBLIC NON-GOVERNMENT ORGANIZATIONS

One of the most influential public organizations is the "Histadrut" (the General Federation of Labor), the largest trade union in Israel. Since its inception in 1920, the "Histadrut" has operated not only as a traditional trade union seeking to improve the salaries and working conditions of its members, but also as a social movement striving to provide a wide array of social, medical, educational, and cultural services for its members. From 1982 to 1992, the "Histadrut" operated an Occupational Welfare Department which encouraged the development of occupational social work (OSW) in workplaces and provided training for occupational welfare workers (Alspector-Caspi, 1994). Until 1995, the "Histadrut" offered its members comprehensive health services through the workers' sick fund.

In recent years, two major developments have weakened the "Histadrut" and caused a significant decline in its membership. First, the National Health Insurance Law, which took effect in 1995, allowed workers to receive medical services from any sick fund without belonging to the union. Second, the new "Histadrut" leadership elected in the early 1990s began to focus on trade union activities and minimized its involvement in social and cultural activities, including development of OSW in workplaces. Despite these changes, the "Histadrut" continues to play a key role in the arena of labor relations.

THE VOLUNTARY SECTOR

Voluntary Service Organizations (VSOs) in Israel provide medical services as well as a wide array of social services for populations such as the elderly, children, the disabled, and their families. These services include hostels and day-care centers, treatment and consultation, educational and recreational programs, vocational training, and referrals to or contact with other services. Many VSOs are at least partially subsidized by the government. In fact, the government has transferred a considerable share of the responsibility for service delivery to VSOs, particularly for segments of the population with severe physical, psychological, or social dysfunction.

While the government views VSOs as an appropriate arm for implementation of certain social programs, they do not function solely as government agencies. In fact, they operate independently in areas where government involvement is limited, and often fill the vacuum created by cutbacks in social services and programs.

In addition to these types of organizations, the private and informal sectors are also involved in the social services arena. While for-profit organizations used to play a minor role in this area, they have been expanding their activities in recent years, particularly in health and personal social services and even in the provison of services funded by the government. The increasing role of the for-profit sector in Israel has apparently been affected by the growing trend toward privatization in Western countries. Informal systems comprised of self-help groups and intimate networks of families, neighbors and friends also constitute a vital source of support, particularly for populations such as the elderly. Thus, a wide range of organizations in Israel provides various types of social and medical services at the local level. This involvement has contributed toward the development of a comprehensive network of agencies offering a wide range of social and medical services to the Israeli population.

How has this sociopolitical context affected the status, development, and growth of OSW in workplaces in Israel? What role have other factors played in shaping the status and function of OSWs? These issues will be discussed in the following section, which will present various aspects of OSW in Israel.

THE PRESENCE OF OSWs IN ISRAELI WORKPLACES

The data in Table 1 is based on the membership list of the OSW Section of the Israel Association of Social Workers (IASW). The list includes an estimated 90% of the professional social workers in Israel. Occupational welfare workers without a degree in social work did not appear on the list, although their number is estimated to be equivalent to that of the professional OSW practitioners. In most workplaces, the OSWs are affiliated with the human resources division, and under the formal supervision of its director. However, as will be shown later, there is evidence that these workers maintain a considerable degree of autonomy. Several findings in the table are noteworthy. Data on the prevalence of OSWs in workplaces in Israel are presented in Table 1.

Out of 18 government ministries in Israel, only 12 employ OSWs. OSWs are involved in only seven of over 200 local authorities in the country. Only 23 OSWs are employed in privately-owned industries and corporations. Of these workers, 13 are employed in large industrial enterprises, while a few other industries use the services of external OSWs. All universities and most banks employ OSWs. Almost all of the OSWs work in settings that employ a large staff. Since most of these employees belong to the "Histadrut," their salaries, working conditions, and social benefits are established in a collective contract signed between the union and the employer. In contrast, almost no OSWs are employed in "unorganized work settings," i.e., settings in which workers are not affiliated with a trade union, many of which are characterized by low salaries and limited social benefits.

Table 2 presents the distribution of OSWs in two work settings, according to sectorial affiliation. Several findings are revealed in the table. About 50% of all OSWs are employed in the government sector (e.g., government ministries and local authorities as well as government-owned corporations, industries, and hospitals). Although this proportion is much higher than the representation of this sector in the Israeli economy, the presence of OSWs in this sector is still limited. OSWs continue to play a minor role in the private sector, with only 23 workers employed in 11 industrial enterprises. Sixteen

TABLE 1. Occupational Social Workers in Workplaces in Israel, by Type of Work Setting (Numbers and Percentages)

Type of Work Setting	No. of Workers	Percentage
Government ministries	12	9.2
Local authorities	7	5.4
Prisons authority, police, army	13	10.0
Government corporations (electric, airlines, communications)	14	10.8
Government-owned industries	9	6.9
Medical services	13	10.0
Universities	10	7.7
Private-owned industries	19	14.6
Private corporations	4	3.0
Banks	13	10.0
Cooperative enterprises	5	3.9
Self-employed	5	3.9
Miscellaneous	6	4.6
TOTAL	130	100.0

TABLE 2. OSWs in Workplaces, by Sectorial Affiliation*

Sector	Number	Percentage
Government	59	47.6
Private-commercial	39	31.4
Voluntary	21	16.0
Cooperative enterprises	5	4.0
TOTAL	124	100.0

* The table does not include independent workers.

percent of the OSWs belong to the voluntary sector, which has been gradually expanding in recent years, and most of them are employed in only two types of organizations–universities and medical organizations. OSW has not yet reached voluntary organizations involved in other areas such as welfare, education, and culture. Although there are dozens of cooperative enterprises in Israel, OSWs are only employed in two.

The findings indicate that OSWs are currently employed in very few workplaces (less than 60), most of which have only one worker serving over 1,000 employees. Only five organizations with branches in different regions of the country employ more than five occupational social workers. To put these findings in perspective, it should be noted that over 30 years ago only a handful of

OSWs were employed in a few workplaces. Consequently, the presence of about 150 OSWs in about 60 organizations may be indicative of significant growth and expansion. However, the fact that OSW has only been introduced in a few workplaces indicates that its expansion and impact are still minimal.

The slow growth and expansion of occupational social work in Israel can be attributed to the simultaneous existence of driving and restraining forces. Four main driving forces have stimulated the entry of OSW into workplaces.

1. The first driving force is the personal initiative of chief executives (mainly directors of human resources divisions) who have acknowledged the importance of involving OSWs in their organizations. Their decision to adopt and implement this idea is motivated by several factors. These include personal acquaintance with social workers, awareness of the activities of OSW in other workplaces, concern for the personal and social needs of their employees, and belief in the ability of OSWs to deal effectively with those needs. The existence of a wide range of welfare and medical services in Israel may have furthered this approach.
2. About 35% of OSWs in Israel work in organizations such as the police, prisons, universities, municipalities, and medical services, which have a long tradition of employing social workers (e.g., schools of social work at universities, and welfare departments of municipalities). In fact, the development of OSW in at least some of these organizations was initiated and encouraged by social workers employed in those settings.
3. The presence of occupational social workers in organizations such as banks, universities, and other specific industries has contributed toward its development in other organizations belonging to the same organizational population.
4. In several workplaces OSWs have been integrated into organizational units, previously run by nonprofessional workers, which handled organization of cultural, social and sports events in the workplace, distribution of gifts to workers, and home visits. Since these units were already part of the workplace, the entry of OSWs was not perceived as a major organizational change but rather as a step toward upgrading and improving current activities.

At the same time, several restraining forces have inhibited or delayed the expansion of OSW in other workplaces.

1. There is no legislation or regulations requiring establishment of OSW units in workplaces, nor is there a provision to this effect in collective contracts between employers and the trade union. An attempt initiated by the occupational welfare department of the "Histadrut" to mandate the employment of OSWs in workplaces failed due to the employers'

opposition. Thus, OSW units are established voluntarily by the organization's management, and are not subject to pressure from workers or other interest groups.
2. Many employers and workers are unaware of the merits and potential contributions of OSW. This situation may be attributed to the absence of academic and research institutions in Israel that focus on investigation of this field and disseminate reliable information about it.
3. Employers may believe that the existence of a comprehensive system of welfare and medical services at the local level relieves them of the responsibility for offering such services in the workplace.

These driving and restraining forces have not only affected the expansion of OSW and its penetration into the workplace, but have also influenced its role, function, and organizational status.

In order to appreciate the role of OSW in Israel, a structured questionnaire was administered to a group of 20 OSWs employed in various types of institutions (government ministries, local authorities, banks, private industries, universities, and government corporations). In addition, open interviews were conducted with several other OSWs. Although this group did not represent the entire population of OSWs, it is assumed that the information obtained is of general relevance, since it is consistent with findings of previous studies on the role and function of OSWs in Israel (Bargal, 1984; Bargal and Shamir, 1980a; Papo, 1995).

THE ROLE AND FUNCTION OF OCCUPATIONAL SOCIAL WORKERS

The respondents were presented with a list of 23 functions and tasks of OSWs, and asked to indicate the amount of time they devote to each task, on a scale ranging from 1 ("no time") to 5 ("a considerable amount of time").

The list covered a broad range of tasks perceived as part of the OSW's role. The respondents were also asked to supplement the list with additional activities in which they are involved, but their response to this request was limited. Table 3 presents the relevant data.

The data indicate that OSWs focus on the needs of individual employees and pay less attention to the employees' families, environmental factors, and organizational context. The time devoted by OSWs to promoting organizational change, mediating between organizational units, and advising directors on organizational issues is minimal. Their contact with individual employees focuses on tasks such as mediating between workers and external services (the National Insurance Institute, local social service bureaus, medical services), short-term care, advocacy, and home visits. Some time is also devoted to tasks such as planning projects to enhance the well-being of employees, marketing OSW in the workplace, and psychological counseling. Thus, OSWs focus on helping individual employees cope with various personal problems and emphasize their role as mediators, advocates, and counselors.

The workers participating in the study were also asked to indicate the amount of time they devote to 12 potential problems of workers, on a scale from 1 ("no time") to 5 ("a considerable amount of time") (see Table 4). The data presented in the table indicate that OSWs focus primarily on physical, mental health, and family problems of employees (e.g., disease, divorce, death). They also deal with material problems (e.g., financial difficulties, housing problems), albeit to a lesser extent, and devote very little time to problems of addiction, which are rarely encountered in workplaces in Israel. These findings are consistent with the information presented in Table 3, and illustrate the OSWs' emphasis on personal problems that are not necessarily related to the workplace but may affect the employee's behavior and morale.

TABLE 3. Amount of Time Devoted by OSWs to Various Tasks and Activities

Rank	Order of Activity	Amount of Time
1.	Mediating between workers and local services	4.26
2.	Contact with other organizations	4.11
3.	Short-range treatment	4.00
4.	Advising directors on personal problems of workers	3.63
5.	Representing workers before agencies	3.63
6.	Supervision of workers	3.53
7.	Home visits	3.53
8.	Marketing OSW in the workplace	3.53
9.	Planning activities and projects	3.53
10.	Psychological counseling for workers	3.32
11.	Group work	3.26
12.	Advising middle-range directors	3.26
13.	Mediating between individual workers and other parties in the workplace	3.26
14.	Providing information about OSWs in the workplace	3.11
15.	Representing workers at external organizations	2.95
16.	Allocating gifts to workers	2.89
17.	Working with employees' families	2.84
18.	Arranging loans for workers	2.68
19.	Long-range treatment	2.63
20.	Advising directors on organizational issues	2.53
21.	Organizational change	2.37
22.	Mediating between organizational units	2.05
23.	Organizing meetings and conferences	1.79

TABLE 4. Amount of Time Devoted by OSWs to Problems of Employees (Averages)

Activity by Rank Order	Amount of Time
1. Physical health	4.53
2. Family problems	4.42
3. Mental health	4.21
4. Employee's death	3.89
5. Employee's retirement	3.84
6. Relations between employees and managers	3.32
7. Financial problems	3.32
8. Relations among employees	2.89
9. Addiction	2.37
10. Working conditions	2.26
11. Problems of new immigrants	2.11
12. Absorption of new employees	1.37

Since many of these needs and problems fall within the domain of local welfare and medical services, mediation is a dominant aspect of the OSWs' role in the workplace. As mentioned, these findings corroborate studies conducted in the early 1980s (Bargal, 1984; Bargal and Shamir, 1980a) and 1990s (Pappo, 1995).

The data indicate that OSWs have created an organizational niche for themselves, characterized by two main features: emphasis on the personal problems and needs of employees; and minimal intervention directed specifically at the organizational and environmental setting of the workplace.

This role structure coincides with the interests and expectations of both the employers' and employees' trade union, and can thus be perceived as a consensual role model. The disengagement of OSWs from functions such as negotiation between employers and employees about salaries and work conditions or promotion of organizational and environmental changes has prevented them from entering domains dominated by the management and the trade union. This had minimized potential conflict and contention between the social workers on the one hand, and between organizational management and workers' representatives on the other.

Occupational social workers' perceptions of their role and functions in the organization will be discussed in the following section.

OCCUPATIONAL SOCIAL WORKERS' PERCEPTIONS OF THEIR INVOLVEMENT IN THE WORKPLACE

The role perceptions of OSWs were examined from three main perspectives: how they feel about their job; difficulties and obstacles that affect their job performance; and their overall satisfaction with the organization that employs them. Respondents were presented with a list of 24 factors that may negatively affect their performance and were asked to rate the influence of each factor on a scale ranging from 1 ("not at all") to 5 ("to a very great extent"). Of the factors on the list, only eight were perceived as having some negative effect on their performance (i.e., a mean score above "2") (see Table 5).

The data indicate that only one factor–"organizational constraints" ("the organization does not provide adequate resources to the OSW unit") received an average score exceeding "3," i.e., that factor was perceived as having a negative effect on their work. Seven other factors were perceived as having either a minimal or partial negative effect. Other items (which are not included in the table) such as managers' attitudes, lack of adequate preparation for the job, limited knowledge, lack of autonomy, lack of support and cooperation from employees, and relations with colleagues, received an average score of less than "2" (i.e., they were perceived as having little or no negative effect on their work).

On the whole, the data indicate that OSWs encounter few obstacles that inhibit proper performance of their tasks. Most of the workers in the study reported that they are highly familiar with their organizational context, that they possess the knowledge and skills required for their work, and that they receive support and cooperation from both managers and employees.

In order to ascertain whether this optimistic view is also reflected in the area of job satisfaction, the participants were presented with a list of 16 variables characterizing different areas of work in organizational contexts,

TABLE 5. Perceived Effect of Various "Inhibiting" Factors (Mean Scores)

Factor	Mean Score
1. Organizational constraints	3.26
2. Discrepancy between employer's expectations and worker's values	2.95
3. Professional isolation	2.79
4. Lack of resources	2.68
5. Difficult problem of employee	2.58
6. Limited opportunities for influence	2.32
7. Inflexible organizational rules	2.11
8. Lack of supervision	2.11

and were asked to indicate the extent of their satisfaction in each area. The items were evaluated on a 5-point scale ranging from 0 ("not at all satisfied") to 5 ("very satisfied") (see Table 6).

In addition, the workers were asked to evaluate their overall satisfaction with their job and with the organization employing them. The average score for job satisfaction was 3.80, and for satisfaction with the organization was 3.25. On the whole, the data reveal medium to high levels of satisfaction. There was no evidence of dissatisfaction or low satisfaction in any of the areas.

The workers expressed high levels of satisfaction with intrinsic factors (e.g., autonomy, contact with employees, utilization of professional knowledge, and type of task), as well as with extrinsic variables (convenient work hours, physical conditions, social benefits). A medium level of satisfaction was expressed in relation to salary, participation in decision-making, supervision, and opportunities for professional advancement. The discrepancy between the levels of overall job satisfaction and satisfaction with the organization may reflect some of the problems faced by OSWs. As shown, the workers expressed high levels of satisfaction in areas related to the job itself, such as: autonomy, interesting work, interaction with employees and managers, social support, and job conditions. Lower levels of satisfaction were expressed in some areas related to the organizational context, such as: salary, supervision, and promotional opportunities. Thus, the lower level of satisfaction with the workplace may be traced, at least in part, to several inherent

TABLE 6. Satisfaction in Various Areas of Work (Mean Scores)

Item	Mean Score
Autonomy at work	4.26
Contact with clients	4.22
Convenient work hours	4.11
Physical conditions	4.00
Social benefits	3.89
Utilization of professional knowledge and skills	3.79
Type of tasks	3.79
Relations with managers	3.79
Challenging and interesting work	3.68
Attainment of professional goals	3.68
Social climate in the workplace	3.47
Opportunities for learning and professional advancement	3.39
Supervision	3.37
Participation in decision-making	3.21
Salary	3.21

characteristics of occupational social work in Israel: professional isolation (most OSWs are the only social workers in the organization); lack of adequate professional supervision (in most cases, supervision is provided by outside workers); and limited promotional opportunities.

These factors are related to the partial institutionalization of occupational social work as a professional field. One of the main indications of this trend is the status of OSW at Israeli schools of social work. This aspect will be discussed in the following section.

EDUCATION AND TRAINING FOR OCCUPATIONAL SOCIAL WORK

Five universities in Israel have schools of social work with undergraduate and graduate programs, and four offer a doctoral program as well. None of the schools offer a specialization program in occupational social work, although some have specific courses related to various aspects of the field, which are not given on a regular or ongoing basis.

This situation may be attributed to two main causes. First, specialization programs are generally initiated by faculty members of a given institution. Few teachers at Israeli schools of social work are interested in OSW. Second, the number of workplaces employing OSWs is limited, and they cannot accommodate enough students for field work placement. Moreover, the existing settings do not meet basic criteria for field work placement, such as: social work units with several professionals (a vital condition for creating a professional culture); workers on the staff who are able to supervise students; and willingness of the management to receive students (in some cases, the management refuses to do so).

Israeli OSWs have academic degrees in social work, either at the bachelor's (BSW) or Masters (MSW) levels. However, these workers are not formally trained in OSW, owing to the lack of specialization programs. Surprisingly, most of the participants in the present study did not believe this "deficiency" negatively affects their professional performance. There are several possible explanations for this finding: First, most of the workers had received relevant practical experience in other settings such as hospitals, rehabilitation services, and local social service departments where they were previously employed. Second, they receive on-the-job training in special seminars and workshops organized by various agencies such as the "Histadrut," the government, and the occupational social workers' section of the Israel Association of Social Workers. Third, many of the occupational social workers hold ongoing formal and informal meetings, which usually focus on professional issues. In addition, the findings indicate that OSWs maintain intensive contact with each other. For example, most of the respondents in the present study reported that when they encounter a problem on the job, they generally consult with another OSW.

It should be noted that many practitioners in other specialized areas of social work lack specialized training. This may be related to the generic orientation of undergraduate social work programs, and to the belief that preparation for a specialized area of practice should be provided by the workplace, e.g., through in-service training programs and supervision.

RESEARCH AND PUBLICATIONS ON OCCUPATIONAL SOCIAL WORK

The uncertain status of OSW in Israeli schools of social work has also affected the scope of research and publications in that area. The lion's share of publications in this field were written by Bargal and Shamir and focused on two topics: theoretical, ethical and practical issues related to introduction of OSW into the workplace; and presentation of empirical studies on the functions of OSWs and their organizational integration (Bargal, 1985; Bargal and Shamir, 1980a, 1980b, 1983a, 1983b, 1984, 1985; Bargal and Karger, 1991; Shamir and Bargal, 1982). Bargal also published a comprehensive monograph on the development of OSW and the role of OSWs in Israel. In addition, Bargal (1993) presented a conceptual framework consisting of factors that affect the development of OSW in work settings, which served as the basis for reviewing the status of OSW in Israel, Australia, Germany, and The Netherlands. Katan and Neikrug (1980) also studied the development of OSW in Israel and other countries, and conducted subsequent comparative research on OSW in Israel and the United States. Another relevant study was conducted by Papo (1995), who examined the personal and organizational factors related to the role of occupational welfare workers, only about half of whom were qualified social workers. A few case studies of OSW and its role in the workplace were conducted by OSWs themselves (Bargal, Back, and Ariav, 1992; Goldschlager and Riv, 1988; Hemmendinger, 1980; Rosenberg, 1990, 1991). Furthermore, Alspector-Caspi (1994) published a comprehensive study on the roles and activities of the Occupational Welfare Department at the "Histadrut."

This review reflects the limited number of scholars engaged in this field and the decline in the number of publications in recent years.

FUTURE PROJECTIONS

The above survey focused on two main issues. First, it described and analyzed the slow development and limited impact of OSW on the labor market in Israel. OSWs are represented in relatively few workplaces, and serve a small population of workers. Second, the findings indicate that OSWs deal primarily with the problems and needs of individual employees and their families, and are much less involved in other aspects such as internal organizational issues and the environment of the workplace.

Regarding prospects for expanding the field of OSW in the future, it seems that any change in the current status of occupational social work in Israel depends largely on the following developments:

1. the declining power and influence of trade unions;
2. the increasing trend toward employment based on personal contracts between employers and employees;
3. the increasing trend toward part-time employment, self-employment, and small enterprises;
4. the increasing trend toward acquisition of services from external organizations (outsourcing);
5. privatization and commercialization, which have heightened competition and increased the tendency to cut "nonessential" expenditures.

Taken together, these developments may weaken employers' commitment and willingness to expand the field of OSW. Nevertheless, although it is difficult to forecast future developments, these trends may be curtailed by measures such as: legislation mandating the introduction of OSW into large workplaces, and establishing an academic/professional center for OSW and specialization programs in the field at schools of social work in Israel.

REFERENCES

Alspector-Caspi, S. (1994). The role of the Occupational Welfare Department at the General Federation of Labor in the development of Occupational Social Work in Israel 1982-1992. Unpublished Doctoral Dissertation, Union Institute Graduate School, Ohio.

Bargal, D. (1984). *Social work in the world of work.* Monograph series. Israeli Council of Schools of Social Work and Akadamon (Hebrew).

Bargal, D. (1993). An international perspective on the development of social work in the workplace. In P.A. Kurzman & S.H. Akabas (eds.), *Work and well-being: The occupational social work advantage* (pp. 372-385). Silverspring-Washington DC: NASW.

Bargal, D., Back, A., & Ariav, P. (1992). Prolonged job insecurity, organizational decline and occupational social work. *Administration in Social Work*, 16 (1), 55-67.

Bargal, D., & Karger, H. (1991). Occupational social work and changing work economic order. *Administration in Social Work*, 15 (4), 95-109.

Bargal, D., & Shamir, B. (1980a). *Social services in work settings: Characteristics and roles.* Jerusalem: The Institute of Labor and Welfare, The Hebrew University of Jerusalem.

Bargal, D., & Shamir, B. (1980b). Social services in work settings: Area of intervention. *Bitahon Soziali (Social Security)*, 20, 167-175 (Hebrew).

Bargal, D., & Shamir, B. (1982). Occupational welfare as an aspect of quality of working life. *Labor and Society*, 7 (3), 255-264.

Bargal, D., & Shamir, B. (1983a). Professional and ethical issues of providing social services in work settings. *International Journal of Sociology and Social Policy*, 1, 37-46.

Bargal, D., & Shamir, B. (1983b). Social work in business and industry: Dilemmas and role characteristics. *Hevra U'Revaha (Society and Welfare)*, 5 (1), 15-25 (Hebrew).

Bargal, D., & Shamir, B. (1984). Job description of occupational welfare: A tool in role development. *Administration in Social Work*, 8, 59-71.

Bargal, D., & Shamir, B. (1985). Personnel directors and welfare officers' views of occupational welfare. *Industrial Social Work Papers*, 19, 56-64.

Goldschlager, A., & Riv, J. (1988). *Employees dismissal: The right way.* Ramat Hasharon, Israel: The Military Industry Human Resources and Occupational Welfare Service (Hebrew).

Hemmendinger, Y. (1980). Social work in a new area. *Hevra U'Revaha (Society and Welfare)*, 3 (1), 100-107 (Hebrew).

Katan, J, & Neikrug, S. (1980). Social work in the world of work. *Hevra U'Revaha (Society and Welfare)*, 3 (2), 171-188 (Hebrew).

Neikrug, S., & Katan, J. (1981). Social work in the world of work: Israel and the United States. *Journal of Applied Social Sciences*, 5 (2), 47-65.

Papo, E. (1995). Personal and organizational factors in the role of occupational welfare workers and their impact on organizational and professional commitment. Master's Thesis, Technion Israel Institute of Technology.

Rosenberg, P. (1991). Organization of social services in the workplace during an emergency. *Human Resources*, January-February, 24-26 (Hebrew).

Rosenberg, P. (1992). The concern for bereaved workers and their families. *Human Resources*, August-September, 24-25 (Hebrew).

Shamir, B., & Bargal, D. (1982). Occupational welfare and organizational effectiveness. *Administration in Social Work*, 6 (4), 43-52.

Shamir, B., & Bargal, D. (1983). Domains of work and methods of work of occupational welfare officers: An exploratory study of an emergency role. *Journal of Social Work Research*, 5 (3-4), 51-70.

Occupational Social Work in South Africa

Angela du Plessis

SUMMARY. This article describes the development and current practices of occupational social work in South Africa. As a means to accomplish this, the author conducted in-depth interviews with social workers employed in work settings throughout South Africa. Workplace practices, education and training and the challenges facing occupational social workers in South Africa are explained and analyzed. *[Article copies available for a fee from The Haworth Document Delivery Service: 1-800-342-9678. E-mail address: <getinfo@haworthpressinc.com> Website: <http://www.HaworthPress.com> © 2001 by The Haworth Press, Inc. All rights reserved.]*

KEYWORDS. Occupational social work in South Africa

THE SOCIETAL AND HISTORICAL CONTEXT OF OCCUPATIONAL SOCIAL WORK IN SOUTH AFRICA

There are two major contexts from which to analyze the development of occupational social work in South Africa. The first is the welfare system, while the second relates to the management of people at work. Both, of course, are linked to economic and ideological trends. The first locates occu-

---

Angela du Plessis, PhD, is former Chair of the Occupational Social Work Program at the University of Witwatersrand, and more recently was Labor Mediator and Arbitrator for the Commission on Conciliation and Arbitration in Johannesburg, South Africa.

[Haworth co-indexing entry note]: "Occupational Social Work in South Africa." du Plessis, Angela. Co-published simultaneously in *Employee Assistance Quarterly* (The Haworth Press, Inc.) Vol. 17, No. 1/2, 2001, pp. 97-118; and: *Global Perspectives of Occupational Social Work* (ed: R. Paul Maiden) The Haworth Press, Inc., 2001, pp. 97-118. Single or multiple copies of this article are available for a fee from The Haworth Document Delivery Service [1-800-342-9678, 9:00 a.m. - 5:00 p.m. (EST). E-mail address: getinfo@haworthpressinc.com].

pational social work within a professional arena, while the second highlights a view of the worker in the workplace, and the acceptance (or not) of social services as necessary and/or desirable management options to support or develop workers.

Many of the issues that are highlighted in a description of the history of welfare in South Africa have affected the development of occupational social work as a field of practice. In looking at the history of the profession of social work, three themes emerge.

First, the formal state welfare system was born out of the massive "poor white" problem in the 1930s; the focus on whites as the primary recipients of welfare services was, of course, entrenched in the system of Apartheid which followed when the Nationalist government came to power in 1948. While African poverty was also a major human welfare problem, the fact that it was treated differently was a powerful force in shaping South Africa's welfare system. Until the election of a democratic government in 1994, services for the different race groups were structurally separated and, in respect of both quantity and quality, whites received the better services (McKendrick, 1990a).

Another consequence of the "poor white problem" was the state's Civilized Labor Policy in which the Nationalist government embarked on a deliberate policy of protecting the positions of skilled whites and providing jobs for poor whites largely in state-run organizations. Such a policy invited social workers into the workplace to offer supportive services. The theme of early service delivery was material aid, which changed over time to focus on personal problems. These posts for professionally qualified social workers were the first at the South African workplace, and in many instances, it was decades before black social workers were employed. An example is the employment of social workers in 1935 within the state-run railway services. The major concern then was to offer a service to white employees many of whom were disadvantaged, poorly educated and recent migrants from the rural areas. The next organization to create social work posts was the state-owned enterprise commissioned to produce oil from coal, SASOL (South African Synthetic Oils Limited). Their professionally qualified white social workers began in 1954. In 1957 a third government-run enterprise producing steel (ISCOR-South African Iron and Steel Corporation) appointed white social workers. It was only around 1969 that ISCOR employed its first black practitioner.

Until the mid-1980s there was still a fair amount of division between black and white practitioners, some reasons practical, but others ideological. At a planning meeting in 1984 which began looking at a professional association for occupational social workers, some mine-based white practitioners refused to allow in black colleagues arguing that black practitioners would "politicize" agenda items. Most of the dozen or so white practitioners rejected this position, and the association did not survive.

The new government is currently addressing the inequity of the welfare system. Equity in access to services, as well as improving standards of services to previously disadvantaged communities, is high on their list of priorities. The point does need to be made that in the majority of occupational social work posts developed since the 1980s, social workers were not limited to offering their services along racial lines and in most cases workplace-based services were accessible to all employees.

The second theme relating to the history of the profession of social work in South Africa which impacted on occupational social work concerns the philosophical underpinning of the old welfare system that led to a focus on therapeutic services which held as its main aim the goal of changing "the person with the problem." Inherent in the Nationalist welfare system was a rejection of the notion of a welfare state. Residual in nature, the welfare system offered services not as a right, but as a privilege. The philosophical underpinnings were based largely on the cultural heritage of whites that emphasized individualism and family independence. Such a philosophy supports the practice of ameliorative, palliative services. Ideologically and practically, space is not created for preventive, developmental and educational services. Thus in South Africa for many decades curative clinical work was the norm. Until 1967 the South African government's subsidization policy for social work posts provided only for casework services.

As will be demonstrated later in this article, the focus on casework was mirrored in occupational social work for many years, although a trend away from this has been noted in the past couple of years.

Focusing primarily on "person-changing" fitted in well with the policies and philosophy of Apartheid. Practicing mainly within a "treatment" perspective limits the opportunities for becoming involved in social action. It did not encourage a critical look at the harsh environments in which the majority of South Africans lived. The assistance which the black masses required was in the form of changing the hostile environment with which they had to transact in order to meet their basic human needs, not help in forcing them to the requirements of an unjust society (McKendrick, 1990b).

The new government is moving away from the focus on casework, and committing itself to developmental, preventive and educational services.

The third and final theme relating to the history of the profession of social work and its impact on occupational social work is its heavy reliance on social work models developed in the Northern Hemisphere countries designed for developed, urbanized and industrialized democracies. Thus, frequently methods and models have not been appropriate to local conditions and in this way much of the social work effort, already limited by lack of resources, was ineffective due to an inappropriate conception of services (McKendrick, 1990b).

Under the old system, social work in South Africa was presented as a first world/third world dichotomy . . . "increasingly black social workers are describing casework as unhelpful or inappropriate in the third world contexts in which they find themselves. Professional casework is unproductive in the face of poverty, disease and unequal distribution of material resources. Black social workers call rather for more community work and macro system change" (Mason, 1990).

In occupational social work, one of the major influences from North America has been the notion of the Employee Assistance Program (EAP). Until North American practitioners visit South Africa, it is hard for them to understand the past imperative for local EAPs to try to become "the social conscience of the organization in which they are ensconced . . . viewed by employees for the most part as an agent of change for social conditions in the work environment" (Maiden, 1992). Thus the usefulness of importing EAP models that focus heavily on clinical work has up until now been limited in the South African context.

Again, the current Department of Welfare is looking critically at methodology from the first world so relied upon up until present times, and is making an effort to move away from specialized care to a more appropriate form of community-based generic care.

Moving away from social work as a professional context for occupational social work, another arena from which social work at the workplace has taken form and content is that of what could loosely be termed human resource management. Much of this is discussed in detail in doctoral research (Du Plessis, 1994) carried out by the author who will be relied on a great deal in this section.

The history of human resource management in South African commerce and industry has not been fully recorded and analyzed. Du Plessis (1994) attempted a description and an analysis, and concluded the section by offering eight factors that have facilitated and hindered occupational social work services to workers within the realm of human resource management.

The first factor is that of individual personalities, interests, idiosyncrasies and preferences. Over the years, individual human resource managers in companies have championed the cause of occupational social work, often because of a personal commitment to the issue of employee care. Many of the pioneers were married to social workers, served on management boards of welfare organizations, or they had a positive experience of social work intervention.

The second factor relates to industrial relations procedures. In the post-Wiehahn era (i.e., since 1979) unions to which black workers belonged were statutorily recognized for the purposes of collective bargaining. Some managers identified social workers as able to deal with such individual concerns, many of which were linked to alcohol abuse. Other managers preferred to deal with the personal problems themselves or failed to link the transgression with a personal concern or chose to dismiss the employee for the offence.

The third factor concerns economic considerations. Simply stated, during times of economic growth and expansion of human resources personnel, some occupational social workers were employed. However, frequently the social workers were retrenched when recessionary times demanded staff cutbacks. Viewed as "nice-to-haves," these social workers were not perceived as representing essential services. Many social workers in the gold mining industry in South Africa lost their posts in this way during the late 1980s.

Another factor that influenced human resource personnel to employ social workers was the approaches by lobbyists. The most striking example of this in South Africa has been the work done by The South African National Council for Alcohol and Drug Abuse (SANCA). From the late 1970s until the present-day, SANCA has encouraged the development of counseling services for alcohol dependent employees by emphasizing and publicizing two important points. The first relates to the hidden cost of alcohol abuse to an organization bottom line. The second is that alcoholism is a treatable illness, not a self-inflicted condition.

Often, such approaches to industry and commerce have resulted in the development of a social work post and/or an EAP. However, this point does rest on the premise that human resource personnel approached are "open" to the message of the lobbyist. An important mediating factor was the attitude of the manager towards the legitimacy of the role of the company in addressing personal problems of employees.

The fifth factor concerns prevailing management views, especially those pertaining to what managers perceive as worker motivators. Paternalism and the will to care for employees have promoted social work at the workplace. However, so does a philosophy that emphasizes productivity. In the early 1980s social workers attempting to enter the workplace used the link between personal concerns and productivity as a central rationale for their services.

The next factor relates to union demands. These have not played a major role as yet in the employment of occupational social workers in South Africa. Management has always aspired to keep a step ahead of union demands. This has been seen in aspects of health and safety at the workplace. Regrettably unions thus far in South Africa have not identified mental health as a priority nor have they identified social workers as the people who could play a role in resolving work-related problems. In general, the social work fraternity in South Africa has not identified with the labor movement and some union representatives are skeptical of services offered by management appointed social workers.

The seventh factor covers the important aspect of sociopolitical changes. In the mid-to-late 1980s, when it was clear that political transformation was under way, certain human resource practitioners did turn to social workers to assist them with change. Here, the "soft" issues, previously often ignored, were highlighted as central to transformation, and the social worker's skills and knowledge in this regard acknowledged. Opportunities for social workers arose in processes such as affirmative action, community development, workplace communication and the promotion of cross-cultural awareness.

In South Africa, legislation both proposed and recently passed will enforce processes in the workplace that reflect the values prevailing in the new democracy: equality and equity, democracy at the workplace, transparency, capacity-building and empowerment are a few examples.

The final factor that has facilitated occupational social work in South Africa in relation to human resource management is the approach by social workers and schools of social work to organizations. In the former case, social workers have attempted to sell services while, in the latter, many posts in industry and commerce were created from student placements negotiated with human resource practitioners. However, the vast majority of schools of social work in South Africa do not offer specialist courses in occupational social work.

DOMAINS OF PRACTICE
IN SOUTH AFRICAN OCCUPATIONAL SOCIAL WORK

In this section, models of service delivery, as well as roles and functions and organizational locality of occupational social workers will be discussed. In the doctoral study (Du Plessis, 1994) mentioned above, two pronounced trends became evident when analyzing the practice of local workplace-based social workers; these trends will form strong themes during the remainder of the article. The first was the heterogeneity of practice while the other was the dominance of casework as a method of practice.

The fact of heterogeneity across settings precludes a neat description of what constitutes occupational social work practice. To begin with the wide diversity of settings, social workers are to be found in banks, factories, insurance companies, police stations, defence force units, retail distributors, computer companies, cement operations, publishing houses and on mines. It has been difficult to count the exact number of practitioners in South Africa. In the late 1980s the author attempted to locate all practitioners in the country, but the number seemed to shift almost on a daily basis. One hundred and forty were identified, but this excluded the Defence Force which was not permitted to share their staff complement with the author. In October 1996 there were 153 social workers in the South African National Defence Force. The original number of 140 did include 35 practitioners from the South African Police. By 1996, the South African Police Services had increased that number to over 200. In the original count, 30% were to be found on gold mines but since then this number has decreased and many mines now do not employ their own social workers but contract the services out to EAP consortiums.

The task of counting occupational social workers is made difficult by a number of factors. Where salaries are low, there is a high staff turnover. Frequently social workers move to positions within the organization to develop their careers and go into training, organizational development or human resource management. Many social workers have entered industry in non-social work positions, such as marketing or public affairs, but still identify with their profession of origin. Finally, there has been in the last few years a proliferation of EAP contractors who may be social workers in private practice, in group practice, or within a specialist division of a welfare agency. Some occupational social workers work within the framework of an EAP while others do not. While social workers appear to be the preferred profession in staffing EAPs, they are certainly not the only ones, as nurses, psychologists and human resource personnel all play a role as well.

Other factors that underscore wide diversity in the field are ages of practitioners, qualifications, background, experiences, length of time in workplace practice, professional identification, to whom social workers report as well as number of employees served.

Further, because social workers offer services as opposed to fixed products, what their work entails will change in response to worker and organizational needs. In a rapidly transforming society this is exacerbated by outside factors that impinge on practice priorities. Analyzing descriptions of occupational social work practice in the literature (Straussner, 1990; Googins and Godfrey, 1987; Akabas and Kurzman, 1982) highlights the wide array of choices in respect of services. Some services are described by method used, such as counseling, group work and resource development. Others are described in terms of issues; here, examples include retirement, alcohol abuse or safety. Role played by the social worker can also outline service as in the cases of advocate, advisor, trainer, educator, broker and consultant. Finally, there is also the dimension of client group involved: women, apprentices, single parents or divorcing employees. The possible permutations and combinations across method, issue, role and client group offer some sense of the variety as well as the richness in the way needs may be addressed at the workplace.

In the study done during the late 1980s and early 1990s (Du Plessis, 1994), there was no doubt that personal counseling/casework dominated. Amongst the group of 70 social workers interviewed, over 50% of the sample spent more than half their time on casework. In addition, for 78.6% of the respondents, casework represented the task on which they spent the single most amount of time.

Some of the social workers who spent a significant chunk of time on it defended this. They offered a number of explanations that included a lack of accessible and trusted community resources and the fact that employees' expectation of the service, often in the context of a hostile anonymous organization, was of a confidential individualized service in which they were heard. In addition, some social workers saw their core competency as therapeutic work and made the point that if they ventured out of this domain into work-related problems, boundaries with other professionals would become blurred.

Other social workers in the study were frustrated with the focus on casework and wished to change this. Their overwhelming desire was to move into preventive work, especially where their caseloads highlighted collective problems that could be addressed by preventive strategies. Reasons for why they did not change their focus included personal and professional limitations and the fact that they felt sanctioned primarily as individual change agents in the work setting.

However, practice was not entirely limited to casework/counseling. Other examples included preventive and educational groups, training courses on relationship skills and communication, as well as community work inside and outside the workplace. Some became involved in policy development as well as advice and guidance on workplace issues such as affirmative action, worker representation and the like.

The majority of the respondents reported to industrial relations or human resource managers. Where social workers were part of large teams, they may have reported to more senior social workers. In some instances in South African practice, social workers work within a health center and may report to medical practitioners. In most cases, there is little if no formal and regular professional supervision or consultation.

There has been for some time heated debate amongst occupational social work practitioners about where they should be located in the hierarchy and with what department they should be identified. The results from the study are interesting and have been confirmed repeatedly in conversations with social workers over the years: Effective practice does not have to depend on your formal place in the hierarchy; rather, it appears to be a function of the social worker's ability to negotiate access across all levels of the organization depending on the task at hand. This confirms that so much success as a social worker, in an "unaccustomed" secondary setting, depends on the practitioner's relationship skills and the ability to deal with all people, despite their hierarchical positions.

CONTINUUM OF OCCUPATIONAL PRACTICE

The idea that there is a continuum of practice from micro to macro intervention which reflects intervening with individuals at one end to organizational intervention (as well as societal intervention) has greatly influenced the teaching and practice of occupational social work in South Africa. Two models have been especially useful. There are similarities between the two, and the thrusts within the models are equivalent. Ozawa's model has four stages in the analysis of social services in the workplace. These are single service orientation, comprehensive services, organizational intervention and, finally, community building (Ozawa, 1980). She makes the point and illustrates how evolvement across the stages means a developing skill and knowledge base for the practitioner as well as changes in the values held, especially as regards a view of worker motivation and relationships at the workplace.

Googins' model outlines five stages that describe the history, current practice and possible future development of occupational social work in the United States. His assertion is that "the more occupational social work takes root and matures, the more complex becomes the practice." The five stages in this model comprise the following: welfare capitalism, personal problem orientation, the service model, the prevention model and, lastly, organizational change (Googins, 1987).

Between 1986 and 1995, the author shared these models with hundreds of students and practitioners in the occupational field, and both received full support in that they were so effective not only in describing local practice, but they also contained the aspirations of local social workers when they thought of how they would anticipate their practice developing. They were also very useful in helping social workers identify and understand factors that discouraged evolvement to the next stage of practice, and thus assisted enormously in strategizing future options.

As the study on occupational social work (Du Plessis, 1994) demonstrated, a great deal of practice was "stuck" at the early stages of the models. This was also confirmed during 1995 when the author and a colleague held seminars with over 90 occupational social workers throughout the country, none of whom had participated in the research project. Throughout research and teaching commitments, efforts have been made to identify what some of the factors are that prohibit evolvement of practice, along the lines of the two models. Before going on to that, the point should be made that the importance of clinical work in occupational social work practice in South Africa has not been negated. This is especially true because of the lack of adequate and accessible community resources to which employees and their families may be referred. Thus an evolvement of practice from a micro to a macro orientation does not preclude the offering of clinical services. It includes some clinical work, but not a dominance of it for inappropriate reasons. Such reasons may include lack of skill or courage on the part of the social workers and lack of organizational commitment or sanction to move away from a preponderance of clinical services.

Some of the reasons for the acceptance of the thesis that occupational social work needs to evolve from services that center on individual change to ones that include organizational intervention are as follows. Given the ecological base of social work, with its dual attention to the person and the environment and their interface, plus the circumstances peculiar to South Africa which impact on workers in the context of powerful employers, as well as the limited resources in a developing country, casework is not the most effective way of dealing with many of the issues that come to the attention of the occupational social worker. Casework-based practice in the workplace does not represent fully the potential of occupational social work practice and limits the role of the social worker as change agent. This limited role then supports the circumstances in the work setting which, in the first place, work together to produce a focus on casework. In this way the status quo is maintained. However, it should not be surprising that social work in the workplace mirrored the conservative nature of the profession generally.

A full discussion of why social work became "stuck" in casework is beyond the scope of the article, so a limited number of factors that explain this trend will be presented.

Two concepts that have been very useful in analyzing occupational social work in South Africa are the idea of "social work in industry" versus "industrial social work" (Neikrug and Katan, 1981). The other that made such sense to local practitioners is linked to the first and relates to the dichotomy of "employee-as-person" versus "person-as-employee" (Spiegel, 1974).

Neikrug and Katan (1981) pointed out that "field of practice" can refer either to the settings in which social work is practiced, or to the type of practice developed specific to that setting–in other words, the definition may rest on context or methodology. In this way these authors have made the distinction outlined above. In their words, "'social work in industry' emphasizes the industrial setting as a locus for the service delivery . . . it points to the working person-as-employee as being a cohort underrepresented in traditional social welfare programs and indicates the unique contribution that social work can make to this clientele." This is then juxtapositioned with "industrial social work" which they assert "refers to the development of a social work method relevant to the industrial setting." Although Neikrug and Katan (1981) do not develop this concept further, they illustrate it by looking at the practice of social work at the workplace in Israel. Here there are many similarities with South African circumstances. They contend that in Israel (as was the case in South Africa) practitioners fall mainly under the description of "social work in industry" in that their primary focus was not on workplace issues but rather on a wide range of individual problems of employees and their families. Work-related issues such as salaries, working conditions, interpersonal relationships and advancement, for example, were avoided. One explanation proffered for this was that by having a traditional welfare/personal problem orientation, these social workers avoided stepping on the toes of other parties such as management, the union and colleagues in similar workplace service professions. The nature of the practice paralleled that offered in the social service offices of local authorities. There was little evidence of a "special" method or technology adapted to addressing and improving the "human side of the enterprise." Neikrug and Katan (1981) offer as examples of industrial social work activities: advocacy, ombudsmanship, arbitration, labor relations, organizational change and management of work.

The above, as mentioned previously, certainly pertained to occupational social work practice during the 1970s, 1980s and part of the 1990s. Indeed, even today it would aptly describe some practice. However, as will be shown later in the article, some changes have occurred.

One of the main reasons for the "social work in industry" focus in South Africa is the simple fact that social workers entering the workplace came from generic training and previous employment in welfare organizations. It was only in 1986 that a specialist degree was offered in the country. As this is only offered at one university, even today social workers are entering the workplace from a generic training background. What social workers therefore did was transfer largely a casework orientation onto their practice in the occupational setting, and create caseloads as they were used to doing in previous jobs in the welfare sector. Literature on the specialist field of workplace practice was scarce, and many practitioners did not mix with others to explore more creative ways of dealing with the new setting. Very few had access to appropriate consultation and supervision, and therefore their traditional way of practicing remained unchallenged. Because colleagues and managers in industry and commerce identified social workers with individual counseling, they, too, did not expect anything else. Local models of practice did not exist. When in 1980 the author was employed as a social worker in a mining community, she simply, not knowing any better, recreated her practice from a child welfare setting.

Returning to the concept of "employee-as-person" versus "person-as-employee," the division inherent therein corresponds well respectively with "social work in industry" and "industrial social work." In the first conceptualization, the emphasis is on serving the employee in his/her non-work role—such as father, mother, brother, daughter and community member. In the case of "employee-as-person," work roles become the focus of social work concern: for example, a stressed manager, sexually harassed female worker, overloaded apprentice, advancing manager, discriminated against minority group worker and retrenched employee. The study undertaken by the author clearly demonstrated that in the late 1980s and early 1990s, the emphasis of services was on employees' non-work roles. In a section of the research, questions were specifically asked about the respondents' involvement in work-related problems. Some reluctance by the respondents to become involved in such problems was noted. The following list outlines, by giving percentages next to the work-related problem, how many of the respondents agreed that they would become involved should such a circumstance occur: deficient job performance (67%); supervisor/subordinate conflict (55%); shift work issues (53%); perceived unfair disciplinary grievances (52%); organizational stressors (40%); unsafe working conditions (40%); grievances around new technology (39%) and grievances around wages (29%).

As can be seen, the respondents were split as a group in acknowledging a role for social work in work-related problems. In principle there was understanding of the need for some involvement in some problems, but in practice there were many constraints, some within the social workers themselves and some within the organization. For example, where social workers felt specialist technical knowledge was needed, they would not intervene. In some cases there were other professionals who were seen as legitimately "owning" that particular turf. In some instances the social workers said that they would not be allowed to become involved by management while in others, employees simply would not identify the social worker with that problem and therefore not approach them for assistance. A trend noted here, and one that ran throughout the study, was that social workers in the workplace tended to avoid conflict with colleagues and for this reason they did not feel comfortable stepping on others' toes, which often was the case when they ventured out of their familiar turf of dealing with personal and family problems.

Changes have occurred since the study and some of these will be discussed in subsequent sections. There is evidence of occupational social workers meeting unusual challenges and reaching out for creative responses in service delivery. There have been two major reasons for this. One is that social workers in the workplace are acquiring specialist knowledge and skills formally through further study, or informally via contact with other occupational social workers. The other reason is that in the past few years, given the changes both in the society generally, as well as within workplaces, problems and needs expressed in the workplace now go beyond the individual's personal and family concerns.

FACTORS IMPACTING ON PROGRAM DEVELOPMENT

Many of the factors that impact on social work practice at the workplace in South Africa have been covered in the previous three sections. However, there are others that require elaboration.

The heterogeneity of practice has been discussed in some detail previously. The fact of diversity in practice highlights the range of factors that can impact on practice. Some are within the personal realm, such as the motivation, commitment and willingness to risk on the part of the social worker. Courage to be challenging in a sometimes daunting setting where colleagues do not have a social work perspective is needed. For some social workers this is not easy, given the nature of their training and personal propensities. Other factors lie in the realm of professional training and guidance and the requisite knowledge and skills that are needed for program development. Many of the factors impacting on program development have to do with organizational restraints, and by implication, opportunities afforded by the employer to be part of new initiatives at the workplace.

The discussions presented in this section will be divided into three main parts. The first will consider some cultural factors that impact on program development; the second will go on to look at some organizational dynamics affecting services, while the third set of factors to be considered will comprise a number of sociopolitical and economic imperatives in the new South Africa impacting on the workplace and therefore on social work programs.

A thorough discussion of all cultural factors that could impact on social work programs at the workplace is beyond the scope of this article. South Africa is made up of many cultures, and the complexity as a consequence goes far beyond a simplistic separation between "black" and "white." There are enormous divisions among the two groups. Also, South Africa is going through sustained transformation, and new identities are emerging. However, the society has a legacy of white domination and the oppression of black people with concomitant beliefs in the "superiority" of the white culture over the black. This was abetted by the situation of commerce and industry being firmly grounded in "white" culture. Many of these beliefs are correctly being challenged as the new society forms.

The point has already been made that social work in South Africa has been rooted in the traditions of Northern Hemisphere countries, especially Britain and the United States. Given this in the context of Apartheid, it is easy to understand how many of the programs were insensitive to cultural needs and expectations of black workers. In addition, many of the services offered in the workplace were split along racial grounds, both in conception as well as staffing.

Moema (1992) discusses some of the cultural issues in South African EAPs. On the whole, black workers, he contends, "use formal services as an alternative to the network of traditional support systems . . . they deploy as a first choice, a myriad of culturally significant figures of authority around them, such as relatives, home-based peers, senior acquaintances, colleagues, roommates, etc." Other examples of cultural differences which may impact on the development of occupational social work programs are traditional beliefs about the causation of problems (such as the belief in witchcraft) and beliefs about remedies. Many social workers have encouraged the acceptance and subsidization of traditional healers by managers and medical insurance funds. Programs may also have to consider that in all black cultures, wisdom is a function of age, and many older workers struggle to accept the counsel of younger social workers. Attitudes to sex differ from those inherent in the explicit education programs around sexually transmitted diseases. Among many people, the medicinal use of cannabis is accepted, and this may impact on the sort of substance abuse program offered in both form and content.

The second set of factors to be considered pertains to organizational factors that impact on program development. Once more, the list could be endless, and many of them have been directly and indirectly mentioned earlier in the article. It would seem that a great deal of the identity of the occupational social work program is a product of personal characteristics of the practitioner in interaction with organizational dynamics. Some of the latter include what other professionals there are within the organization, the dominant management style, as well as the commitment to the social worker in the form of resources and interest. The discussion on these presented below relies heavily on the research conducted by the author (Du Plessis, 1994).

The number and type of "specialists" within the human resource department appears to have an influence on the types of programs developed. This is related to the issue of turf and who is seen to "own" a problem. Sometimes, in smaller less specialized human resource departments, the social worker has greater leeway to define the parameters and limits of his/her function. Take the issue of HIV/AIDS.[1] If there are medical, training, organizational development, industrial relations and social work personnel, who runs with the HIV/AIDS portfolio? There are no hard and fast rules, and clearly, interpersonal relationships are important in respect to the sort of teamwork and collective effort that such a broad and complex issue requires. It is often the issue of turf that encourages social workers to stick to counseling as that is seen by others as their core competency, and claiming that turf as theirs will not ruffle feathers.

Dominant management style will also influence the boundaries that social workers practicing in the workplace will be allowed to draw. In the occupational setting, some cultures are more authoritarian than others, and this affects the leeway social workers are able to have in setting their own goals and encouraging workers to participate in the planning of services. As will be seen in the following section, there are changes in management style that will affect social work services to a large extent.

Management commitment to the social work service is of vital importance, just as, of course, is the acceptance of the social worker by employees. Many occupational social workers in South Africa find that, despite being employed by the organization, their efforts to justify themselves have to remain a continuous priority. This can be very demotivating if there is no progress and social workers have left posts because of this. If the job was created because of one person's commitment to the idea of a social worker, and that person leaves, the support base may disappear.

In the study concerning occupational social work practice in South Africa, management ignorance and apathy were highlighted by some practitioners as negatively affecting their work. Non-support of the social work function was experienced as delays in obtaining sanction as well as the non-referral of employees to the service. Another theme to emerge was that management ignorance limited the social worker's scope of impact through non-integration into the organization. Thus the social work service could become marginalized as a peripheral unit and the potential to impact on the person-environment interface limited.

Another area in which management commitment was expressed was in the evaluation of the service. Clearly, evaluation of the social work effort affects program development for a number of reasons. While 67 out of the 70 respondents undertook some form of evaluation of their work, in 29 cases management did not require this evaluation. For the majority of these social workers, management never asked for assessments of their work and this presented to the social workers as disinterest. Overall, in respect of evaluation, there was little evidence of systematized and formalized effort, and what work was done concentrated on the assessment of output, as opposed to input.

Commitment to the social work function and the sanctioning of resources for the social worker go hand in hand. They directly affect programs developed for the reason of extending capacity in service delivery. Some social workers have been well resourced while others have battled with this. It is unusual for the social worker to have a budget of his/her own, and there tends to be the perception that what the social worker will do will either cost nothing, or so little that money can be obtained from others' budgets. In this way the direct and indirect costs of the social work function in many settings are unable to be calculated. For some practitioners this could be an advantage, while for others it could prevent them from having an organizational profile.

Outsourcing the EAP/occupational social work function has become more and more popular in South Africa. In response, a range of individual practitioners and group profit and not-for-profit organizations have been initiated.

Services in this position have direct costs associated with them. By implication, there would be a higher degree of accountability, and this could have positive spinoffs for evaluation of services and program developments.

The final section of this discussion on the factors which affect program development is perhaps, at this time in South Africa's history, the most significant. It deals with some of the sociopolitical and economic imperatives facing the country. For the purposes of this discussion, some major trends in South African workplaces will be described. These trends include three interrelated factors: the values/cultural change at the workplace; productivity and motivation in the context of world class manufacturing; and the "new relationships" envisaged by the Labor Relations Act of 1995 between employers and employees. Inherent in these trends are opportunities for creative occupational social workers to build services because many of the values and processes that have been espoused by social workers for many decades are currently being placed at center stage. At the same time many other professionals, not from the social work fraternity, are taking the opportunity to offer to industry, commerce and labor their interpretation of the world of work. Thus, coming through the doors of a manager's office to sell programs may be an occupational social worker, industrial or clinical psychologist, industrial sociologist, or corporate anthropologist. In some respects it would seem that defining the "culture" of the workplace is "up for grabs"; no one has the monopoly on describing and prescribing the nature of change at the workplace and as the depth of the change is profound and complex, every view has merit.

There are two major thrusts which lie at the heart of current change at the South African workplace. One is the nature of change preceding and following the introduction of a democratic order in the country. At the center of this lies the concern for a culture of human rights; the other is the change seen internationally in business. This deals with the need for increased competition in view of the "global village" perspective. The latter trend is thrown into sharper relief in South Africa as former economic protections from the period of sanctions and isolation are removed. In most industries, South Africa is not generally internationally competitive especially when compared with similarly developing countries.

The point made by a business consultant (Madi, 1995), offering some thoughts on "Africanizing your EAP," is that transformation of the business culture needed in South Africa parallels the sociopolitical changes. Some of the trends he noted were changes from an authoritarian culture to a more participative one; from an exclusive to an inclusive style; from secrecy to transparency in dealings, and from a withholding to an empowering modus operandi. As far as workers are concerned, some changes envisaged at the workplace include a movement away from an alienating environment to one of belonging; away from an adversarial mood to one of cooperation; a movement from blind obedience to one of involvement in decision-making.

Productivity has for a long time been a contentious issue in South Africa. The question was often raised why workers should be expected to commit to productivity when they had no stake in the business. Indeed, many of the factors that would promote productivity were artificially regulated by laws–access to education, job advancement, ability to own property in urban areas–and all of this in the circumstance of the majority of workers being denied the right to vote. For many workers, discrimination in the workplace reflected discrimination in the general society, and to commit to productivity did not present as a fair expectation. Now that South Africa has reentered the global economy, the damage done during the Apartheid era has become even more apparent. South African goods, for a number of historical reasons, are priced out of the international markets and many forecasts, while relatively optimistic about political change, are more wary with respect to the growth of the economy. It is acknowledged that productivity is a crucial issue facing local stakeholders.

It is obvious that in order to institute and sustain the sort of changes mentioned above, a new set of relationships are necessary at the workplace. Many of these are explicit and implicit within the new Labor Relations Act passed in November of 1996. Indeed, this was the first piece of labor legislation negotiated by the three "social partners": labor, business and government. It is perceived as ushering in a new era by increasing union and worker rights. In the words of the Minister of Labor (Mboweni, 1996): "An educated, productive and well-treated workforce can become a national asset." Some of the main objectives of the new Act are to promote employee participation in decision-making through the establishment of workplace forums and to extend rights to workers in the agricultural and domestic sectors previously not covered by legislation. It also aims to mediate the majority of disputes as opposed to dealing with them through the adversarial court system. This has been done in the spirit of commitment from all parties to allow the economy to grow and create the jobs necessary to counter poverty, unemployment and discrimination.

Needless to say, the new dispensation has been greeted with some suspicion from both labor and business. Small and medium-sized enterprises believe that they cannot afford many of the rights given to workers. Some unions are cynical of the new relationships which need to be forged at the workplace, seeing them as a method of co-opting workers to give more for less; indeed, some of the conditions for becoming "world class manufacturers" would seem, at least in the short term, to place workers' job security at risk: Some concepts here include rightsizing, re-engineering, outsourcing, and the like.

The implications for the occupational social work agenda of the above would seem obvious, and the response needed goes far beyond a narrow agenda of casework, although, as will be seen in the final section, individual clinical services may once again be placed at the heart of the occupational social work intervention.

CLINICAL ISSUES IN SOUTH AFRICAN OCCUPATIONAL SOCIAL WORK

The point has already been made at length about the focus on individual intervention in local practice. This was encouraged by the introduction of Employee Assistance Programs influenced by the United States experience as well as by the fact that many social work programs were established at the workplace because of a concern for alcohol abuse.

There has been lively debate amongst EAP and occupational social work practitioners in South Africa as to what the "correct" percentage of substance abuse should be in respect of problem identification in program usage. At the beginning of many programs the percentage was over 50%, but over time this dropped to 20% or lower. The reasons for this differ according to the interests of the person relating the drop-off. Those working in the field of substance abuse claim that practitioners are misdiagnosing, or allowing substance abuse to fall off the agendas of their programs. Those with a different point of view maintain that other problems have come to the fore (such as post-trauma debriefing), or that they identify problems before they reach the stage of substance abuse–hence the increase in problems around relationships and depression. It is difficult to say which opinion is more accurate. In May 1995, one large company which runs an in-house program reported that the number of alcohol-related cases had increased from 12.5% of reported problems to 18% between 1992 and 1994. Four other companies at that meeting of practitioners shared their percentages as well for alcohol/substance abuse within their EAPs, and these were 12%, 6.5%, 2.9% and 2%.

On the whole, over the past few decades, mental health per se has not been a national priority. While it was accepted that the policies of Apartheid contributed to mental health problems, a focus on the abuse of human rights as a collective issue seemed to preclude a focus on mental health problems themselves. For people dealing with gross violation of human rights and poverty, unemployment and a poor education system, looking at issues such as depression presented almost as a "luxury." The major battle for unions was, and remains, a living wage and other conditions of service. There was little space on their agendas for mental health. As one unionist remarked to the author in 1987, "Our role is to get the alcohol dependent person's job back. We simply do not have the time to deal with the problem itself."

There have been some changes in this regard for a number of reasons over the past few years. The changes which have happened have highlighted some mental health concerns. Posttraumatic stress has been identified as a national concern because of the experiences of ex-detainees, families of murdered political activists, an increasing awareness of abuse within the family, and the dramatic rise in violent crime outside of the townships where the rate has always been high. Depression has been repeatedly discussed in the popular media and is not as "hidden" any more.

Looking at the sorts of problems within five companies which shared statistics at an EAP meeting in Johannesburg in 1995, family, marital and general relationship problems appear the highest. Health issues such as HIV/AIDS and sexually transmitted diseases are on the increase. Financial problems also occur and the process of trauma debriefing is gaining more attention in such programs.

As a matter of interest, the utilization rates of seven programs shared at the meeting ranged from 5.4% to 38%. The latter figure is unusually high, but it represents a program which focuses primarily on housing problems of black employees and their families. The next highest figure is 13.3% that pertains to a mining company which has a relatively large team of full-time social workers.

When compared with the programs in the United States, one of the biggest challenges faced by local practitioners has been the unavailability of accessible and appropriate community resources to which to refer employees and their families. Some of the child and family agencies have fairly long waiting lists, while private services are out of the reach of many. Social workers in private practice–a growing field in South Africa–are being used more because, if they are registered, part of the costs are borne by the employee's medical insurance. There are specialist in- and outpatient facilities for psychiatric problems and addictions, but certainly not on the scale seen in the Unites States. Health services generally in South Africa are facing crises due to escalating costs and reduced manpower.

EDUCATION AND TRAINING FOR OCCUPATIONAL SOCIAL WORK

There is only one university currently offering a specialist course in occupational social work. The program began in 1986 at the University of the Witwatersrand and until 1990 was at a fourth-year level of the Bachelor's degree. However, when the training period for social work returned to four years, the South African Council for Social Work decreed that students had to undergo a fourth year of generic training as opposed to specialist courses. The program was then offered from 1991 as a part-time Masters degree for social workers practicing at the workplace. Teaching and internships cover interventions at all three of the levels–micro, meso and macro. Students are required to undertake a dissertation of limited scope, and thus there is a growing body of local research.

Some other universities offer undergraduate students occupational placements and some theory input. At the University of Pretoria, a module on EAPs is taught as part of a Masters degree in Supervision. What is lacking, however, at all local universities, are undergraduate courses on work and human development.

There are two support groups in Johannesburg which cater to the needs of occupational social workers in South Africa. One is the Forum for Occupational Social Work which is an informal support and education-oriented group that meets in Johannesburg every second month. Attendance is usually restricted to social workers. The group was formed in 1984 and continues to function.

The second group is also an unconstituted body that has a rotational chairperson. It is called the Southern Gauteng EAP Workgroup and is open to all EAP practitioners. This group also meets six times per year and remains extremely active. There are a number of similar groups in four other cities, and all are affiliated with a National EAP group situated in the Institute for Personnel Management. This Committee is made up of EAP practitioners who serve on it in a voluntary capacity. They hold annual conferences, conduct research and have recently explored a link with EAPA in the United States for the purposes of accrediting South African practitioners.

The purposes of the EAP Workgroup are mutual support and education. Some of the topics covered by the various workgroups during 1994 and 1995 included: EAPs and the Reconstruction and Development Program; sexual harassment; co-dependency; alternative therapies and traditional healers; input from several community resources; employees with financial problems; domestic violence and trauma counseling; coping with divorce; caring for the caregiver, and managing change at the workplace.

FUTURE DIRECTIONS AND CHALLENGES

Many of the future directions and challenges facing occupational social workers in South Africa have been dealt with in the previous sections. The heterogeneity of practice circumstances, linked to the different needs of organizations, prevents any attempt at a neat prediction about the future of social work at the workplace. In some settings it will continue to flourish and grow. In others, services will be outsourced. In an effort to diversify programs and to deal with the threat of reduced state subsidies, many welfare organizations are now offering services to industry and commerce. Such services include trauma debriefing and life skills training. There is an enormous potential for programs assisting organizations and workers to cope with change although social workers do not have a monopoly on such interventions.

There has definitely been a move away from casework by those practicing full-time within organizations in order to free up time to look at bigger system change. Also, private practitioners on a contract basis can do counseling. Examples of some current projects among the occupational social work fraternity are the training of primary health care workers for the community in which the organization operates; stress management programs; sexual harassment policy development; team building and change management. Occupational social workers have begun to assume a major role in employee education and prevention training in the area of HIV/AIDS, the presenting problem in close to 50% of the cases seen by some EAPs in South Africa.

As mentioned earlier in the article, change is acknowledged as a central dynamic in all activities at the workplace. Many different professionals are dealing with this and some larger companies have separate specialist departments working on preparing people to face new challenges. It could be argued that occupational social workers may return to a focus on clinical work because frequently that is precisely what is missing from the skills brought by the various human resource practitioners. In order to survive as a member of a human resource team, each one has to provide a core competency. Exactly what the core competency of the social worker is has been hard to define. Some social workers have commented that they do not want to become diluted organizational change agents or "half-baked" trainers in situations where they have fuzzy boundaries with colleagues in related fields. What these social workers have said is that they would like to "stick to their knitting," and this means excellence in counseling all employees. Also, as South African society changes and the spirit of democracy grows, some of the "watchdog" functions that social workers claimed in the occupational setting may recede.

While some social workers at the workplace can debate future directions and a strategy for an evolvement of practice, others are still struggling to market their services and have them accepted. It is therefore difficult to proffer a description of how the field will develop as practitioners are at very different stages. However, during the national set of seminars run by the author and a colleague in 1995 that involved over 90 practitioners, there was agreement that, perhaps as never before, the time for occupational social work had arrived. Opportunities abounded for creative responses to a range of challenges thrown up in the new South Africa. The question that was posed, however, was whether social workers were ready to meet the challenges. In all of the discussion groups, practitioners acknowledged that they had a great deal to do in terms of honing up their skills and knowledge base, and finding ways to create and sustain their capacity to take risks and be courageous as they faced the road ahead.

NOTE

1. After this article was written the issue of HIV\AIDS in South Africa took on international ramifications. See Helen Epstein, "The Mystery of AIDS in South Africa," *The New York Review of Books,* Vol. XLVII, No. 12, pp. 50-55.

REFERENCES

Akabas, S. H. & Kurzman, P. (1982). "The Industrial Social Welfare Specialist: What's So Special?" in S. H. Akabas & P. Kurzman (eds.), *Work, Worker and Work Organizations: A View from Social Work.* Englewood Cliffs, NJ: 195-235.

Du Plessis, A. W. (1994). Issue Resolution in the Evolvement of Occupational Social Work Practice in South Africa. PhD Dissertation, School of Social Work, University of the Witwatersrand, Johannesburg.

Googins, B. (1987). "Occupational Social Work: A Developmental Perspective." *Employee Assistance Quarterly,* 2 (3): 37-53.

Googins, B. & Godfrey, J. (1987). *Occupational Social Work.* Englewood Cliffs, NJ: Prentice Hall.

Madi, P. (1995). "Africanise Your EAP." Paper presented at the National Employee Assistance Programme Committee's Annual Conference, Pretoria.

Maiden, R. P. (ed.) (1992). *Employee Assistance Programmes in South Africa.* New York: The Haworth Press, Inc.

Mason, J. B. (1990). "Social Work with Individuals and Families," in B. W. McKendrick (ed.), *Introduction to Social Work in South Africa.* Pretoria: Haum Tertiary.

Mboweni, T. (1996). "A New Labour Dispensation." Address by the Minister of Labour, 19 September 1996.

McKendrick, B. W. (1990a). "The South African Social Welfare System," in B.W. McKendrick (ed.), *Introduction to Social Work in South Africa.* Pretoria: Haum Tertiary: 20-43.

McKendrick, B. W. (1990b). "Introduction" in B. W. McKendrick (ed.), *Social Work in Action.* Pretoria: Haum Tertiary: xii-xvi.

Moema, M. S. (1992). "Cultural Issues in South African EAPs: The Perspective of the Black Client," in R. P. Maiden (ed.), *Employee Assistance Programmes in South Africa.* New York: The Haworth Press, Inc.

Neikrug, S. M. & Katan, J. (1981). "Social Work in the World of Work: Israel and the United States." *Journal of Applied Social Sciences,* 5 (2): 47-65.

Spiegel, I. (1994). *Not for Work Alone: Services at the Workplace.* New York: Urban Research Center, Hunter College.

Straussner, S. L. A. (1990). "Occupational Social Work Today: An Overview," in S. L. A. Straussner (ed.), *Occupational Social Work Today.* New York: The Haworth Press, Inc.: 1-17.

The Evolution and Practice of Occupational Social Work in the United States

R. Paul Maiden

SUMMARY. Occupational social work was first introduced in the United States at the dawn of the 20th Century in response to heightened industrialization, rapid urbanization and an influx of immigrants with numerous social needs. In the absence of institutionalized social welfare services and increasing consumer demands, leading industrialists of the era assumed the role in the provision of social welfare services. While paternalistic in its approach, these early employer sponsored social services set the tone for the workplace programs that have evolved over the past 100 years. While these services have been offered under many different auspices such as unions, large corporations, small employers, federal, state and local government agencies, drug and alcohol treatment programs, hospital and related health care services, the military, and by major health insurers, social workers have played a pivotal role in the evolution of workplace human services. This article traces the journey of the occupational social worker in the U.S. and the evolution of work related delivery systems. It also examines the unique perspective that social workers bring to the world of work and the resiliency with which they have been able to assist workers and work organizations respond and adapt to a rapidly changing workplace and environment. This article also explores the roles social workers play in the areas of adapting to technological and organizational change, under-

---

R. Paul Maiden, PhD, is Associate Professor, School of Social Work, University of Central Florida in Orlando. He coordinates the MSW program and the graduate addictions certificate program and is a faculty member of the PhD in Public Affairs program.

[Haworth co-indexing entry note]: "The Evolution and Practice of Occupational Social Work in the United States." Maiden, R. Paul. Co-published simultaneously in *Employee Assistance Quarterly* (The Haworth Press, Inc.) Vol. 17, No. 1/2, 2001, pp. 119-161; and: *Global Perspectives of Occupational Social Work* (ed: R. Paul Maiden) The Haworth Press, Inc., 2001, pp. 119-161. Single or multiple copies of this article are available for a fee from The Haworth Document Delivery Service [1-800-342-9678, 9:00 a.m. - 5:00 p.m. (EST). E-mail address: getinfo@haworthpressinc.com].

© 2001 by The Haworth Press, Inc. All rights reserved.

standing and accepting diversity, health care cost containment, economic fluctuations and job insecurity, work induced stress and illness, managing trauma, conflict and violence, work and family issues, and the recent infusion of public welfare recipients into the workplace. *[Article copies available for a fee from The Haworth Document Delivery Service: 1-800-342-9678. E-mail address: <getinfo@haworthpressinc.com> Website: <http://www.HaworthPress.com> © 2001 by The Haworth Press, Inc. All rights reserved.]*

KEYWORDS. Occupational social work in the United States

THE SOCIETAL AND HISTORICAL CONTEXT OF OCCUPATIONAL SOCIAL WORK IN THE UNITED STATES

Occupational social work was one of the earliest domains of practice in social work in the United States. The emergence of social services in the late 1800s and early 1900s was a response in part of the early welfare movement in American industry. In the late 19th Century, businessmen were faced with a number of labor problems that were viewed by management as threats to the paternalistic and autocratic style that they had been accustomed to for so long.

In an effort to deal with these problems businessmen began, in the late 1800s, policies and programs that marked the early efforts of welfare capitalism. This resulted in the hiring of personnel who were charged with the development of a wide range of services for employees that had not existed before and were not available in the community where social agencies were yet to be established (Popple, 1981).

The Industrial Revolution in America

Northern States Power and H. J. Heinz were among the first companies to hire the early period occupational social worker, commonly called social welfare secretaries. Aggie Dunn, hired in 1875, was H. J. Heinz's first occupational social worker. For the next fifty years, "Mother" Dunn interviewed, hired, counseled, and generally watched over her 1,200 charges in the Pittsburgh pickle factory. Although a blatant form of institutional sexism, Heinz's effort was aimed at a large number of female employees. From these earlier gender-bound functions, the early occupational social workers broadened their practice to serve entire work groups and acted as a bridge between employer and employee. An example of services they oversaw were: medical examinations, washing and bathing facilities, lunch rooms, loans, insurance, savings plans, entertainment and concerts, job training, citizenship training for immigrants, housing, recreation, and family care (Fleisher, 1917).

Other programs developed after the turn of the century were more sophisticated. One such program was Macy's department store's Department of Social Services (Evans, 1944).

The occupational social worker employed by Macy's had a multi-faceted role: informational, societal, and psychiatric. She held the belief that as caseworkers, she and her counterparts in other companies should provide workers with comprehensive information about social service agencies and community resources. She also felt that as a caseworker she should be able to recognize conditions in an employee's living situation requiring assistance through financial intervention such as loans and grants. Lastly, she expected social workers in the workplace to provide personal counseling and guidance to workers about problems and solutions (Masi, 1982).

Early occupational social work did not maintain a footing in the workplace, however. There were a number of factors that contributed to their decline. The primary function of the welfare worker as a socializing influence revealed a downside as welfare capitalists began to react to the growing threat of organized labor and unionization efforts. As these early work based social welfare programs became identified as management's tool to avert unionization, the welfare secretary began to be viewed with distrust by workers. This laid the foundation for the animosity that developed and has been sustained throughout the past decades regarding the inappropriateness of social workers in occupational settings. Unfortunately, the emerging social work profession also contributed to this view by the position taken regarding social work's involvement in the workplace.

Social workers were unsure that work in business and industry was an appropriate domain of practice for this newly emerging profession. After the Flexner report in 1915, the social work profession attempted to narrow the domain of practice to a point where knowledge could be developed and expertise claimed (Flexner, 1915). A series of studies of social work and social work education done in the 1920s all mention social work in business and industry, but all agree that it was more appropriately a field of business administration. There was a general consensus that the ethics and values they perceived as being held by business and industry were not conducive to the practice of social work in these settings (Tufts, 1923; Walker, 1928; Steiner, 1921). Consequently, there was no place for industry in psychosocial casework.

This view continued to be held for several decades as suggested in a paper presented at a 1958 Columbia University School of Social Work alumni conference titled, "Is There a Place for Social Work in Industry?" The presenter differentiated between social "workers" in industry and social "work" in industry. Acknowledging the presence of social workers in business settings, but stating that in most cases they were performing non-social work functions, they did not see social work in industry as being part of the immediate future (Masi, 1982). It is historically noteworthy that this conference took place at Columbia University School of Social Work as it was one of the first schools to develop an industrial social work concentration a few decades later.

World War II

Industrial social workers reemerged briefly again during World War II. One of the best known programs was the joint project of the National Maritime Union and United Seaman's Service in which a social worker supervised a group of caseworkers. The program was set up for seamen and their families who needed help in making claims for death, injuries or losses, assisting bereaved families, procuring ration books, and locating sailors stranded in foreign countries (Reynolds, 1951). This program was particularly significant because Bertha Capen Reynolds, a social worker who played a significant role in conceptualizing social work practice, headed it. The services offered through the Seaman's Service were provided to all members regardless of need. Reynolds noted:

> The sense each applicant had of belonging (without having to face acceptance or rejection at the door) eliminated much resistance which social agencies expect to find, and talk was usually spontaneous, savings hours of time establishing rapport. The casework tradition that it is important to sift out as quickly as possible those who are not eligible to receive what they asked was not applicable in this setting. Here, nobody was "out," and a person who could not be given one type of service might be helped in some other way. To concentrate on saying no was to miss important clues to real service that could be given. (Reynolds, 1951)

Reynolds noted that the services offered by her group of caseworkers were considered to be very successful by the Seaman's Service because they were provided in a context where individuals and families who received service were provided that service through an organization to which they "belonged." She presents several cases of clients who were identified and given aid because they belonged to the organization and were identified through organizational channels. She contends that some of these cases would have raised serious questions by commonly adhered to standards of determining eligibility for casework service from private agencies. She also questioned whether a social service agency would invest the time "to give service to a person who did not know how to formulate his problem, who disliked social workers and was not appreciative, and who did not even cooperate very well" (Reynolds, 1951).

The scenarios described by Reynolds present situations where social services are provided to individuals in the context of a work organization; services that were devoid of the stigma commonly associated with means tests and eligibility requirements that are often demeaning and dehumanizing to individuals seeking assistance from public welfare agencies. Reynolds' work in this occupational setting was determined successful but ended shortly after the war.

Another significant but largely unrecognized wartime era effort was undertaken by numerous Jewish organizations throughout the world which involved the relocation, resettlement, training and job placement of thousands of displaced European Jews and Holocaust survivors. These efforts had much to do with transplanting early industrial social work concepts developed in the United States to Europe and beyond. The efforts of member agencies of the Jewish Federation in the resettlement and naturalization of Eastern European Jews, especially those from the Soviet Union, are also acknowledged as their work contributed to the early conceptualization of occupational social work. These early efforts also had a substantial impact in North America. In 1938 Jewish communal groups created the Jewish Labor Committee to address discrimination against Jewish workers, including their exclusion from many areas of employment (Morris and Freund, 1966). In 1939 a national coordinating committee for the care of refugees from Germany was formed (Lowenstein, 1939). In an effort to minimize the Christian community's fears of European Jewish refugee immigration to the United States, Jewish social workers took the lead in distributing new immigrants across the country and providing aid in job placement and the amelioration of job related problems (Goldsmith, 1940).

The efforts of U.S. Army Public Affairs Division and Jewish Joint Distribution Committee social workers led directly to the emergence of modern industrial social work in Europe and Israel, and Jewish social workers dealing with refugees set long neglected precedents for occupational social workers in North America (McClellan, 2000).

Occupational Social Work Reemerges in the 1970s

There was little in the way of occupational social work activity until the 1970s which saw development of employee assistance programs (EAPs). Increasingly widespread over the past few decades, the advent of this program resulted in a resurgence of workplace human service delivery. Occupational alcoholism programs (OAPs), begun in the 1940s, were the predecessors to EAPs. Companies initially established programs of confrontation and intervention staffed by recovering alcoholics to deal with alcoholic employees. This was the beginning of a new era of social service programming in the workplace, although somewhat limited, because of what was generally viewed as a spasmodic effort to deal with a growing problem. Employee assistance programs overcame these limitations by broadening the scope of services and the basis for intervention and treatment. Consequently, occupational social workers began to assume positions in EAPs in significant numbers and are now generally considered the profession of choice to staff workplace programs (Tanner, 1991). Although EAPs continue to be the primary area of employment for occupational social workers in the United States, they are gradually entering other workplace programs such as human resources management, corporate social responsibility, occupational health and safety, family work life programs, affirmative action, downsizing and retrenchment efforts, labor relations, military social work, and employer sponsored eldercare and day care programs (Eskin, 1989; Foster and Shore, 1990; Googins and Burden, 1987; Gonyea, 1993; Lewis, 1990; Ortiz and Bassoff, 1987; Seck, 1992; Shanker, 1983; Weinstein, 1990).

It is important to note that the reemergence of occupational social work did not evolve out of any purposefully conceived models or conceptualizations on the part of the social work profession. The foresight and persistence of a handful of innovative practitioners and educators are primarily responsible for what is now called occupational social work (Googins and Godfrey, 1985). The social work profession was not at the forefront of this new era of workplace human service delivery. This is demonstrated by the fact that there was no organized professional response until 1979 when the National Association of Social Workers (the professional association for social work practitioners in the U.S.) and the Council on Social Work Education (the national accrediting organization for schools of social work and membership organization for social work academicians) co-sponsored a project that represented a major commitment by the profession to further the development of occupational social work education and practice. Furthermore, it was not until 1982 that NASW formed the National Occupational Social Work Task Force, which had as its agenda: "Assessing job functions of occupational social workers and the knowledge, skills and abilities needed to perform those functions; reviewing recent trends in the use of occupational social workers; and projecting how and what settings they are likely to be employed in, in the future; recommending to NASW how to respond to current and future practice needs; and recommending curriculum development for occupational social work training to the Council on Social Work Education and continuing education providers" (NASW, 1984).

As a growing number of social workers began to enter workplace programs suspicions again arose regarding the appropriateness of social work practice in work settings. The response ranged from mild questioning to outright disapproval of occupational social work as being antithetical to the nature and mission of social work. Googins and Godfrey (1987) suggest that with the reemergence of occupational social work there were three persistent questions regarding the appropriateness of workplace practice. They were:

1. Is the workplace an appropriate setting for social workers?
2. Is occupational social work really social work?
3. Can occupational social work achieve macro as well as micro change?

In addressing each of these questions, Googins and Godfrey (1987) turn to the ideology and change orientation espoused by the profession, contained in the NASW Code of Ethics and shared by "all" social workers regardless of practice setting. They present scenarios in response to these questions that can and do occur in both occupational and traditional practice settings. There still remains, however, certain uneasiness that the goals and ethics of the social work profession are being compromised. Googins and Godfrey (1987) maintain that the persistence of social work professionals who are pioneers in the work setting, the growing sophistication of some faculty members in schools of social work, and a developing body of knowledge that encompasses the nature of work, culture and human development have changed this perspective. While work-focused social work has earned a place of legitimacy, its ability to serve at-risk populations still comes into question.

A CONCEPTUAL FRAMEWORK FOR OCCUPATIONAL SOCIAL WORK

While occupational social work began to reemerge as a viable field of practice in the late 1960s in the U.S., it was not fully addressed by the profession (National Association of Social Workers and Council on Social Work Education) until the mid to late 1970s when the National Occupational Social Work Committee was formed. The committee was comprised of leading practicing occupational social workers of the day and was charged with conceptualizing this newly reemerging field of social work practice. This committee was primarily responsible for developing the Occupational Social Work policy statement adopted by the National Delegate Assembly of the National Association of Social Workers (1984). The following is a summary of this position statement (NASW, 1984).

> Work is viewed as a significant aspect of the lives of more than 100 million employed Americans. Work is important to the person's self-esteem, economic well-being, and status in the community. This perspective is systemic in its conceptualization and suggests that problems that occur at work have a special meaning to people and are often reflected in problems that develop at home or in the community. Similarly, the opposite also occurs; problems that occur at home are conveyed by individuals to their work. The work setting is an important arena for helping individuals to gain access to the helping process (counseling,

advocacy, information, and referral). Management and labor and social work practitioners are becoming more aware of the common agenda they share. This awareness has resulted in the entry of the social worker into occupational settings. There are many reasons why the social work profession actively supports the development of occupational social work as a designated field of practice. First, social workers recognize the critical importance of work, work-related benefits, and the impact of problems on the well-being of the individual, the family and the community. Social workers are knowledgeable about benefit entitlements. They can apply their knowledge, skills, and experience to enable systems to function more smoothly, to advocate on behalf of workers, or to identify new approaches to management that value employees' rights, to providing expert information about human service needs of employees, and to link them to a variety of services.

Occupational social work also allows the practitioner to fill the unique role of generalist. At various times, the social workers will provide direct service to individuals and families, consult with managers and supervisors, assist with organizational development, train staff, and help with the administration of programs and the analysis of policies. Occupational social workers can analyze aspects of corporate social responsibility to the community at large. Finally, the social change role of the occupational social worker can operate in this important human service environment, the workplace. Occupational social work is a field of practice defined by the setting in which services are provided, the workplace, and the auspices under which they are offered, e.g., management or unions in public and private employment settings. Occupational social work as a field of practice incorporates traditional social work skills and abilities: services to individuals, families, groups, and special populations as well as policy formulation, administration and community organization. The cultural context of the workplace determines the manner in which these services are delivered.

Three categories of occupational social work can be described:

- *Policy, planning, and administration,* which involves no direct counseling, such as coordination of employee assistance programs, functions within corporate social responsibility departments, training, the formulation of policies for career path advancement, and the administration of affirmative action programs.
- *Direct practice with individuals, families, and special populations,* such as crisis intervention, the assessment of personal problems, and the referral for treatment of alcohol, drug and mental health problems, short-

term counseling for personal problems, child and eldercare in a company or union program, retirement counseling and relocation services.
- *Practice that combines direct service and administration/policy formulation.* Occupational social work practice focuses on individual workers and their dependents as well as employing organizations. Social work is not the only profession that has entered the workplace, but the qualifications of the social work professional are particularly well-suited for effective practice in the workplace. The focus is on person-in-environment. This concept is basic to helping the individual at work. Occupational social work includes a variety of skills and services traditionally offered in other settings. What makes this practice setting unique is the impact of the organizational structure and culture on delivery of services. Occupational social work occurs in corporations, small businesses, unions, hospitals, schools, military units, government (federal, state, regional and local) and so forth.

The social work profession has long been concerned about workers, the conditions of employment, and unemployment. However, occupational social work as a specific field of practice was reconceptualized in the late 1960s when the following trends and social issues converged:

- The reaction to the compartmentalization of life, paralleled by renewed appreciation of the connections among work, family and community.
- Interest in the importance of work, not only because of economic benefits, but also because of its function in ascribing meaning and value to life.
- Identification of the cost of human problems on work productivity, particularly, but not exclusively, the problem of chemical dependence.
- The renewed attention in the social work profession to person-in-environment as the focus of practice and interest in a non-stigmatizing approach to service delivery.
- The identification of the emotional stress and physical dangers created by the work environment.
- Rapid societal and environmental changes that accentuated individual stress in the workplace and the community.
- The entrance into the workplace of new groups with special concerns.
- The consumer movement, equal rights, and worker entitlements that have resulted in legislation including the Family and Medical Leave Act, the Americans with Disabilities Act, the Occupational Safety and Health Act, the Employee Retirement Income Security Act, the Age Discrimination in Employment Act and the Civil Rights Act.
- The identification by unions of job satisfaction and job security as important issues beyond wages.

- Changes in the role of women as wage earners, new family structures that lessen the separation between workplace and the home.
- The interest of management in increasing proficiency and productivity as a way of lowering costs and raising profits.
- The interest in corporate social responsibility and its impact on the community.

The Practice Continuum

Occupational social work is based on a continuum of practice from micro (clinical) to macro (organizational) interventions which reflects intervening with individuals on one end to organizational change on the other end of the continuum. Models described by Ozawa (1980) and Googins (1987) have been helpful in conceptualizing the occupational social work continuum. Ozawa proposes a four stage model to analyze social work services in work settings. They are the: (1) single service orientation, (2) comprehensive services, (3) organizational intervention, and (4) community building. She suggests that the stages are progressive in their scope and influence within the workplace. Googins proposes a five stage model and suggests that the more occupational social work becomes entrenched and institutionalized in work settings, the more complex the practice becomes. His five stage model spans the century of occupational social welfare's evolution and includes welfare capitalism, personal problem orientation, the service model, the prevention model and, at full maturity, organizational change. A related study examining the growth, development and trends in employee assistance programs supports the notion of evolving workplace programs. The programs studied suggest a transition from "benefiting the employee" to "benefiting the employer" (McClellan and Miller, 1988). Another study of industrial social work practices in Canada suggests that offering work based social services to employees is a good start toward demonstrating an increased sense of social responsibility. While the motivation for a program began with a primary focus on alcohol problems, the program was implemented with a broader agenda. The services grew from being offered at work to include several off-site locations for the convenience of family members. As a result of the success enjoyed by the occupational social workers, they were later asked to serve on a joint labor management group to help foster the development of other work enhancement programs both at work and in the community (Chandler et al., 1988). The study supported the notion that the organization was moving toward stage four (community building) of the Ozawa model (1980).

Whether or not occupational social work can or will fully evolve in either of Ozawa's or Googin's models and have a real and lasting impact on the workplace is a continued area of debate in the social work profession (Bakalinsky, 1980; Kurzman and Akabas, 1993; Maiden, 1987a, 1987b; Masi, 1982; Ozawa, 1980).

SERVING AT-RISK POPULATIONS IN THE WORKPLACE

Occupational social work serves a diverse population including women and racial and ethnic minorities in work settings. Although occupational social work programs provide service to a diverse clientele who represent both ends of the economic scale, the occupational social worker provides services to at-risk populations including single parents, many of whom are at or near the poverty line, working poor, the recently unemployed, substance abusers, mentally ill workers, older retired workers, the handicapped and developmentally disabled, persons with HIV/AIDS and family members of each of these groups.

In many instances, the only defining difference between clients seen by occupational social workers and social workers in other settings is that the occupational social work clients are employed. In this setting, the occupational social worker often plays an essential role in helping individuals retain employment, which keeps them from slipping into the ranks of the unemployed.

Occupational social workers are oftentimes the advocates in the workplace for populations at-risk. Their advocacy work includes development of sexual harassment policies and ensuring compliance with work related policies such as the Americans with Disabilities Act, the Civil Rights Act, the Drug Free Workplace Act and the Family and Medical Leave Act. They are also involved in promoting the development of adequate mental health benefits and coverage of services for families.

Occupational social workers also play a significant role in sensitizing the workplace to issues of domestic violence and random criminal violence which is the leading cause of death of women at the U.S. workplace. Other work includes drug, alcohol and mental health counseling as well as assisting clients with posttraumatic stress counseling for workplace accidents to deter mental disabilities, assistance in day care and elder care services, budgeting, single parenting and career management, and adolescent and family counseling.

Occupational social workers provide a wide range of training, much of which addresses issues of gender, multi-culturalism, ethnic and racial diversity, and sexual orientation. Occupational social workers also have substantial responsibility for managing the costs and quality of mental health benefits and ensuring that adequate treatment is provided in community programs that are often used for more extensive interventions. In many instances, the occupational social worker is the last line of defense in helping clients resolve personal problems that threaten their jobs. Furthermore, the social worker in the workplace is the first and sometimes only contact with an advocate or mental health professional. This is the case as oftentimes the employees and family members are ineligible for community services because they are still employed and do not access other mental health professionals because low incomes and/or inadequate health care coverage do not pay for the cost of care.

Legislation that mandates welfare recipients to leave the welfare roles within five years and gain employment are considered a particularly high-risk population, as they will bring a myriad of personal problems to the work setting. These problems include long histories of alcohol and drug abuse frequently coupled with domestic violence, mental and emotional problems, child care and transportation issues, job skill development, developing and maintaining appropriate workplace practices related to dress, timeliness, and developing appropriate co-worker and supervisor interaction skills. Given the enormity of the new welfare-to-work initiatives, one can assume that this group of new workers will also be the new clients for occupational social workers in the future as discussed in a later section of this article on new opportunities for occupational social workers.

Occupational social workers have gained access to a broad cross section of urban work settings, although only a few job areas have emerged as the predominant practice area. For many people in work settings, the occupational social worker is often the only thing between self-sufficiency and personal fulfillment and unemployment and mental illness.

CURRENT PRACTICE SETTINGS IN THE U.S.

Social workers are employed in a range of workplace settings, but there are only a few specific types of jobs that have emerged as predominant areas of employment for the occupational social worker. This section will provide an overview of jobs held by occupational social workers and tasks and responsibilities of occupational social workers in these specific jobs.

Social Work in Employee Assistance Programs

Employee assistance programs (EAPs) are by far the predominant practice arenas for occupational social workers. Employee assistance programs emerged in the U.S. during the 1970s and were the successor to an earlier model of workplace intervention known as occupational alcoholism programs (OAP). The OAP model evolved in the 1940s and for the next few decades provided the predominant form of workplace services that focused primarily on intervening with employees with alcohol problems.

Staffed by recovering alcoholics, these programs were viewed as innovators of work based social intervention. Although there was substantial growth over a 20-year period these programs also proved to be quite limiting in that they focused primarily on employee alcoholism, often detected problem employees when they had reached a latter stage of alcoholism, and were staffed by recovering alcoholics. Although quite effective in intervening with the alcoholic employee, the recovering alcoholic counselors were not skilled in other mental or social problem areas that surfaced during intervention with the alcoholic employee. This cadre of recovering alcoholic employees/counselors were the pioneers of workplace intervention and set the stage for the subsequent emergence and rapid growth of the employee assistance field. Employee Assistance Programs built on the interventions of the OAP but overcame many of the OAP's limitations by broadening the scope of services and the basis for intervention and treatment.

Drawing on a recognition of the interrelationship between personal problems and job performance, the EAP acknowledged the breadth of employee problems and focused on deteriorating work performance as the legitimate basis for intervention and treatment, and broadened services to include emotional, marital, and behavioral problems. Today, the general thrust of EAPs is to deal with any employee problem that affects or has the potential to negatively impact job performance and productivity. This approach assumes a more preventative orientation through early intervention, while the early model occupational alcoholism program was more curative in nature as the intervention commonly occurred after the employee had suffered through years of alcohol abuse.

Assessment and Referral and Short-Term Counseling

The tasks of the occupational social worker are both clinical and administrative although not always equally balanced between the two. From a clinical perspective, the occupational social workers are engaged in clinical assessments of employees to determine the nature and severity of the problem. Once this two-to-three session assessment is completed, it then becomes incumbent on the social worker to determine if the problem can be resolved in a series of four-to-six counseling sessions carried out by the occupational social worker. If not, a referral to a community resource is indicated. It then becomes the responsibility of the occupational social worker to identify an appropriate clinical provider such as inpatient, intensive outpatient or outpatient counseling depending on needs of the employee. This also requires that the occupational social worker develop and maintain collegial relationships with a wide range of referral resources as employees often present with a myriad of personal and psychological problems including mental and emotional problems, drug and alcohol abuse, marital and family problems, and legal and financial difficulties, each of which can significantly impact productivity and performance.

Supervisor Training and Management Consultation

Another equally important responsibility of the occupational social worker in an EAP is to provide supervisor training and ongoing management consultation to help management deal with employee problems impacting their jobs. This involves conducting periodic training to sensitize managers to signs and symptoms of job deterioration while recognizing the value of offering assistance, counseling and rehabilitative services as a means of restoring employees to productivity. Through the management consultation process the occupational social worker also guides the supervisor through the process of confrontation and intervention with the problem employee, and consultation in reintegrating employees to the workplace once they have completed a recommended course of treatment. The ongoing training and consultation is also used to develop awareness among managers of the relevant social policies in the U.S. that apply to the workplace such as the Americans with Disabilities Act, the Drug Free Workplace Act, the Civil Rights Act, and the Family and Medical Leave Act. Some parts of this legislation significantly affect the workplace and can result in substantial penalties if employers fail to comply.

Employee Education

Occupational social workers also provide the employing organization with a wide range of training on issues related to work and family life, racial and ethnic sensitivity, gender issues, accommodation of handicapped employees and the like. Similarly, the occupational social worker is also charged with educating employees in these and other areas including workplace violence, HIV/AIDS, health and wellness, stress management, day care, elder care, and single parent and dual career management, to name a few. The goal is to enlighten the workforce while marketing the services of the EAP that can help employees deal with these problems when they arise. Some of these problems have become significant issues for both employer and employee alike. For instance, domestic violence and other acts of random violence have emerged as the leading cause of death for women in the workplace (Maiden, 1996). Training in areas such as this is critical to protect the well-being of the employee and promote the development of a safe working environment. Another area that has achieved prominence is that of critical incident stress debriefing as a means of reducing the long-term effects of workplace trauma such as accidents, injuries and deaths that occur in the workplace.

This shift to a more comprehensive program model has led to the employment of occupational social workers in employee assistance programs. EAPs also served to legitimize the concept of intervening and treating personal and social problems in the mainstream workforce in the U.S. Perhaps most importantly, the evolution and considerable growth of EAPs has served as a gateway to the development of other employer sponsored health and human service programs.

Social Workers in Unions and Member Assistance Programs

The social work profession has maintained a lengthy but somewhat ambivalent relationship with unions stemming back to the early 1900s. The role of social worker has shifted from that of the welfare secretary in the early part of the decade mentioned previously to labor organizers and clinically licensed professionals providing counseling services through member assistance programs, the commonly-referred-to counterpart of the organization sponsored EAP.

As social workers moved into the public sector to help fill the human and social concerns accompanying the Great Depression of the 1930s, they were freed from the constraints of private voluntary agencies that were generally dependent on the largesse of private corporations for financial support. With a new (and more autonomous) public base of financial support and a growing conviction that micro interventions had to give way to macro interventions, social workers' relationship with labor achieved more clarity and the ambivalence faded. The newly emerging themes of collective action and systemic social change were much more compatible with that of organized labor. Leading social workers of the day such as Jane Addams and Harry Hopkins were vocal supporters of unionized workforces and lent all their skills and efforts to help workers in the collective bargaining process with their employers. Social workers in the public sector were also joining labor unions and organizing their own locals at their places of work. Although many social workers now belong to diverse unions, as public sector employees, the majority hold union membership with the American Federation of State, County and Municipal Employees (AFSCME), the Service Employees International Union (SEIU), Communication Workers of America (CWA) and the Drug, Hospital and Health Care Employees Union (Molloy and Kurzman, 1993).

Occupational social workers have also provided direct services to workers and their families for many years. The first of these was Bertha Reynolds and her cadre of social workers with the National Maritime Union, discussed previously. Other prominent programs have been developed by the AFL-CIO under social work pioneer Leo Perlis and unions such as Amalgamated Clothing Workers of America, Communication Workers of America, the Steel Workers, and the United Auto Workers.

Leo Perlis was the founder and director of the AFL-CIO's Community Services department. Originally a member of the Amalgamated Clothing and Textile Workers Union (ACTWU), by the start of World War II he was the unofficial director of community service for the CIO. In 1942, as a member of the War Production Board, he first unveiled his idea for a "union counselor" program to help workers who had personal problems that adversely affected their work. Later, as director of the CIO's War Relief Committee, Perlis established a role for the union counselor. Union counselors have been a recognized part of organized labor's community services programs ever since (McClellan, 1986; Presnall, 1986). His later writings on the role of labor and human services in the organized workplace are seminal to the field of occupational social work (Perlis, 1977).

The American Federation of State, County and Municipal Employees (AFSCME) has also provided services to their members for a number of years. In Chicago, Illinois, for example, AFSCME negotiated a contract with Central Management Services, the State of Illinois' personnel division, to provide member assistance services to all state employees who are union members. Called the Personal Support Program, AFSCME hired a number of seasoned mental health and substance abuse professionals, including social workers, to provide counseling services to its members. Occupational social work interns from the University of Illinois have also helped staff the program from its inception and were the primary source of social workers hired to work with union members in this program.

The Personal Support Program also provides training and consultation to union stewards dealing with members' personal problems and who are at risk of losing their jobs. The Personal Support Program was so well received by state employees and the State of Illinois that AFSCME was able to negotiate services to County and City of Chicago employees as part of their collective bargaining agreements.

Historically, many union sponsored assistance programs were not staffed by social work professionals. They were developed through the initiative of peer counselors who were unpaid volunteers. When unions began to organize workers in the early 1900s, the role of the welfare secretaries ceased to be of value to employers. This, however, created a void, which was filled by peer counselors. The peer counselors assumed many of the same responsibilities of the welfare secretary, albeit from a labor perspective. They were advocates of the worker rather than the employer. The peer counselor was also particularly needed to assist union members and their families during periods of prolonged strikes. In these instances they helped members secure a range of social services such as money, food, clothing, medical care and other essentials that were in short supply when members went on strike.

During the 1960s and 1970s, the role of the counselor in the unionized setting received considerable professional attention through the development of professional social work education at Columbia University and Hunter College in New York City. Both universities developed "World of Work" fields of practice and trained some of the first graduate social workers for employment in a wide range of union settings. While a number of union based programs continue to be staffed by paraprofessional helpers, a growing number of social workers and other mental health professionals are securing jobs in unions to staff member support programs.

Another initiative was undertaken by the AFL-CIO Department of Community Services. The *Union Counselor Program* was a nationwide effort sponsored by the United Way and accredited by Cornell University's School of Industrial and Labor Relations. The goal of this initiative was to facilitate social outreach for organized labor and to prepare union members to play an active role in peer assistance (Miller and Metz, 1991).

In addition to industrial unions offering services to their members, trade unions also developed outreach programs to their members. What started as alcohol intervention programs soon evolved into full service, trade union sponsored member assistance programs (Roberts-DeGenarro, Larazolo and Phillips, 1986). While industrial union members were employed in factories such as textile mills and auto plants, trade unions function as a primary network for building, construction, electrical, plumbing, etc. In many industries, trade unions function as a primary source of hiring and health and welfare benefits. The trade union network can gain access to more workers faster and probably better than the employers who hire or contract with workers at a building or construction site (McClellan, 1982).

Joint labor-management employee assistance programs are another service delivery model where occupational social workers are employed. The labor-management model typically has a governing board consisting of elected union members and human resource managers. The focus on assisting the troubled employee is the same, but each member represents the interests of his or her constituency. Labor-management programs are typically found in workforces that employ large numbers of blue collar and semi-skilled workers. Some of the most successful joint labor-management assistance programs in the U.S. are the GM-UAW (General Motors-United Auto Workers), Ford-UAW and AT&T-CWA (Communication Workers of America).

Integrating Employee Assistance and Managed Care

EAPs promote easy access to care for troubled employees, and early identification of and intervention into job performance problems (Robbins, Gerson and Moore, 1992). Effective EAPs provide alternatives to termination, along with short-term counseling and educational and prevention components to reduce hospitalization as the first option for mental health and substance abuse problems. Conversely, EAPs have done little else in the way of controlling actual behavioral health care costs. Companies have responded by contracting with MBC vendors to check the rising cost of care. Managed behavioral care programs aggressively oversee mental health care in order to contain costs, while continuing to coordinate all facets of client treatment. Unfortunately, clients often have not been satisfied with restrictions to higher levels of care. Huge profits realized by MBCs over the last decade are suspect and may occur at the expense of effective treatment of the employee. The amicable solution would be for the EAP and MBC to cooperate and perform those functions in which they have the greatest expertise. This integrated partnership would enhance the qualities of both programs, while ultimately benefiting all areas of the work organization.

Managed Behavioral Health Care

Managed behavioral health care (MBHC) is closely related to employee assistance programs as it requires occupational social workers to play a significant role in managing the quality and costs of care of mental health and substance abuse treatment.

Managed care is defined as any form of health care plan that initiates selective contracting as a means of channeling patients to a limited or set number of providers. It refers to a variety of market-driven systems and strategies to control costs by monitoring and controlling the utilization of health related services. Managed behavioral care (MBC) refers to a system that generates and uses a plan to organize and quantify the delivery of behavioral care through specific providers, to minimize the costs of care. Organizations purchasing MBC contracts expect to pay smaller plan premiums to cover their employees, as a result of MBC vendors being able to control mental health costs.

There are three distinct historical events that helped shape the face of MBC today (Winegar, 1996). The first was the gradual development of prepaid health care coverage. During the late 1930s and early 1940s, industrialist Henry J. Kaiser and physician Sydney Garfield established the first HMOs in Oregon and California. The most prominent feature of this model was that the consumer paid one monthly fee and then received all health care services from selected providers at little or no cost. The success of these first organizations, designed specifically to serve the health care needs of Kaiser's employees, was the basis for the nation's largest group model HMO, Kaiser-Permanente HMO. Nevertheless, opposition from physician and hospital groups stunted the development of HMOs in the country until President Nixon signed the HMO Act of 1973. The law required employers of twenty-five or more people to offer an HMO option, if an HMO is in operation in their locale, and if requested by the HMO to do so. Though there was a large increase in enrollment and continued growth, rising health care costs made the entire industry struggle financially during the 1980s. The 1990s brought a financial turnaround in the industry and the success of HMOs has spurred the development of other managed care systems such as preferred provider organizations (PPOs). Currently HMOs make up nearly 22% of all employee health benefits across the nation (Tolnai, 1996).

In 1975 the Diagnostic Related Group system (DRG) was developed at Yale University (Winegar, 1996). The federal government began using the DRG system for Medicare patients in order to contain costs and share financial risk with hospitals. Hospitals received maximum amounts based upon the DRG diagnosis given to the patient, no matter what the length of stay required. Though DRGs were used for medical hospital care, they were not applied to psychiatric diagnoses due to lack of professional consensus on treatment. Reduced profits in medical care motivated hospital management to shift expansion into specialty areas of mental health and substance abuse in the 1970s through the 1980s. The magnitude of this shift became overwhelming. Winegar (1996) reports that the incidence of teenage hospitalization went up 350% between 1982 and 1986, but the total adolescent population declined. Inpatient substance abuse and teenage treatment units proliferated, providing intensive and costly behavioral care. Hospital personnel aggressively marketed their inpatient units to EAP staff and psychiatrists, who could make direct referrals to them.

Another development that influenced managed behavioral care (MBC) was the expansion and divergence of the counseling professions (Masi, 1994). Before the 1960s, most insurance carriers reimbursed services provided only by psychiatrists. As the public's attitude toward therapy for emotional and substance abuse changed, the number of counseling professions and professionals expanded. The American Psychological Association (APA) and the National Association of Social Workers (NASW) successfully lobbied for legal recognition as providers of treatment services. Currently psychologists have achieved regulatory status in all fifty states and social work is regulated in forty-eight states. Other professions have statutory recognition as mental health providers in fewer numbers of states. Consumers flocked to the newer counseling professions, resulting in increased service utilization and increased mental health care costs. Insurance companies passed on these cost increases and their associated risks to the employers.

Struggling to contain the rising cost of health care on their profits, most of the nation's largest employers followed IBM's lead in the early 1980s (Winegar, 1996). They either developed or expanded their EAPs in the search for ways to provide appropriate, cost-effective care for employees' mental health and substance abuse treatments. Many of these employers already had managed health care in the form of HMOs and PPOs. These organizations gratefully resolved employers' questions on how to provide adequate mental health and substance abuse care while containing escalating costs by bringing managed care to the forefront.

A number of major employers also explored other ways to manage and/or contain employee health care through development of health promotion programs (Shain, Suurvali and Boutilier, 1986). Many of the efforts focused on reducing stress and hypertension which, when left unchecked, often leads to more severe and long-lasting physical illness. One study undertaken by Ford Motor Company sought to test and compare the effects of different hypertension-control interventions. Some of these interventions were more extensive than others and were also offered on-site at one of four auto plants. Findings from the study suggested that more involvement in care such as screening and referral, frequent follow-up and aftercare led to a higher level of adherence to hypertension management. The results showed lower blood pressure of up to 90% among closely monitored employees as compared to only 21% by those who were only screened but not closely monitored (Foote and Erfurt, 1978).

Another study examined increased stress levels of female workers who were juggling the demand of jobs and family responsibilities. The research suggested that while work may have a beneficial effect on mental health, certain types of jobs in combination with family responsibilities may lead to increased risk or actual development of cardiovascular disease (Haw, 1982).

The health promotion, wellness and lifestyle management programs of the late 1970s and early-to-mid 1980s were some of the first efforts on the part of employers to improve health care of employees in an effort to reduce associated costs (Shain, Suuvali and Boutilier, 1986).

Managed behavioral health care represents a paradigm shift in both the delivery of behavioral health services and the outcome measures expected of occupational social workers in employee assistance programs.

Managed behavioral health care has intensified the occupational social worker's responsibility for managing quality and cost of care. There are a number of operational parallels between EAP and managed care that place the occupational social worker in line to assume new responsibilities in benefits management on behalf of the employer. The initial EAP intake assessment has become more intensified. In the traditional EAP the occupational social worker assesses the client's needs and identifies an appropriate community referral source thus relying on the agency to develop a treatment plan. Under the managed care model an in-depth diagnostic assessment is required to determine an appropriate course of treatment. Rather than a periodic follow-up to measure client satisfaction with treatment, the occupational social worker now has the added responsibility of closely monitoring the quality and extent of care and the clinical effectiveness of the treatment. The community resources developed by the EAP can be characterized as a loose network of collegial associates that were used to refer clients with a range of presenting problems.

The new managed care model called for the development of a contracted preferred provider network consisting of licensed mental health professionals whose clinical performance and credentials are verified and periodically reviewed. Furthermore, preferred providers by nature of their preferred referral status have a preset pricing structure for delivery of all levels of care and agree to be subject to utilization review protocols developed by the EAP/managed care organization.

Finally, the traditional EAP model relies on periodic follow-up with the client to determine problem resolution. Oftentimes the severity of the problems determined the extent of the follow-up. A minor financial problem might warrant a follow-up phone call a month or so after the referral is made. On the other hand, an EAP client who has been in off work during treatment will receive workplace reintegration counseling and regular face-to-face follow-up counseling sessions for up to a year as a means of monitoring for relapse prevention.

Under the managed care model, a more structured case management approach is used. The more serious the problem and the higher the use of mental health benefits, the more intensive the case management. The aim is to monitor progress after completion of initial treatment and ensure that appropriate aftercare or ongoing counseling services are offered where appropriate and are a cost efficient means of managing the mental health care needs of the client. This intensified managed care process is oriented to clinical outcomes and sets the stage for determining the cost benefit and/or cost effectiveness of EAP and managed care services.

These newfound responsibilities have served to enhance the role of occupational social workers in the American workplace. Their job responsibilities have grown beyond that of assisting employees with work related problems to clinical and financial management of mental health benefits. Managed behavioral health care has positioned the occupational social worker to advocate for the expansion of mental health benefits beyond the traditional hospital based care. Health coverage for alternative levels of care such as intensive outpatient, day treatment, evening and weekend treatment programs and community based care has helped reduce mental health care costs. Many of these service delivery models fall on the preventative rather than the curative end of continuum of care which is most often associated with inpatient hospitalization. On the other hand, managed behavioral health care has stymied the occupational social workers' role limiting them to clinical service delivery (micro) in the workplace as opposed to organizational development and change (mezzo and/or macro) opportunities.

Employee assistance and managed behavioral health care are the dominant domains of practice for the occupational social worker in the United States. Other areas in the workplace arena where social workers have begun to make some limited inroads are described below.

Occupational Health and Safety

Occupational health and safety is an area of practice related to the workplace, which is concerned with the identification and treatment for the victim of job related hazards–both injuries and illness. United States Department of Labor, Bureau of Statistics figures paint a dismal picture of the increase in reported illness and death from accidents and toxic wastes at the workplace. This suggests a need for occupational social workers to increase their knowledge of this specific area of service where they could make a real contribution. Working with victims of workplace hazards presupposes a knowledge of the symptomology of occupational illness, concern for prevention, coordination of the total plan for treatment of the victims in their environment, and the ability to work with an inter-disciplinary team of doctors, lawyers, and other specialists in order to provide the complete service.

In order to handle such a program competently, the occupational social worker must know how to take an in-depth work history, must understand the workers' compensation law and other appropriate benefit systems, the regulatory agencies concerned with health and safety at the workplace, contract requirements which may affect the worker's ability to return to work at his former level, etc. All of these factors need to be considered in the total planning for the injured worker(s). In view of the rapid growth of clinics and outpatient hospital services under the umbrella of occupational medicine, occupational social workers are challenged with utilizing their total range of social work intervention and advocacy skills in treating their worker-clients.

The presence of occupational social workers in the health and safety arena is not widespread in the United States. However, there are several notable instances where occupational social workers have had a significant impact in advocating corrections of workplace hazards. An example of one such case involved an occupational social worker who was part of a team of medical professionals at a major university hospital's occupational medicine program studying work-related illnesses. A worker reported to the clinic complaining of nausea, stomach pain, and headaches. When tests eliminated a flu virus or other similar ailments, doctors began to suspect conditions at his job, a fabric-coating factory where he worked pouring solvents. A non-infectious form of hepatitis was eventually diagnosed. In subsequent weeks, other factory workers reported to the clinic complaining of similar symptoms. Eventually tests showed that 10 factory workers had the same non-infectious hepatitis, and another 20 of the factory's 50 employees showed liver damage. The occupational social worker's response in the early stages of the outbreak provided traditional, direct services to workers and their families, helping them apply for benefits and find other employment. However, the occupational social worker grew concerned with the lack of corrective action on the part of the factory. The occupational medicine clinic sent industrial hygienists and physicians to tour the factory with no objection from the owners. Empty chemical drums littered the overgrown, trash-strewn yard. The factory located in the basement of an aging building was crowded, poorly ventilated, hot from ovens with chemical odors everywhere, making some workers vomit. Workers dipped chemicals from open vats with ladles. They did not have protective clothing, gloves, respirators, or training in handling dangerous substances. Clinic doctors suggested improvements that the factory owners made.

Occupational social workers, however, felt that simply working privately with the factory owners was not enough and informed their coworkers that factory workers should be informed of their right to contact federal investigators from the U.S. government's Occupational Safety and Health Administration. Occupational social workers and other organizers felt that the workers, mostly poor undocumented immigrants who spoke little English, should be helped to take action themselves. Even though the factory was working with the clinic to take corrective action, the employees were still left without guaranteed protection that kept them dependent on the clinic and the factory owners' good graces. In addition, while the factory was complying with recommended changes in conditions, it continued to deny employees' worker compensation benefits, claiming that their illnesses were not linked to working conditions.

The occupational social worker tried working within the clinic program but was eventually told by the clinic director to seek support in the community. Having already set up a labor advisory board for the clinic, the social worker invited a union organizer from the International Ladies Garment Workers Union to speak about the union's experience with minority workers. The social worker also told the ill workers about the union organizer, and they asked to meet him. Within 72 hours the union had organized the workers and called a strike against the factory. At the same time the union also involved the Occupational Safety and Health Administration, state Department of Environment officials and the state chief attorney, the health department, the media and an organization of neighbors who wanted the hazardous factory shut down. Investigators found that the factory had violated air-quality standards and hazardous waste laws, allowed improper food storage and consumption, failed to provide adequate protective equipment for workers, and failed to adequately train workers in safety procedures. More than half a million dollars in fines were levied against the company. After a four-month strike, the union negotiated the contract with the factory.

This is the occupational social work perspective of empowering clients, and it may differ from the perspective of other health professionals, suggests the occupational social worker who advocated for the workers at this factory.

The social worker believed that advocacy, especially in work situations where people are at risk, is vital (NASW, 1987).

Corporate Social Responsibility

Occupational social work practice in corporate social responsibility (CSR) is designed to assist organizations in making a commitment to the economic and social well-being of the communities in which they operate (deSilva et al., 1982). Corporate social responsibility is in the context of a relationship between business and society. It involves deciding how business is to function in establishing priorities, and considering the larger community as a factor in arranging those priorities (Masi, 1982). Corporate social responsibility is another aspect of business in which occupational social workers can make a professional contribution.

Occupational social workers bring community organization skills to their corporation's staff such as the ability to locate and work with community leaders, and knowledge of community organizations. Occupational social workers both influence and educate corporations about critical, timely human service needs in their own organization and in the larger social and political environment. They can guide corporations in how to respond to these environments through the distribution of money and human resources. Their abilities in administrative and program analysis are often used to evaluate and analyze budgets and requests for contributions, and to conduct internal and external needs assessments (Weinstein, 1995).

The skills and activities relevant to social work practice in corporate social responsibility were conceptualized by occupational social workers in the 1970s (Feinstein and Brown, 1979). Similar to the skills needed by social workers engaged in community organization work, the skills needed for occupational social workers engaged in corporate social responsibility include the following seven categories:

1. organizing;
2. planning and policy making;
3. political and legislative skills;
4. interpersonal and small group skills;
5. administration skills;
6. strategy design and implementation;
7. promotion and communication.

Feinstein and Brown also list CSR activities sponsored by organizations that occupational social workers perform. These include:

- community development and activities related to community improvements;

- developing coalitions to coordinate youth and family services;
- participating in economic development planning;
- working with financial planners to rehabilitate multi-family buildings;
- involvement in expanding minority business ownership opportunities;
- issues related to needs of disabled women;
- corporate contributions.

In the 1980s, social workers showed initial interest in CSR when descriptive models and conceptualizations of CSR services began to appear in the social work literature (Weinstein, 1995). One early development model in the social work literature on CSR, juxtaposed commonly associated areas and tasks with comparable social work skills (Presbury, 1989). The Corporate Public Involvement model relates social work practice to assisting corporations in making commitments to the economic and social well-being of the communities in which they operate (deSilva et al., 1990). This model recognizes the impact of business operations on local tax rates, employment opportunities, housing costs, demands for educational services and on the lives of community residents (deSilva et al., 1990). Another model of CSR includes the following roles and activities of occupational social workers:

- consultation on human resources, policy, donations to tax exempt activities;
- analyze legislation;
- administer health and welfare benefits;
- social research;
- community development; linkage between social service, social policy and corporate interests;
- consultation;
- data management–collecting and analyzing data for decision-making policies;
- administrator;
- community planner (Shank, 1995).

The customer service model expanded occupational social workers' traditional concern with employees and their families (deSilva, 1988). This model studied the larger population of customers or consumers who needed services resulting from their interaction with and/or dependence on organizations. De Shank pointed out that occupational social work interventions are particularly suited for organizations whose clients, customers or consumers are vulnerable or at-risk populations. Specific services offered through customer assistance services reflected the unique nature of the organization. Examples of these services include the provision of consumer education activities, financial counseling for payment for the organization's service or products and referrals.

Another framework identifies five discrete areas in which occupational social workers may function (Straussner, 1990). An assumption of this model is that occupational social workers focus on identifying and assisting corporations to make a commitment to the social and economic well-being of the community in which they operate. The titles and responsibilities of social workers in these functions may include charitable allocations analyst, urban affairs advisor, CSR director, community relations' consultant, and community services coordinator. The roles and skills included in this model are community analyst and planner, budget allocator, program developer, broker, advocate and negotiator.

The work-related public policy model is conceptualized in terms of formulation, identification, analysis and advocacy for public and governmental policies, programs and services which affect the world of work (Straussner, 1990). For example, unemployment as a social work issue is addressed in this model as part of fundamental human rights with profound human costs. Unemployment and underemployment are CSR issues dealt with in terms of policy planning and analysis, program development, advocacy, coalition building and networking (Foster and Shore, 1989; Sheraden, 1985).

The efforts of occupational social workers employed in corporate social responsibility positions in the U.S. are aimed either internally at employees or externally at the community. Examples of these are an occupational social worker employed by a large pharmaceutical firm who managed a program designed to provide financial aid to employees for a range of needs. Grants are given to employees to assist with college tuition. Other employees may receive assistance because of a financial setback resulting from medical bills not covered by insurance, assistance with care for an elderly parent, day care assistance, or relief from a bad debt. Employees make application to the fund, which is then reviewed by the occupational social worker who in turn makes a recommendation for assistance to the members of a board of a foundation established by the company. In those instances where employees have created financial hardships for themselves due to gambling debt or poor money management, seeking counseling from the company's employee assistance program may be a contingency of receiving financial aid.

A second example is of an occupational social worker who serves as director of the manufacturing company's foundation. This company sets aside a percent of its net annual profits for the purpose of funding a broad range of health, social, arts, educational and community development programs. In this position, the occupational social worker has the responsibility of soliciting applications from community agencies to fund various projects. Once the project applications are received, the occupational social worker reviews the proposals and makes funding recommendations to the foundation board. Board members are appointed from the ranks of executives in the company. When the community agency accepts funds from the foundation, it does so with the understanding that the occupational social worker will monitor the progress and expenditures of the project, thus placing the occupational social worker directly in the community.

Generally speaking, practice in the area of corporate social responsibility is an untapped resource for occupational social workers. It is, however, an expanding one and is growing to include areas of work/family life, literacy training, services to indigent workers, business ethics, employee education and career development, and environment and ecology issues.

Military Social Work

Social work practice in the military has generally not been equated as occupational social work because of the association with uniformed personnel, soldiering, war and national defense. In reality, however, military social work is very much a part of occupational social work. The military is simply another type of work setting and is essentially non-civilian employee assistance services.

The U.S. has a long history of providing aid and comfort to its soldiers. The commitment to support soldiers and the beginnings of social services in the military can be traced to the Civil War, when volunteers visited hospitalized Union soldiers (McNellis, 1987). This same commitment was also documented during World War I when social work services were provided by the Salvation Army, the YMCA and the Red Cross which continued to staff military hospitals with social workers until the end of World War II (Masi, 1982). Following the onset of World War II, the civilian social work community established liaisons with military psychiatrists to determine the most effective use of professional social workers who were entering the Army. This effort resulted in the establishment of the army's first Mental Hygiene Consultative Service staff by military social workers. At this point, psychiatric social work was recognized by the army as a legitimate occupation relevant to the military mission (Ross, 1946).

By the end of World War II, 711 social workers had served in enlisted status. In June 1945, the military social work program was incorporated into the Army's Surgeon General's office. In 1946, the first social worker was commissioned an Army officer, and uniformed social work officers began to staff military hospitals. In 1947 the Air Force became a separate service, and in 1952 it instituted the Air Force social work program. The Navy had no social workers in uniform until 1980. Before then, the program was staffed by the Red Cross and civilian social workers. During the 1960s and 1970s, Army social workers attempted to broaden the scope of their practice from its psychiatric-medical base. They were instrumental in establishing the non-medical occupational social work services called Army Community Service (ACS). In that role social workers undertook activities in race relations, organizational effectiveness, correctional rehabilitation, drug and alcohol prevention programs and child advocacy. Social workers now serve in all combat arenas and have proved to be particularly valuable working with traumatized soldiers during and after the conflict in Vietnam. They have also served with multinational peacekeeping forces on the Sinai Peninsula, in Grenada and in Panama. Most recently they also served in the Persian Gulf war (Harris, 1993).

"Military life" is a term often referred to as the culture of the military. Here lies the uniqueness of occupational social work practice in the military. Their clients are military personnel and their families. Their lives revolve around and are directed by the military.

Occupational social workers in the military are both civilian and enlisted personnel. They typically hold a masters degree and provide clinical and social services. While most military social workers hold masters degrees, a number also hold doctorates in social work. Some are high-ranking officers and have substantial administrative and management responsibilities.

Military life can be stressful in war and peace alike. Military exercises involve war, global peacekeeping, regional stabilization and many other related activities where there is often a massive deployment of troops from military bases throughout the United States and around the globe. Oftentimes these deployments occur rapidly with little time for emotional adjustment. They are often accompanied by prolonged separation and fear of loss.

There are different sets of stressors during peacetime. Situations such as relocation, uncertain and ever changing duty hours, spousal and parental absence due to temporary duty assignments along with the myriad of other personal, emotional, marital and family problems that the general population experiences are no less stressful. Armed services personnel are expected to be in a state of military preparedness at all times. Consequently, the role of the social worker is primarily one of helping military personnel and their families maintain mental and emotional stability and assisting them in recovering from the ravages of combat.

Military social workers are employed in a broad range of roles throughout the armed forces. These include medical social workers in hospitals, counselors in family services centers, therapists in substance abuse treatment centers, psychiatric social workers, health promotion, family support groups during times of military crisis, trauma counseling and crisis debriefing during national emergencies and in combat situations to help military personnel deal with unresolved issues around their battlefield experiences (Harris, 1993). In many of these capacities the military social worker is a member of a service team including psychiatrists, psychologists, nurses, rehabilitation counselors or physical therapists depending on their work setting.

Social work in the armed services focuses on military preparedness while social work in the civilian workplace focuses on productivity. Similarly, some military social workers are fellow soldiers and officers while others are civilian personnel, just as some social workers in EAPs are employed by the organization to staff internal programs while others are external vendors delivering services under contract to a specific workforce.

EDUCATION AND TRAINING IN OCCUPATIONAL SOCIAL WORK

The first degree granting programs with specializations in occupational social work were not offered until the 1970s. Occupational social work offerings are typically available at the masters degree level and are completed as a specific field of practice or taken as elective course work while pursuing a masters of social work degree. If completing a full occupational social work concentration, the student also completes a substantial internship (three days per week for nine months) in an employment setting where they receive supervision by a qualified occupational social worker.

Occupational Social Work Curriculum

An earlier study of occupational curriculum offerings in schools of social work in the United States found that 39 of 74 graduate degree programs responding had occupational social work courses (Maiden and Hardcastle, 1986). Of these, 17 said they had a specific occupational concentration. Twenty-two others offered occupational electives only. It was also determined that 55 of the 74 graduate schools responding were located in metropolitan areas. This finding was not surprising, since occupational internships are typically found in areas where there is major industry–usually located in more densely populated regions of the country. Occupational social work curriculum offerings were identified in six content areas: (1) Social policy, (2) Administration, community organization, (3) Clinical, (4) Research, (5) Human behavior, and (6) Other. Some programs focused specifically on social work practice in employee assistance programs with courses like: Introduction to EAPs, Administering EAPs, and Clinical Intervention in EAPs. Other course offerings appeared to have a broader occupational focus demonstrated by such offerings as: Occupational Social Welfare Policy and Services, Essential Knowledge of Social Workers in the Workplace, and Management and Organizational Issues in Occupational Social Work. The various course offerings suggest that while some schools have focused on practice in EAPs, others have assumed a broader stance of practice in the work setting, which in most instances includes EAPs.

Almost without exception, courses on substance abuse and treatment of chemical dependency were prevalent in the curriculum content. This demonstrates the recognition of the importance of understanding alcohol and drug abuse and its impact on the U.S. workforce.

Internship Opportunities

A second year advanced field experience is part of all specialized curricula in schools of social work as a requirement for completion of the degree. Field placements usually have either a clinical or an administrative/organizational emphasis, depending on the student's chosen concentration. Internship opportunities in major urban areas abound. They are located in private sector companies and corporations, with EAP vendors delivering services to employers, and federal, state, county and municipal governments.

Placements are direct practice, where students are involved in clinical intervention with troubled employees, as well as administration/organizing experiences. In the administrative placements, students are primarily involved in program and policy development, and managerial aspects of service delivery. Placement with an organizing component is characteristic of a union's community service department, in which students are involved in advocating for the development of workplace services through union/management agreements.

Occupational social work internships include diverse settings such as public utilities, airlines, newspapers, universities, unions, construction companies, automobile plants, banks, schools, hospitals, electronic manufacturing firms, pharmaceutical companies, police departments and railroads.

Status of Occupational Training

A recent study of workplace curricula in higher education shows a decline in the number of schools offering occupational coursework (Harney and Frissell, 1996). This can be attributed to several factors such as inadequate faculty, lack of enrollment, occupational curricula established outside of large urban areas, with limited appropriate field placements. A more significant contributing factor, however, may be attributed to the decline in qualified faculty to teach occupational content. In an earlier study of occupational curriculum development it was determined that job market needs and faculty interest were the leading reasons given for developing curriculum (Maiden and Hardcastle, 1986). Faculty expertise, however, was rated as the primary factor in enabling schools to develop occupational curricula. Similarly, lack of faculty expertise was given as the basis for the decision by those schools that had not developed curricula and courses, indicating a reluctance on the part of social work education programs to attempt occupational specialization when they lacked expertise.

It should also be noted that the reemergence of occupational social work as a viable field of practice began anew in the 1970s with social work entrepreneurs who recognized the opportunity for new employment in a dynamic and growing field. The development of occupational social work was not initiated or supported in schools of social work unless one of these occupational social work entrepreneurs joined a social work faculty on a full- or part-time basis with the express purpose of developing courses. Where this occurred, it was, for the most part, due to the effort of a single faculty member. This made the occupational program vulnerable if the faculty member relocated or retired or chose to pursue more lucrative employment outside of an educational institution. Additionally, unless the faculty member holds a doctorate in the discipline and chose academia as his or her career, there is little likelihood of long-term employment and instructional continuity and continued development of the occupational curriculum. In all likelihood, this is one of the primary reasons for the decline of recognized occupational social work concentrations in social work. The table following is a listing of universities with established occupational social work specializations (Harney and Frissell, 1996). There are approximately 15 other U.S. universities that offer employee assistance specific coursework not affiliated with a school of social work and a number that offer occasional elective courses in occupational social work.

OCCUPATIONAL SOCIAL WORK CONCENTRATIONS IN THE U.S.

University and Location	Year Established
Columbia University - New York	1979
Hunter College - New York	1974
University of Illinois - Chicago*	1986 to 1999
University of Maryland - Baltimore	1984
Syracuse University - New York	1985
University of Southern California - Los Angeles	1982

* The University of Illinois-Chicago occupational social work program was discontinued when the author, who was the program chair, left the university. A replacement was not recruited.

NEW OPPORTUNITIES AND CHALLENGES FOR OCCUPATIONAL SOCIAL WORKERS IN A GLOBAL ECONOMY

As we enter the 21st century we are experiencing an unrelenting move towards a technologically proficient global economy. The U.S. is also experiencing its most robust economy in several decades and with it, an unemployment rate that has dipped below 5%. This has created a critical demand for more technologically proficient workers.

National and global economic forces are associated with widespread worker dislocation and disadvantage, particularly among the poor inner city populace. First, technological advancements and reductions in entry-level manufacturing positions continue to necessitate a more educated workforce. Second, expanded foreign policy production sites have lowered labor needs and opportunities in the United States for both entry-level and middle-management workers. Third, in recent decades, the post-industrial economic structure has changed from manufacturing to an information service economy. This change has resulted in a new strata of workers who work either part time, temporary or time limited contractual jobs, many without benefit of health and disability insurance, and lower wages (Iversen, 1998). These demands are creating new challenges and opportunities for occupational social workers as they will have to develop creative ideas in service delivery that exceed what they currently do through employee assistance programs and other workplace services described previously.

Perhaps the most significant challenge facing American occupational social workers in the new millennium will be their ability to assist work organizations to accept and adjust to the influx of new workers who are being released from federal and state public assistance roles resulting from a major change in welfare policy in the U.S. While there have been numerous federal initiatives over the past two decades that have sought to reduce the number of individuals receiving public assistance and help them to gain employment, the most significant of these has been more recent legislation mandating welfare recipients to secure employment.

From Welfare to Work

The Personal Responsibility and Work Opportunity Reconciliation Act (P.L. 104-193), commonly referred to as welfare to work, is the United States' most recent attempt to address the issue of how to assist families who receive government resources. When signed into law by President Clinton in August 1996, the law abolished existing welfare policy and dramatically changed the way in which welfare services are provided in the U.S. Prior to P.L. 104-193, needy families were provided financial assistance through Aid to Families with Dependent Children (AFDC, Title IV of the Social Security Act), an open-ended Federal (with State matching funds) entitlement program with no time limits. Although the eligible population remained essentially unchanged from previous policy (the large majority of benefits recipients being single-parent families headed by women of child-bearing age), the emphasis of Temporary Aid to Needy Families (TANF) is on *temporary* support to families, and contains an explicit social contract between the government and the benefits recipients that requires transition off welfare within a specified time period. This social contract is "enforced" through time limits on benefits. Thus, TANF is far more proscriptive than previous welfare policy and mandates employment.

Each state must develop a plan for the use of TANF funds. Though each plan is unique, the Federal government has established certain expectations regarding work, which all states must meet. These expectations of work under TANF are threefold:

- Cash assistance is time limited, with the expectation that families will move towards work. States may not use Federal funds to provide assistance to families who have received cash assistance for five cumulative years.
- Families receiving cash assistance are expected to participate in work activities (including subsidized or unsubsidized work, training, or community service) 20 hours per week if headed by a single parent, and 35 hours per week if a two-parent family.
- Families that do not meet this expectation may have their cash assistance reduced via sanctions.

A Profile of the Welfare-to-Work Population

A profile of the TANF population suggests that many TANF recipients will need assistance beyond those specified in the TANF law. Among the barriers to employment are lack of child care and transportation resources, children with health or behavioral difficulties, family dysfunctional behaviors (Bush and Kraft, 1998; Woolis, 1998; Pavetti and Duke, 1995; Urban Institute, 1998), housing instability, past criminal histories, and domestic violence (Quint, Fink, and Rowser, 1991; Young and Gardner, 1998; Woolis, 1998).

The most common barrier which substantially contributes to the difficulty of obtaining and sustaining employment is the lack of or low basic skills (Pavetti, 1993). Seventy-five percent (75%) of the TANF population in Project Match needed remedial education and lacked basic skills necessary to enter the work force (Kelly, 1997). United States Department of Health and Human Services (USDHHS) (1994) reported 25% to 40% of TANF recipients have undiagnosed learning disabilities. Psychological issues and mental health problems also impinge upon the ability of TANF recipients to perform adequately in the work force. Recent literature indicates between 27% to 50% of TANF recipients are clinically depressed (Kelly, 1997). Another study reported that 42% of welfare recipients in Georgia had clinically significant levels of depression (Moore, Zaslow, Coiro, and Miller, 1996). Seventeen percent (17%) of participants in the Gain program (the California model of the JOBS program) in Riverside, California were deferred because they were identified as having substantial mental health or emotional difficulties (Maynard, 1995).

Additional problems encountered *after* participants enter the workplace include the lack of suitable clothing, the insensitivity of other employees and employers in addressing the needs of this group, the need for additional social support (Bush and Kraft, 1998), and the lack of awareness and understanding of workplace norms and culture (Ranagarajan, 1996). Each of these factors contributes to the difficulty in maintaining employment.

TANF's emphasis on rapid entry into the work force presents particular challenges for families where an adult is affected by substance abuse. Many TANF recipients have significant problems with alcohol and other drugs that are likely to impair their ability to secure and maintain a job. Recent estimates of the number of TANF recipients with alcohol and/or drug problems indicate that the range is broad: 5% (Strawn, 1997), 16% to 37% (CASA, 1996), and 25% (Young and Gardner, 1998). Merill (1994) reports that approximately 25% of recipients are so severely addicted that they cannot maintain employment. CASA reports that 20% of AFDC recipients have such severe alcohol and/or drug problems that they will require treatment before they can benefit from or engage in employment. Forty percent (40%) of homeless TANF recipients are thought to have a problem with alcohol and drugs (Young and Gardner, 1998).

Obtaining accurate estimates is difficult because many states (approximately 40%) currently do not screen or assess for alcohol and drug problems. The under-identification of women substance abusers by professionals (i.e., physicians, social workers, EAP counselors, etc.) (Beckman, 1994; Pape, 1993), the under-reporting that occurs in surveys and personal interviews due to possible stigma and judgment, and inconsistent definitions of the problem of alcohol and drug misuse all contribute to the underestimation of this problem (USDHHS, 1994).

Many TANF recipients entering the work force, some for the first time, will experience a great deal of anxiety and stress. Although policy makers recognize that employment is critical in breaking the cycle of dependency, they have not considered, nor fully anticipated, how fragmentation and lack of services will create undue challenges and stresses for this population. Chronic stressors and anxiety are both associated with higher levels of substance use and abuse (Moos, Brennan, Fondacaro, and Moos, 1990). Many TANF participants are likely to cope with these new stressors through increased use of substances, and repeat the failure of previously attempted welfare reform which indicated that 40% to 50% returned to welfare within one year. This fact from the earlier welfare reform literature has ominous implications for the current TANF populations due to the time limited nature of this "reform" (Rangarajan, 1996).

Preliminary Results of Welfare-to-Work

Public assistance roles have dropped drastically since the implementation of welfare-to-work initiatives. Florida leads the nation's eight largest states in reducing its welfare caseload. For families subject to time limits, caseloads have declined almost 75% from September, 1996 to October, 1999 (Jonas, 1999).

Research on the effects of welfare reform suggests that its main effect so far has been to increase the ranks of the working poor. These working poor are mostly single mothers working long hours at low paying jobs, many of whom are trying to raise young children. While most former recipients are finding jobs, many are not earning enough to bring their families out of poverty. In a study of 500 adult former welfare recipients, three out of every five were employed, working an average of 34 hours a week, and making $6.34 per hour. Of those not working, 20% said they could not find a job, another 17% reported lack of child care, 15% had an injury or illness, and 12% lacked transportation. When asked further about providing for their families while off welfare versus on it, 50% said they currently were behind in paying their rent or utilities, versus 39% when they were on welfare; 14% now could not pay for medical care, versus 3% while on welfare; and 16% said they now had periods without enough money to buy food, versus 7% while on welfare (Albelda, 1999).

Many supporters of welfare reform suggest that the initiative is successful because of the large number of mothers who now have paid jobs. In their enthusiasm, they fail to point out that a vast majority of these mothers and their children are still poor. In one Florida city, for example, three quarters of former and current welfare recipients made less than $7.00 per hour. In Minnesota the average wage for former recipients was $6.55 an hour while in Portland, Oregon the average was $7.34; and in South Carolina the average wage was $6.44 per hour (Albelda, 1999).

In addition to low wages, most recipients who find jobs do not receive paid or sick leave from their employer or employer-sponsored health insurance. Many such workers also will not be covered by the federal Family and Medical Leave Act (FMLA) which requires employers to provide up to 12 weeks of unpaid leave for employees who need time off for certain reasons such as to care for a child with a serious health condition or to attend to their own serious health condition.

Implications for Occupational Social Workers

Occupational social workers have made substantial inroads into the American workplace over the past three decades. A review of the literature suggests, however, that their practice has focused primarily on the needs of employed workers (Googins and Godfrey, 1985; Kurzman and Akabas, 1993; Maiden, 1996; Masi, 1982). Occupational social workers should systematically apply the specialized knowledge and skills they have accumulated in workplace practice to practice in welfare-to-work settings (Iverson, 1998). This occupational practitioner would enact multiple work-specific roles concurrently at multiple systems levels. Although this reformulation focuses occupational social work practice on the work related needs of unemployed or newly employed people, such practice would also pertain to the work needs of underemployed, dislocated and working poor people, as well as the needs of those who are comfortably employed.

The latest U.S. welfare reform initiative presents occupational social workers with a series of new and challenging opportunities to work with a population that is viewed as particularly high risk. The need for work based case management services is self-evident. As many of these former welfare recipients join the work force, there will be a substantial need for counseling and mentoring programs to help them maintain substance free lifestyles and develop new coping strategies to help them manage the demands and pressures of the workplace. One such approach would be to take the employee assistance program described earlier and evolve it to a case management model that would provide ongoing services to help former welfare recipients as they transition from welfare to work. This type of program could also lead to employment retention and increased job satisfaction. Positive results in these areas might also lead to better jobs, increased pay and a reduction in poverty among welfare recipients. The components of a "case management employee assistance program" are described below.

Work Based Case Management Services for Former Welfare Recipients

There is an increasing body of literature suggesting that addressing alcohol and other drug problems is a critical component of interventions directed at improving employment related outcomes for alcohol and other drug using welfare recipients. Data from four national studies (Young and Gardner, 1997) suggests that the proportion of welfare recipients in need of substance abuse treatment or intervention ranges from 15% to 39%. Under the new TANF law (PL 104-193), participation in the work force by welfare recipients is mandatory, with a goal of economic self-sufficiency, and with a lifetime eligibility limit of five years. Therefore, there is considerable pressure on all of the serving agencies to promote early and lasting employment among welfare recipients.

The Employee Assistance Program (EAP) model is increasingly recognized as being a cost-effective way to address employee related problems in the workplace, resulting in increases in performance productivity, and reductions in tardiness/absenteeism and turnover. However, traditional EAP services are not as well suited for alcohol and drug abuse problems because the services are often short-term in nature (e.g., 3 to 5 "visits" or sessions per referral), and they are less often available among small businesses where the majority of TANF/Work First participants are likely to be employed.

An innovative variation on traditional EAP programs is proposed that provides support to welfare-to-work participants in two ways. First, it provides support to Work First participants who are not job-ready, due to their use of alcohol and other drugs. Second, it provides long-term (1 to 2 years) support to welfare-to-work participants in the workplace, through biweekly client contact and aftercare directed at relapse prevention. This "case management" EAP model would employ gender-sensitive assessments (the large majority of welfare recipients are women), and would work collaboratively with Work First service providers, such as state child and family services case managers, therapists and substance abuse counselors.

The case management model expands traditional EAP services to provide support to former welfare recipients who are identified as having problems with the abuse of alcohol and drugs that might interfere with their job performance. This model would provide services within a framework that views addiction as a complex, progressive social problem that has biological, psychological, sociological, and behavioral components. The underlying premise of the case management model EAP is that substance abuse is a chronic, relapsing condition requiring long-term support; substance abuse impacts on many aspects of a woman's life, thus requiring a holistic approach to treatment; there are special needs of women substance abusers, and gender specific services are needed which include such issues as child care, domestic violence, etc. An integrated approach to substance abuse treatment and work is required thereby linking the two experiences to reinforce sobriety and maximize success at work and ensure ongoing employment.

The case management model EAP is designed to promote job retention by offering an EAP with the four enhanced services:

1. The case manager would assume a more proactive approach in his or her involvement with the welfare-to-work participant. The aim of the case management EAP is to provide long-term follow-up services to the new employee to monitor adjustment to the work environment and provide assistance in resolving work related or personal problems that might negatively impact employment retention. Case management follow-ups would typically be provided on a biweekly basis to all welfare-to-work participants for at least one calendar year following job placement. Follow-up contacts could occur by telephone or in person, de-

pending on the needs of the participant and could be determined at the discretion of the EAP case manager and supervisor.
2. The EAP case manager would provide general support and mentoring to enhance the welfare-to-work participant's transition from welfare to permanent employment. Mentoring has been found to be a critical component in helping women and minorities make significant advancements in the corporate world. The mentoring program is designed to provide support, direction, skill building, and encouragement to overcome obstacles related to the workplace.
3. The EAP case manager would monitor participants' involvement in job performance through a defined process of introductory supervisor training and ongoing management consultation involving both the direct supervisor and the participant. The intent of the introductory training is to educate the supervisor about the welfare-to-work initiative and to sensitize him/her to some of the issues specific to the welfare population. Ongoing management consultation would be available to supervisors on an as-needed basis, should participants encounter work or personal problems that may threaten job retention. In addition to optional consultation services, the EAP case manager would also conduct monthly follow-ups with a supervisor to monitor work related issues including timeliness, attendance, compliance, conformity to work norms, response to supervision, co-worker interaction and performance and productivity. The intent is to detect and resolve potential problems and minimize the occurrence of disciplinary action.
4. In addition to providing access to traditional EAP services, a broader range of EAP services would be provided that could include ongoing counseling and expanded referrals to community resources such as locating suitable transportation and housing and other services that would promote employment retention.

CONCLUSIONS

In many ways, the case management employee assistance program proposed here brings occupational social workers in the United States full circle as they enter a new century. In the late 1800s and early 1900s the early occupational social workers (welfare secretaries) worked primarily with the working poor and other at-risk populations. Since their introduction to the workplace, they have made significant inroads and progress in employee assistance programs, managed mental health care, working with unions, occupational health and safety, corporate social responsibility, and social work practice in the military. Through the development of welfare-to-work initiatives, occupational social workers are presented with a substantial opportunity to assist former welfare recipients to move towards successful employment and self-sufficiency and hopefully away from poverty and dependency, endeavors that are in full alignment with the social work professional's mission of service to the poor, the at-risk and the oppressed.

REFERENCES

Albelda, R. (1999). What welfare reform has wrought. *Dollars and Sense Magazine*, Jan./Feb.

Bakalinsky, R. (1980). People vs. profits: Social work in industry. *Social Work*, July, 471-475.

Beckman, L. (1994). Treatment needs of women with alcohol problems. Special focus: Women and alcohol. *Alcohol Health and Research World*, 18 (3), 206-211.

Browning, C. and Browning, B. (1995). *How to Partner with Managed Care*. Independence, MO: Herald House Press, 6.

Bush, I.R. and Kraft, M.K. (1998). The voices of welfare reform. *Journal of the American Public Welfare Association*, Winter, 11-21.

Chandler, R.G., Krocker, B.J., Fynn, M., and MacDonald, D.A. (1988). Establishing and evaluating an industrial social work programme: The Seagram, Amherstburg experience. *Employee Assistance Quarterly*, 3 (3/4), 243-254.

deSilva, G. (1990). *Work and Social Work*. National Association of Social Workers. Greenwich, CT: JAI Press.

deSilva, G. (1988). Services to customers: Customer assistance programs. In G.M. Gould and M.L. Smith (eds.), *Social Work in the Workplace: Practice and Principles*. G.M. Gould and M.L. Smith (eds.), New York: Springer Publ., 283-298.

Eskin, M. (1989). The role of the EAP counselor as a deterrent to sexual harassment. *EAPA Exchange*, 19 (6), 30-34.

Evans, E. (1944). A business enterprise and social work. *The Compass*, January 11-15.

Feinstein, B. and Brown, E. (1982). *The New Partnership: Human Services, Business, and Industry*. Cambridge, MA: Schenkman Publishing Co.

Fleisher, A. (1917). Welfare services for employees. *Annals of the American Academy of Political and Social Science*, 69, 50-57.

Flexner, A. (1915). Is social work a profession? *Proceedings, National Conference of Charities and Corrections*. Baltimore: Sage, 576-590.

Foote, A. and Erfurt, J. (1978). Hypertension control at the work site: Comparison of screening and referral alone, referral and follow-up, and onsite treatment. *New England Journal of Medicine*, 308, 804-813.

Foster, B. and Shore, L. (1990). Job loss and the occupational social worker. *Employee Assistance Quarterly*, 5, 77-96.

Goldsmith, S. (1940). Local organization for refugee service. *Jewish Social Service Quarterly*, 17 (1), September, 119-131.

Gonyea, J. (1993). Family responsibilities and family-oriented policies: Assessing their impacts on the work place. *Employee Assistance Quarterly*, 9 (1), 1-29.

Googins, B. (1987). Occupational social work: A developmental perspective. *Employee Assistance Quarterly*, 2 (3), 37-53.

Googins, B. and Burden, D. (1987). Vulnerability of working parents: Balancing work and home roles. *Social Work*, 34 (4), 295-300.

Googins, B. and Godfrey, J. (1987). *Occupational Social Work Today*. New Jersey: Prentice Hall.

Harney, P. and Frizell, S. (1996). An update to EAP curricula in higher education. *EAPA Exchange*, 26 (1), 10-14.

Harris, J. (1993). Military social work as occupational practice. In P. Kurzman and S. Akabas (eds.). *Work and Well-Being: The Occupational Social Work Advantage*. Washington, DC: NASW Press.

Haw, M.A. (1982). Women, work and stress: A review and agenda for the future. *Journal of Health and Social Behavior*, 23, 132-44.

Iversen, R.R. (1998). Occupational social work in the 21st century. *Social Work*, 43 (6), 551-566.

Jonas, D. (1999). Business of welfare reform a success in Florida. *Orlando Sentinel*, October 6, A-13.

Kelly, J.S. (1997). *Working with and Motivating Welfare Recipients*. Cygnet Associates.

Lewis, B. (1990). Social worker's role in promoting occupational safety and health. *Employee Assistance Quarterly*, 5, 99-117.

Lowenstein, S. (1939). Changes in Jewish social structure under the impact of refugees problem. *Jewish Social Services Quarterly*, 15 (3), March, 313-316.

Maiden, R.P. (1996). The incidence of domestic violence among alcoholic EAP clients before and after treatment. *Employee Assistance Quarterly*, 11 (3), 21-46.

Maiden, R.P. (1988). Employee assistance evaluation in a federal government agency. *Employee Assistance Quarterly*, 3 (4), 191-203.

Maiden, R.P. (1987a). Employee assistance programs: Issues for social work practice. *Social Casework*, 68 (8), 503-506.

Maiden, R.P. (1987b). Ethical issues in occupational social work: Implications for practice. *Journal of Independent Social Work*, 1 (4), 31-40.

Maiden, R.P. and Hardcastle, D. (1986). Social work education: Professionalizing EAPs. *EAP Digest*, Nov/Dec, 63-66.

Malloy, D. and Kurzman, P. (1993). Practice with unions: Collaborating toward an empowerment model. In P. Kurzman and S. Akabas (eds.). *Work and Well-Being: The Occupational Social Work Advantage*. Washington, DC: NASW Press.

Masi, D. (1982). *Human Services in Industry*. MA: Lexington Books.

Maynard, R.A. (1995). Subsidized employment and non-labor market alternatives for welfare recipients. In Demetria Smith Nightingale and Robert H. Havemen, (eds.). *Work Alternative: Welfare Reform and the Realities of the Labor Market*. Washington, DC: The Urban Institute Press.

McClellan, K. (2000). The contribution of Jewish support for displaced persons in the aftermath of World War II to industrial social work: An initial exploration. Unpublished manuscript.

McClellan, K. and Miller, R. (1988). EAPs in transition: Purpose and scope of services. *Employee Assistance Quarterly*, 3 (3/4), 25-42.

McClellan, K. (1986). Leo Perlis remembered as EAP pioneer. *U.S. Journal of Drug and Alcohol Dependence*, 10 (6), 9.

McClellan, K. (1982). An overview of occupational alcoholism programs for the 80's. *Journal of Drug Education*, 12 (1), 1-27.

McDonnell Douglas Corporation and Alexander and Alexander Consulting Group. (1990). *McDonnell Douglas Corporation Employee Assistance Program Financial Offset Study, 1985-1989*. Bridgeton, MO: McDonnell Douglas Corporation and Westport, CT: Alexander and Alexander Consulting Group.

McNellis, P. (1987). Military social work. In A. Minahan (ed.-in-chief). *Encyclopedia of Social Work*, 18th edition (Vol. 2, 154-161). Silver Spring, MD: National Association of Social Workers.

Merrill, J.C. (1994). *Substance Abuse and Women on Welfare*. New York: Center on Addiction and Substance Abuse at Columbia University (CASA).

Miller, R. and Metz, G. (1991). Union counseling as peer assistance. *Employee Assistance Quarterly*, 6 (4), 1-22.

Moore, K.A., Zaslow, M.J., Coiro, M. and Miller, S.M. (1996). *How Well Are They Faring? AFDC Families with Preschool-Aged Children in Atlanta at the Outset of the JOBS Evaluation*. Washington, DC: US Department of Health and Human Services, Office of the Assistance Secretary for Planning and Evaluation.

Moos, R., Brennan, P., Fondacaro, M., and Moos, B. (1990). Approach and avoidance coping responses among older problem and non-problem drinkers. *Psychology and Aging*, 5 (1), 31-40.

Morris, R. and Freund, M. (eds.). (1966). *Trends and Issues in Jewish Social Welfare in the United States, 1899-1952*. Philadelphia: The Jewish Publication Society of the United States, 358.

NASW. (1984). *Occupational Social Work*, Policy statement adopted by the 1984 National Delegate Assembly of the National Association of Social Workers.

Ortiz, E.T. and Bassoff, B.Z. (1987). Military EAPs: Emerging military family service roles for social workers. *Employee Assistance Quarterly*, 2 (3), 55-67.

Ozawa, M. (1985). Economics of occupational social workers. *Social Work*, 30, 442-444.

Pape, P. (1993). Issues in assessment and interventions with alcohol and drug abusing women. *Special Issues and Special Populations: Alcohol and Drug Abusing Women*, 251-269.

Pavetti, L.A. (1993). *The Dynamics of Welfare and Work: Exploring the Process by Which Women Work Their Way Off of Welfare*. Cambridge, MA: Harvard University.

Pavetti, L.A. and Duke, K.E. (1995). *Increasing Participation in Work and Work-Related Activities: Lessons from Five-State Welfare Reform Demonstration Projects*. Report prepared for the Office of the Assistance Secretary for Planning and Evaluation. U.S. Department of Health and Human Services. Washington, DC: The Urban Institute.

Perlis, L. (1977). The human contract in the organized workplace. *Social Thought*, Winter, 29-35.

Popple, P. (1981). Social work practice in business and industry. *Social Service Review*, June, 257-269.

Prenall, L. (1986). Letter to the editor: Perlis eulogy missed key date. *U.S. Journal of Drug and Alcohol Dependence*, 10 (8).

Presbury, C. (1981). Monograph, Chase Manhattan Bank, Community Department, New York.

Quint, J.D., Fink, B.L., and Rowser, S.L. (1991). *New Chance: Implementing a Comprehensive Program for Disadvantaged Young Mothers and Their Children.* New York: Manpower Demonstration Research Corporation.

Rangarajan, A. (1996). *Taking the First Steps: Helping Welfare Recipients Who Get Jobs Keep Them.* Report submitted to the State of Illinois, Division of Planning and Community Services, Department of Public Aid. Princeton, NJ: Mathematica Policy Research, Inc.

Reynolds, B.C. (1951). *Social Work and Social Living*, New York: Citadel Press, 53-56. For another account of the project see *Reynolds an Uncharted Journey*, New York: Citadel Press, 1963.

Roberts-DeGennaro, M., Larazolo, G., and Phillips, W. (1986). A human needs assessment of a trade union: The need for a union-managed EAP. *Employee Assistance Quarterly*, 1 (4), 29-42.

Ross, E. (1946). *Psychiatric Social Work* (Technical Bulletin No. 154). Washington, D.C. U.S. Department of the Army. In Harris, J. *Military Social Work as Occupational Practice.* In P. Kurzman and S. Akabas (eds.). *Work and Well-Being: The Occupational Social Work Advantage.* Washington, DC: NASW Press.

Seck, E.T. (1992). Social work intervention with displaced workers. *Employee Assistance Quarterly*, 7 (4), 77-100.

Shain, M., Suurvali, H., and Boutilier, M. (1986). *Healthier Workers: Health Promotion and Employee Assistance Programs.* Lexington, MA: DC Heath.

Shank, B. (1985). Considering a career in occupational social work? *EAP Digest*, 5, 54-62.

Shanker, R. (1983). Occupational disease, workers' compensation, and the social work advocate. *Social Work*, 28 (1), 24-27.

Sherraden, M.W. (1985). Chronic unemployment: A social work perspective. *Social Work*, 30, 403-408.

Steiner, J. (1921). Education for social work. *American Journal of Sociology*, 26, 475-518.

Straussner, S.A. (1990). *Occupational Social Work Today: An Overview.* New York: The Haworth Press, Inc.

Strawn, J. (1997). Substance abuse and welfare reform policy. Welfare Information Network, http://www.welfarewatch.orglcgibiniprintreport.cgi?18

Tanner, R.M. (1991). Social work: The profession of choice for EAPs. *Employee Assistance Quarterly*, 6 (3), 71-83.

Tufts, J.A. (1923). *Education and Training for Social Work.* New York: Sage, 61-62.

U.S. Dept of Health and Human Services National Institute on Drug Abuse. (1994). *Patterns of Substance Abuse and Substance-Related Impairment Among Participants in the Aid to Families with Dependent Children Program.* Washington, DC.

Urban Institute. (1997). *Personal and Family Challenges to the Successful Transition from Welfare to Work.* Executive Summary. Prepared for the Office of the Assistance Secretary for Planning and Evaluation and the Administration for Children and Families, Contract No. 100-95-0021, Task Order No. 6.

Walker, S.H. (1928). *Social Work and the Training of Social Workers.* Raleigh: University of North Carolina, 576-90.

Weinstein, S. (1995). Corporate social responsibility: How it is defined by occupational social workers and corporate leaders. University of Illinois-Chicago unpublished doctoral dissertation.

Weinstein, S. (1990). Matching EAP expertise and corporate social responsibility. *EAP Digest*, 11 (1), 52-58.

Woolis, D. (1998). Family works: Substance abuse treatment and welfare reform. *Journal of the American Public Welfare Association*, Winter, 24-31.

Young, N.K. and Gardner, S.L. (1997). *Implementing Welfare Reform: Solutions to the Substance Abuse Problem*. Washington, DC: Drug Strategies.

Index

Aboriginals, support for, 8
Absenteeism, social workers and, 45,57
Accident Insurance, German trade union movement and, 18
ACTWU. *See* Amalgamated Clothing and Textile Workers Union (ACTWU)
Addams, Jane, leading social worker, United States, 133
Addiction. *See also* Chemical dependency; Drug abuse
  alcohol, intervention strategy for, 57
  rare in Israel, 89
Addiction at Work, theme of congresses, 34
Addiction support program. *See also* Alcohol Working Group, The
  continuing education programs and, 33
  limitations of, 33-34
  outcomes of, 34
  preventative measures and, 33
  reasons for success of, 32-33
Advocates, occupational social workers as, 129
AFL-CIO
  Community Services department, history of, 133-134
  programs developed under, 133
AFSCME. *See* American Federation of State, County and Municipal Employees (AFSCME)
Age Discrimination Act, occupational social work and, United States, 127
Agricultural workers (India), lack of welfare amenities for, 44
Aid to Families with Dependent Children, 150

Alcohol and drug abuse. *See also* Addiction; Substance abuse
  case management model and, 154-155
  EAPs and, 11
  South African National Council for Alcohol and Drug Abuse (SANCA) and, 101
Alcohol at Work, conference (Germany), 31-32
Alcohol intervention and treatment programs, successful, 17
Alcohol use
  employer-sponsored programs not trusted, 3
  Germany, 30-32
    consumption at work, 31
  welfare recipients and, 154
Alcohol Working Group, The. *See also* Addiction support program
  program description, 32
  program developed in Germany, 31-32
  program implementation, 32-33
  training provided for, 32-33
Alcoholics Anonymous, role in German program development, 31
Alcoholism
  costs of, 30-31
  German workforce and, 30-31
  OAPs and, 130-131
  programs for, 123
  social workers and, 45
Amalgamated Clothing and Textile Workers Union (ACTWU), 133
Amalgamated Clothing Workers of America, programs developed under, 133

© 2001 by The Haworth Press, Inc. All rights reserved. *163*

American Federation of State, County and Municipal Employees (AFSCME)
Personal Support Program, 134
services provided to members, 134
social workers belonging to, 133
American Psychological Association (APA), counseling profession and, 137
Americans with Disabilites Act, management training and, United States, 132
Americans with Disabilities Act
compliance with, occupational social workers' role in, 129
occupational social work and, 127
APA. *See* American Psychological Association (APA)
Apartheid
mental health problems and, 114
practice within treatment perspective and, 99
social work programs affected by, 109
welfare system, poor white problem and, 98
Arbeitsgemeinschaft Betriebliche Sozialarbeit. *See* Workers community of occupational social work
Arbeitskreis Alkohol. *See* Alcohol Working Group, The
Arbeitskreis Sucht. *See* Working Group Addictions
Army Community Service (ACS), occupational social work services, United States, 145-146
AT&T-CWA (Communication Workers of America), labor-management programs and, 135
At-risk populations. *See also* Welfare-to-work
United States
advocacy of, 129
served by occupational social workers, 129-130
Australia Association of Social Workers Newsletter, comments on privatization, 7
Australia Post, social worker employment by, 4
Australian Council of Trade Unions, employer/employee disputes and, 3-4
Autonomy, attraction of occupational social work and, 38-39

Barrington Commission of Enquiry into Safety, Health and Welfare at Work, report of, 70
Basic state assistance (Germany)
funded by taxpayers, 22
government guarantees and, 22
Behavioral health care costs, managing, United States, 135-136
Betriebsfürsorgeinnen. *See* Occupational social work
Black masses, assistance in changing hostile environment, need for, 99
Black social workers, views of, 100
Bombay Labor Institute
industrial social welfare and, 43
Labor Welfare study, 53-54
Welfare Officer study, 53-54
British in India, legislation in favor of Indian workers and, 46
Business culture, transformation of, South Africa, 112-113

Career transitioning, occupational social workers and, 9-10
Case management Employee Assistance Programs
conclusions regarding, United States, 156-157

welfare-to-work, opportunities presented by, 156-157
Case management models
 EAP services expanded for, 156
 Employee Assistance Programs (EAPs) and, 154-155
 job retention promoted by, 155-156
 role of case manager, 155-156
Casework, dominating social work, South Africa, 104
Casework-based practice
 limits role of social worker as change agent, 106
 trend away from, South Africa, 117
Causation of problems, beliefs about, program development and, 110
Central Employers' Organizations (India), views on welfare officer roles, 51-52
Change management
 occupational social workers' roles in, 119-120
 survival skill training and, 9-10
Chemical dependency. *See also* Addiction; Alcoholism
 education and training courses on, 147-148
Child care, social work profession and, 2
Child labor
 First Factories Act and, 46
 industrialization and, 45-46
Child labor laws (India), industrialization and, 43
Child-care programs (Australia), contract workers and, 13-14
CIO, War Relief Committee, union counselor within, 133-134
Cities, occupational social work in, 25
Civil Rights Act (United States)
 compliance with, occupational social workers' role in, 129
 management training and, 132
 occupational social work and, 127
Civil Service Departments (Ireland), welfare officers from, 69
Civilized Labor Policy, poor white problem and, South Africa, 98
Client numbers, Australia, 8
Clinical issues, Australia, 6-10
Clinical work, curative as norm, South Africa, 99
Code of ethics, Irish Association of Welfare/Employee Assistance Counselors and, 74
Collaborative research, privatization's effect on present social problems and, 11-12
Collective wage agreements (Germany), present economic situation and, 21-22
Colonies, for employees, 58
Committee on Labor Welfare, India, 50
 recommendations of, 44,55,61
 satisfaction for welfare officers and, 54-55
Commonweath Government Health and Social Security Department (Australia), history of, 2
Communication Workers of America (CWA)
 programs developed under, 133
 social workers belonging to, 133
Community organization, corporate social responsiblity (CSR) and, 142
Community work, industrial social work and, 58
Community-based welfare services, occupational social workers and (Australia), 8
Competition, global village perspective and, South Africa, 112
Confederation of Irish Industry
 Employee Assistance Programs (EAPs) support, 71
 public health expenditure and, 70

Confidentiality, of social workers (Germany), 28
Continuing education programs, alcoholism programs and, 33
Contract practitioners (Australia)
  relationship with management and, 12-13
  training programs and, 12
Contract workers, equal employment opportunity infrastructures forged by, 13
Corporate Public Involvement model, corporate social responsiblity (CSR) and, 143
Corporate social responsibility (CSR)
  activities sponsored by, 142-143
  models of service, 143-145
  occupational social work practice in, 142-145
  skills relevant to social work practice in, 142
Cost management
  need for reduction of costs, 24
  occupational social worker as responsible for, United States, 138
Council on Social Work Education, United States, 124
Counseling profession, managed behavioral care (MBC) and, 137
Counselors, unionized setting (United States), role of, 134-135
CSR. *See* Corporate social responsibility (CSR)
Cultural factors, program development, South Africa, 109
Cultural issues, EAPs and, South Africa, 109-110
Customer service model, corporate social responsibility (CSR) and, 143
CWA. *See* Communication Workers of America (CWA)

Data protection (Germany), 28-29
Defence Force (Australia), social worker employment by, 4
Delivery systems, work-related, United States, 119
Department of Welfare, critical look at methodology and, South Africa, 100
Depression, as issue, South Africa, 115
Deutsche Arbeitsfront. *See* German Worker's Front
Developed nations, institutionalized model of welfare, 62
Diabetes, intervention strategy and, 57
Diagnostic Related Group (DRG) system, development and use of, United States, 137
Disability benefits, contributions toward, Ireland, 66
Disadvantaged, fear of increased dispossession of, privatization and, 5-6
Drug abuse
  case management model and, 154-155
  employer-sponsored programs not trusted, 3
  social workers and, 45
  welfare recipients and, 154
Drug Free Workplace Act
  compliance with, occupational social workers' role in, 129
  management training and, United States, 132
Drug, Hospital and Health Care Employees Union, social workers belonging to, 133
Dunn, Aggie, social welfare secretary, 120
Duties, occupational social workers, 26-27

EAPs. *See* Employee Assistance Programs (EAPs)
Economic imperatives, program

development, South Africa,
109,112-114
Economy (German)
present difficulties in, 21-22
structural change to, 21-22
Education and training. *See also*
Employee education
Australia, issues, 10-11
core social work content,
specialization and, 59-60
Germany
objectives, 20
programs for occupational social
work, 34-35
degree specialization
available in, 35
degrees for, 35
India
emphasis of, 63-64
human resource management
training and, 59-60
occupational social work, 59-60
occupational social workers, 43
specialization courses in, 59-60
inertia as factor in, 10
Ireland
courses, 72-73
institutions providing, 72-73
occupational social work
development and, 76
welfare officers, 67
Israel, 81
informal, 93-94
institutions providing, 93
schools of social work, 93
managerial roles and, 62
occupational social work, status of,
148
program development and, 109
recommendations of Sri Ram
Centre for Industrial
Relations on, 52
South Africa, 115-116,117
degree conferred, 115
formal and informal, 108

institutions providing, 115-116
occupational social workers, 97
support groups for occupational
social workers, 116
specialization and, 76
United States
Council on Social Work
Education, 124
degree-granting programs, 147
institutions providing,
134-135,149
internship opportunities, 148
occupational social work
curriculum, 147-148
Educational choices, Federal
Professional Association of
Occupational Social Work
(EPAOSW) and, 37-38
Employee as person, *versus* person as
employee, 107-108
Employee assistance, continuously
developing field, 75
Employee Assistance Officers,
Employee Assistance
Programs (EAPs) and, 72
Employee Assistance Program (EAP)
practitioners
backgrounds of, 72
diversity of, 72
Employee Assistance Programs
(EAPs). *See also* Case
management models
Africanizing, 112
as model, cost-effective, 154-155
challenges faced by, South Africa
compared with United States,
115
complementary views and, 11
comprehensiveness of model and,
United States, 132-133
concept association with welfare
concept, Ireland, 74
Confederation of Irish Industry
support, 71
consortiums, social work services
contracted by, 103

cultural issues and, South Africa, 109-110
development of, 70-71
  Ireland, 72-73
  United States, 71, 123-125
distinguished from managed care model, 138-139
emphasis of, United States, 131
focus on alcohol and drug abuse and, 11
influence from North America, South Africa, 100
Ireland, 65
issues of (Australia), 7-8
joint labor-management, service delivery model, 135
managed behavioral care programs and, United States, 135-136
occupational social work field development, 70
outsourcing, 111-112
practice area, United States, 130-133
program elements, 71
service delivery model, Ireland, 71-73
statistics on problems, South Africa, 115
training available for, Ireland, 72-73
trends in, United States, 128-129
United States experience, influence in South Africa, 114
Employee counseling, 26-27
Employee education, provided by occupational social workers, United States, 132-133
Employee problems, social workers and, 45
Employee productivity, worker satisfaction and, 68-69
Employee Retirement Income Security Act (United States), occupational social work and, 127
Employee well-being, EAPs focusing on, 74
Employee work practices, linked with theoretical positions, 11
Employees
  focus of occupational social workers on individual, Israel, 88
  only individual needs addressed, Israel, 95
  problems of, Israel, 89-90
Employer's Association (Germany), collective wage agreements and, 21-22
Employer-sponsored services, United States, 119
Employers
  Germany, relations with unions strained, 22
  responsibility of, 75
  South Africa, powerful, 106
ENOS. See European Network of Occupational Social Workers
Environment, change to hostile needed, for black masses, 99
Equal employment opportunity infrastructures (Australia), contract workers and, 13-14
Eurocontrol, social workers employed by, 70
Europe, modern industrial social work and, 123
European Community Directives
  impact of, 65
  legislative framework of, 75
  occupational safety and health protection and, 70
European Foundation for the Improvement of Living and Working Conditions
  conclusions of, 75
  criticisms by, 73
  review of health promotion activities of, 73
European Network of Occupational Social Workers (ENOS)

founding of, 38
Irish social workers and, 74
Evaluation of social work, program development and, 111

Fabrikpflegerinnen (factory nurses). *See also* Factory nurses
  history of, 19
Factories (Germany), helping women adjust to entering workforce, 17
Factories Act
  India
    First, 46
    Model Rules under, 49-50
    provisions of, 48-49
    social workers and, 47-48
  Ireland, 69
Factory nurses. *See also* Fabrikpflegerinnen (factory nurses)
  Nazi ideology and, 19
  objectives of, 19
  responsibilities of, 19
  title changes of, 19
Family, as unit, change with industrialization, 18
Family and Medical Leave Act (FMLA) (United States)
  compliance with, occupational social workers' role in, 129
  management training and, 132
  occupational social work and, 127
  workers not covered by, 153
Family problems, EAPs and, South Africa, 115
Fatal Accident Act (India), passage of, 46
Federal Assistance Law (Germany), unemployment insurance and, 22
Federal Professional Association of Occupational Social Work (FPAOSW)
  founding of, 37
  objectives of, 37-38
Federal Professional Association of Occupational Social Work (FPASOW), Germany, 25
Federal state administrations (Germany), occupational social work in, 25
Fee-for-service, occupational social workers and (Australia), 3
Fee-for-service EAP consulting organizations, development of (Australia), 7-8
Female workers (Germany), factory nurses and, 19
Fieldwork placements, undergraduate programs (Australia), 12
FMLA. *See* Family and Medical Leave Act (FMLA) (United States)
For-profit organizations, increasing role of, Israel, 84-85
Ford-UAW. *See* Ford-United Auto Workers (Ford-UAW)
Ford-United Auto Workers (Ford-UAW), labor-management programs and, 135
Forum for Occupational Social Work, support group, South Africa, 116
Foster care services, social work profession and, 2
FPAOSW. *See* Federal Professional Association of Occupational Social Work (FPAOSW)
Freelance social workers, Germany, 25
Funding
  arrangements (Australia), public to private professional practice, 7
  focus of practice (Australia), 8-9

General Federation of Labor, influence of, Israel, 83-84
General Motors-United Auto Workers (GM-UAW),

labor-management programs and, 135
Generic practitioners (Australia), occupational social workers and, 15
German Worker's Front
factory nurse training and, 19
factory nurses, objectives under, 19
GM-UAM. *See* General Motors-United Auto Workers (GM-UAW)
Googins' model, stages of, 105,128
Governesses, factory placement (Germany)
Nazi ideology and, 17
post WWI, 17
Governmental structures, Israel, 81

H. J. Heinz, use of occupational social worker, 120
Hawthorne experiments, employee productivity and, 68-69
Health and wellness, education in workplace about, United States, 132
Health care
cost containment, occupational social workers' roles in, 119-120
Germany, structure of, 22-24
Health care costs
Employee Assistance Programs (EAPs) and, 137
health promotion programs and, 137-138
HMOs and, 137
PPOs and, 137
Health care service, comprehensive, Ireland, 66
Health care system, Israel, 81
Health insurance (Germany)
higher income groups and, 23
national, 23-24
private, 23-24
self-employed and, 23
streams of, 23
Health Insurance scheme, German trade union movement and, 18
Health issues, HIV/AIDS, South Africa, 115
Health management organizations (HMOs), MBC programs and, 136-137
Health promotion activities
EAPs and, 70
in workplace, 75-76
study of European, 75
Health services
crises faced by, South Africa, 115
high costs of German, 24
Higher income groups (Germany), health insurance and, 23
Histadrut. *See also* General Federation of Labor
Israel, 83-84
occupational social workers and, 85
Occupational Welfare Department of, study published by, 94
occupational welfare department of, mandating employment of occupational social workers, 87-88
training by, 93
Historical context, occupational social work (Australia), 2-3
HIV/AIDS
education and prevention, occupational social workers role in, 117
social workers and, 110
South Africa, 115
United States, education in workplace about, 132-133
HMO Act (United States), development of HMOs and, 136-137
Home care, social work profession and, 2
Hopkins, Harry, leading social worker,

United States, 133
Hospital Benefit and Medical Funds
    (Australia), professional fees
    and, 3
Hospitals (Australia), occupational
    social workers role in, 6-7
Human relations, approach to
    management, 68-69
  occupational welfare services and,
    69-71
Human relations movement
  impact on industrial social work,
    Ireland, 65
  roots of occupational social work
    and, 70-71
Human resource development,
    industrial social work,
    institutional model and,
    57-58
Human resource management, South
    Africa
  factors affecting, 100-102
  history of, 100
  personal commitment and, 100
Human rights
  abuse, South Africa, focus on, 114
  South Africa, culture of, 112
Human service agencies
  funding of (Australia), 8
  non-governmental organizations
    (Australia), 8

ILO, establishment of, 47
In-house wage agreements,
    restructuring in German
    economy and, 21
Income maintenance benefits,
    National Insurance Institute
    (NII) and, 82
Indian Factories (Amendment Act), 47
Indian Mines Act, 47
Individual counseling, occupational
    social workers and, 20
Industrial Law, skills needed in
    (Australia), 6

Industrial managerial social workers,
    demand in India, 63
Industrial organizations, occupational
    social work services
    developed in, Irish, 69
Industrial Relations, skills needed in
    (Australia), 6
Industrial Relations Commission
    (Australia),
    employer/employee disputes
    and, 3-4
Industrial relations law (Germany),
    application to public sector
    and, 22
Industrial relations officers/managers.
    See Social workers
Industrial relations procedures, black
    unions and, South Africa,
    100-101
Industrial social welfare, reemergence
    of, Ireland, 69-71
Industrial social welfare officers
    (India)
  responsibilities of, 43
  role of, 43
Industrial social work. *See also*
    Occupational social work
  community based model
    objectives of, 58
    role of social worker in, 58
  definition of, 62
  future of, 63
  India
    domains of, 44
    history of, 62
  institutional model
    human resource development
      functions in, 57-58
    non-statutory welfare functions
      in, 57
    statutory welfare functions in,
      56-57
  Ireland, original concept, 66
Industrial social workers, programs
    during WWII, United States,
    122-123

Industrial unions, services offered to members, United States, 135
Industrial working population (India), reforms and, 46-47
Industrialization
　effect on working life, 18
　India
　　child labor laws and, 43
　　industries involved with, 45-46
　　worker protection laws and, 43
　United States, 120-122
　　occupational social work and, 119
Industries
　Australia, union movement and, 6
　Germany
　　job cuts in, 24
　　occupational social work tradition in, 24-25
　increase in number in India, 46
Institute of Personnel Management, certificate courses, 72
Institutionalized model of welfare, developed nations, 62
Insurance. *See also* Health insurance
　Ireland, 66
International Labor Conventions, ratification in India, 47
International Ladies Garment Workers Union, workplace hazards and, 141
Invalid and Old Age Pension Insurance, German trade union movement and, 18
Irish Association of Welfare/Employee Assistance Counselors, code of ethics in counseling and, 74
Irish Civil Service, welfare officers employed by, 69
ISCOR. *See* South African Iron and Steel Corporation (ISCOR)
Israel, modern industrial social work and, 123
Israel Association of Social Workers (IASW)
　membership of, 85, 86
　training by, 93

Jacobs biscuit factory, Dublin, enlightened attitude shown toward, 68
Jewish Federation, early efforts of, 123
Jewish Joint Distribution Committee, modern industrial social work and, 123
Jewish Labor Committee, discrimination against Jewish workers, addressing, 123
Jewish organizations, social services provided by, wartime era effort, 123
Job Link Program (Australia), addressing unemployment, 9
Job retention, case management model EAP and, 155-156
Job satisfaction, occupational social workers and, Israel, 92-93
Job security
　occupational social workers' roles in, 119-120
　world-class manufacturers and, South Africa, 113
Job security laws (Germany), occupational social work and, 25
Job-related hazards, occupational health and safety, United States, 140

Labor conditions
　industrialization and, 45-46
　social awareness regarding, 46
Labor Investigation Committee (India), 47
　recommendations of, 48-49
Labor legislation
　India, 47
　South Africa, Labor Relations Act, 113

Labor protection laws (Germany), occupational social work and, 25
Labor relations, Histadrut's role in, 84
Labor Relations Act, South Africa, 112
　workplace relationships required by, 113
Labor welfare, need for management's cooperation, 53
Labor welfare measures, progress of, 46
Labor welfare officers. *See also* Welfare officers
　recommendations of Sri Ram Centre for Industrial Relations on, 52-53
　role of, recommendations of Sri Ram Centre for Industrial Relations on, 52-53
Labor-management conflict, Australia's history of, 3
Lean management, restructuring in German economy and, 21
Lean production, restructuring in German economy and, 21
Legislation. *See also* Labor legislation
　in favor of Indian workers, 46
　Ireland, 70
　United States
　　health care, 136-137
　　occupational social work and, 127
Living conditions (Germany), industrialization and, 18
Local governments, department of social services within, Israel, 83

Macy's department store, Department of Social Services, role of occupational social worker, 121
Managed behavioral care (MBC), influences on, 136-137
Managed behavioral care (MBC) programs
　Employee Assistance Programs (EAPs) and, United States, 135-136
　role of, United States, 135-136
Managed behavioral health care (MBHC). *See also* Managed care model
　HMOs and, 136
　occupational social worker and, 138
　outcomes expected and, 138
　services delivery and, 138
　system of, United States, 135-139
Managed care model, distinguished from Employee Assistance Programs (EAPs), 138-139
Management, nature of social work practice and, 55
Management commitment, importance of, 111
Management style, social work services affected by, 110-111
Management views, paternalism and social work promotion, South Africa, 101
Marital problems, EAPs and, South Africa, 115
Marketing, duty of occupational social worker, 27
Mass poverty, social work practice, 64
Maternity Benefit Act, 47
MBC programs. *See* Managed behavioral care (MBC) programs
MBHC. *See* Managed behavioral health care (MBHC)
Mediation, occupational social workers and, Israel, 90
Medical model, occupational social workers and, 6-7
Member assistance programs (United States), counseling through, 133-135
Men, retrenched middle-aged (Australia), 6
Mental Hygiene Consultative Service, US Army and, 145

Middle class, problems of, 2-3
Middle-class clients, social workers attitudes toward working with, 10
Migrant groups, safe havens provided by social work profession, 13
Migrant workers, minority (Australia), 6
Migration
　industrialization and, community-based social work and, 58
　rural to urban, 18
　to urban areas, India, 58
　urban ills and, 2-3
Military life, stress of, social work and, 146
Military social work, United States, 145-147
　history of, 145
Military social workers, roles of, 146-147
Mines Act (India), provisions of, 49
Minimum wage levels, India, Committee on Labor Welfare and, 61
Minimum wages, First Factories Act and, 46
Minister of Labor, South Africa, 113
Ministry of Education, Israel, 83
Ministry of Health, National Health Insurance Law (Israel), 83
Ministry of Housing (Israel), 83
Ministry of Immigrant Absorption (Israel), 83
Ministry of Labor and Social Affairs (Israel)
　funding of services for local governments and, 83
　personal social services and, 82-83
　role of, 82-83
Model Rules, labor laws in India and, 49
Models. *See also* Googins' model; Ozawa's model
　Employee Assistance Programs (EAPs) as, 154-155
　of practice, South Africa, 107

social services, corporate social responsibility and, 143-145
Montage Chelmsford Reforms (India), industrial working population and, 46-47

NASW. *See* National Association of Social Workers (NASW)
National Association of Social Workers (NASW) (United States), 124
　Code of Ethics, practice setting, 125
　counseling profession and, 137
National Authority for Health and Safety (Ireland), 75
National Cash Register Company, welfare work in American industry and, 68
National Delegate Assembly of the National Association of Social Workers, policy statement adopted by, 125-126
National Electricity Supply Board, welfare services established by, 69
National Health and Safety Authority (Ireland), establishment of, 70
National health insurance. *See also* Health insurance
　Germany, funding of, 23-24
National Health Insurance Law (Israel)
　basket of medical services for citizens and, 83
　Histadrut and, 84
National Institute of EAPs, health promotion programs and, 70
National Insurance Institute (NII) (Israel)
　legislative status of, 82
　occupational social workers role with, 88
　operation of, 82

National Maritime Union and United
    Seaman's Service
  casework program, 122-123
  direct services to workers and, 133
National Occupational Social Work
    Committee (United States),
    formation of, 125
National Occupational Social Work
    Task Force (United States),
    agenda of, 124
National socialist beliefs (Germany),
    infiltration of, 19
Nationalist government (South Africa),
    welfare system and, 98
Nazi ideology, governesses in factories
    (Germany) and, 17
Network of agencies, development of,
    Israel, 84-85
NGOs. *See* Non-government
    organizations (NGOs)
NII. *See* National Insurance Institute
    (NII) (Israel)
Non-government organizations
    (NGOs)
  India, workers issues and, 44
  public, Histadrut, 83-84
Northern Ireland, distinguished from
    Republic of Ireland, 65-66
Northern States Power, use of
    occupational social worker, 120

OAPs. *See* Occupational alcoholism
    programs (OAPs)
Occupational alcoholism programs
    (OAPs)
  model of, 130-131
  predecessors of EAPs, 123
Occupational health and safety, United
    States, 140-142
  skills needed to work in, 140
Occupational medicine, occupational
    social workers and, 140
Occupational programs (Germany),
    in-house, 25
Occupational Safety and Health Act
    (United States), occupational
    social work and, 127
Occupational Safety and Health
    Administration (United
    States), 141
Occupational social welfare services,
    reemergence of, Ireland, 65
Occupational social work. *See also*
    Industrial social work
  ambivalent attitude toward, 10
  as industrial social work, 106-108
  as social work in industry, 106-108
  Australia
    current practice, 1
    development, 1
    generalist and, 11
    historical context, 2
    issues of current practice, 11-13
    societal context, 2-3
  categories of
    combination of direct practice
      and administration/policy
      formulation, 127
    direct practice, 126-127
    policy, planning, and
      administration, 126
  community focus of, 61
  concepts for analysis of
    industrial social work, 106-108
    social work in industry, 106-108
  development of addiction support
    program and, 32
  discounted by unions after fall of
    Third Reich, 19-20
  evolution of, 106
  Germany
    challenges to, 39-40
    changing nature of, 39-40
    company counseling, 26
    domains of practice, 24-26
    education programs of, 34-36
    financial costs and, 39
    future perspectives, 39-40
    historical context, 18-21
      research and publication on
        limited, 18

limited possibilities in field, 35
marketing strategies needed for, 39
objectives of, changes to, 20-21
personal qualifications needed
   for, 35-46
political ramifications of, 24
professional culture of, 36-37
professional profile developing
   for, 36
profile needed in, 40
quality of, 25
social framework of, 21-22
societal context, 18-21
standards needed in, 40
tasks of, 25
titles assigned to, 19-20
training in, 20,34-36
   objectives of, 20
globalization and, 61
implications for South African
   agenda, 113-114
India
   current practice, 60-61
   education and training, 59-60
   future directions, 60-61
   historical context, 43-48
   scope of, 43-44
   societal context, 43-48
   term defined, 44
interventions, models for providing,
   143-145
Ireland
   current practice, 65
   development, 65
   future directions, 75-76
   historical context, 65-66
   origins, 66-68
   societal context, 65-66
Israel
   degrees for, 93
   developments necessary for
      expansion of field, 95
   historical context, 81-82
   reasons for slow growth of, 87
   research and publications on, 94
   societal context, 81-82

models of
   Googins' model, 105,128
   Ozawa's model, 105,128
post-graduate training for, 10-11
practice of, continuum of
   interventions, 1298
presence in Israeli workplaces,
   85-88
programs in, 29
reemergence as viable field of
   practice, effects on education
   and training, 149
role in Working Group Addictions,
   34
South Africa
   approach to organizations, 102
   challenges, 116-117
   clinical issues in, 114-115
   continuum of practice, 105-108
   diversity in field, 103
   domains of practice, 102-105
   emphasis, 107
   focus on, 114
   future directions, 116-117
   historical context, 97-102
   individual intervention focus,
      114
   influences from North America,
      100
   management at work, 97-98
   problems confronted by, 115
   program diversification and,
      116-117
   societal context, 97-102
   study on, 108
   welfare system and, 97-98
trends in West compared with
   India, 44-45
United States
   conceptual framework for,
      125-129
   historical context, 120-125
   history of, 119
   paternalistic early approach, 119
   reconceptualization of, 127
   reemergence of, 124

societal context, 120-125
support as a designated field of practice, 126
trends and issues confronted, 127-128
values and ethics in, 38-39
Occupational social work duties, Germany, no rules for, 25
Occupational social work function. *See also* Social work function
outsourcing, 111-112
Occupational social work limitations, Germany, no rules for, 25
Occupational Social Work policy statement, position statement summary, 125-126
Occupational social work practice
future development of, Ireland, 76
models for, 56-59
nature of, 56-59
Occupational social work programs
Ireland
organizations with, 69-70
service delivery model, 73-75
training available for, 73
South Africa, cultural differences and, 110
Occupational social work services, Ireland, evolution in urban areas, 66
Occupational social work standards (Germany), no rules for, 25
Occupational social workers
as partners of organizational change, 28-29
as referral resources, 131
at-risk populations served by, 129-130
Australia
challenges facing, 1
changing roles of, 4-5
crisis of confidence among, 7
downsizing of, 4
employment opportunities for, 5
focus of, 8-9
health and safety workplace agreements and, 4
outside public system, 7
policy development and, 4-5
privatization, 4
privatization of social service system and, 1
resource information and, 4
united front with generic social workers needed, 13
worker-to-worker dispute mediation and, 4
corporate social responsibility and, 142
corporate social responsibility positions
aims of, 144
examples of, 144-145
responsibilities of, 144
Germany
attractive field to men, 20
change in duties of, 20
current practices of, 17
development of, 17
duties, 26-27
fabrikpflegerinnen (factory nurses) as precursors of, 19
increase in pay and, 20
objectives of, 20
Professional Association of Occupational Social Workers and, 17
resources used by, 26-27
roles of, 26-27
impact on workplace hazards, examples in United States, 140-142
India
education and training for, 43
future challenges of, 43
practice models for, 43
Israel
focus of, 88
functions of, 81, 88-91
future projections, 94-95
perceptions of, 81

perceptions of involvement in workplace, 91-93
prevalence in workplaces, 85,86
questionnaire administered to, 88-93
role perceptions of, 91-93
roles of, 81,87-91
study of, 88-93
tasks performed by, 88-89
time per task, 89-90
types of organizations that employ, 86
work settings, 85, 86
workplaces, 87-88
managed behavioral health care and, 138
occupational medicine and, 140
organizational niche, features of, 90
problems addressed by, 74
ratio of worker to employees, 86-87
responsibilities of, 25
role of, Macy's department store, 121
roles of, 73-74
United States, 126
scope of practice, 74
skills employed by, 2
South Africa
  challenges facing, 97
  changing functions of, 117
  creative responses in service delivery, 108
  location in hierarchy, 104-105
  meet unusual challenges, 108
  number of, 102-103
  training, 108
  workplace practices, 97
supervisor training and management consultation, 132
threat to profession of, 60
United States
  advocacy role of, 141-142
  challenges and new opportunities for, 149-156
  changing role of, 121
  current practice settings, 130-147
  domains of practice, 139
  EAPs as primary area of employment, 124
  early decline of, 121
  empowering clients and, 141-142
  evolution of, 119
  health and safety arena, 140
  importance to individuals, 130
  responsibilities of, 131-133
  social welfare secretaries, 120
  welfare-to-work settings and, 153-154
Occupational Welfare Department, Histadrut operated, 84
Occupational welfare services, development of, Irish organizations, 69-71
Old age pension scheme (Germany), guarantees of, 24
Organization-related measures, duty of occupational social worker, 27
Organizational affiliations, effect on occupational social work, 28-29
Organizational factors, program development and, South Africa, 110-111
Organizational restraints, program development, 109
Organizational social workers, as facilitators, 8
Organizations, occupational social work in, 25
Organized labor, community services programs, United States, 133-134
OSW. *See* Occupational social work
Ozawa's model, stages of, 105,128

Patterson, John Henry
  attitude toward welfare officers, 68
  welfare work in United States and, 68

Index

Peer counselors, unionized setting, United States, 134
Pension provisions, contributions toward, Ireland, 66
Perlis, Leo, founder of AFL-CIO's Community Services department, 133-134
Person, general status of, 46
Person as employee, *versus* employee as person, 107-108
Person-in-environment, focus of occupational social work, United States, 127
Personal realm, social work practice, development and, 109
Personal Responsiblity and Work Opportunity Reconciliation Act. *See also* Welfare-to-work
emphasis of, 150
Personal Support Program, American Federation of State, County and Municipal Employees (AFSCME) and, 134
Personnel departments
Germany, occupational social work and, 28
organizational structure of, 59
welfare officers and, 51,55
Personnel work, as disciplinary function, 54
Personnel/human resources managers. *See* Social workers
Plantations Act (India), provisions of, 48-49
Political centralization, Israel, 81-82
Political parties and organizations, dominance of, Israel, 81-82
Poor white problem, consequences of, South Africa, 98
Post-industrial society (Australia), traditional way of life attacked by, 13
Posttraumatic stress, national concern, South Africa, 114-115
Poverty

as target for inadequate resources, 2
targeting of social resources and, 2
Practice development, factors impacting (Australia), 5-6
Preventative measures
addiction support program and, 33
alcoholism programs and, 33
Private consultants (Australia), competition between for public contracts, 5
Private sector, occupational social work and, 40
Private social work practitioners (Australia), emergence of, 3
Privatization
dispossession of disadvantaged and, 5-6
for-profit organizations and, 84-85
threat to minorities (Australia), 5-6
Productivity, contentious issue, South Africa, 113
Professional Association of Occupational Social Workers, efforts to promote recognition, 17
Professional associations (Germany)
for occupational social workers, 36
social work, 36
unions, 36
Professional isolation, job satisfaction and, Israel, 92-93
Professional supervision, job satisfaction and, Israel, 92-93
Professional teams, Promotional Unit (Australia), 9
Program development, factors impacting, South Africa, 109-114
Promotional opportunities, job satisfaction and, Israel, 92-93
Promotional Unit (Australia), development of, 9
Public non-government organizations. *See also* Non-government organizations (NGOs)
Histadrut, 83-84

Public practitioners (Australia),
  occupational social workers
  and, 15
Public relations, duty of occupational
  social worker, 27
Public sector
  Germany, occupational social work
  new in, 25
  occupational social work and, 40
Public service practitioners
  (Australia), middle-class
  concerns and, 3
Public system (Australia), *versus*
  privatization, 7
Public utilities (Australia),
  occupational social workers
  role in, 6-7

Quality assurance, occupational social
  work objectives and, 20-21

Race groups, different services for
  different groups, South
  Africa, 98
Race relations, occupational social
  work services, 145-146
Racial divisions
  among social workers, South
  Africa, 98-99
  ideological basis of some, 98-99
Recruitment and retention policies
  (Australia), contract workers
  and, 13-14
Red Cross, social work services
  provided by, 145
Reemployment process, change
  management and, 9-10
Refugees, Jewish social workers and, 123
Rege, D. V., Labor Investigation
  Committee and, 47-48
Relationship problems, EAPs and,
  South Africa, 115
Republic of Ireland, distinguished
  from Northern Ireland, 65-66

Research on occupational social work.
  See also Studies
  Federal Professional Association of
  Occupational Social Work
  (EPAOSW) and, 37
Resources
  sanctioning for social work, 111
  South Africa
  limited, 106
  unavailability of community, 115
Reynolds, Bertha Capen, social worker
  National Maritime Union and, 133
  significance of, 122-123
Royal Commission on Labor (India), 47
  institution of welfare officer and,
  48-49
  recommendations of, 48-49

Safety measures, industrialization and,
  45-46
Safety, Health and Welfare at Work
  Act (Ireland), 70
  legislative framework of, 75
  training requirements of, 72
Salvation Army, social work services
  provided by, 145
SANCA. *See* South African National
  Council for Alcohol and
  Drug Abuse (SANCA)
Sargent, Miss Violet, first Irish welfare
  officer, 67
SASOL. *See* South African Synthetic
  Oils Limited (SASOL)
Satisfaction, occupational social
  workers and, Israel, 92-93
Schools of Social Work
  Australia, educators in, 10
  emerging (Australia), 2
  India, professional training and, 53
  reactivity of, 10
Seaman's Service, casework program,
  122-123
SEIU. *See* Service Employees
  International Union (SEIU)
Self-employed (Germany), health
  insurance and, 23

Service delivery
  models of, Ireland, 71-75
  work environment and, 14
Service Employees International Union (SEIU), social workers belonging to, 133
Service industry workers, occupational social work and, 44-45
Sexual harassment policies, development of, occupational social workers' role in, 129
Social assistance scheme, supplementary, Ireland, 66
Social change (Australia), women in workforce, 2-3
Social counseling, social work employed by companies, 20-21
Social injustice, targeting of social resources and, 2
Social insurance benefit (Ireland), statutory, 66
Social issues, occupational social work and, United States, 127-128
Social market economy, pillar of German democracy, 21
Social resources, targeting of inadequate (Australia), 2
Social service system (Australia), privatization of, 1
Social services
  Germany, high costs of, 24
  Israel
    delivery of, 81
    government organizations providing, 82-83
    support for government involvement in, 82
  United States
    Army Community Service (ACS) and, 145-146
    provided in context of work organization, 122-123
Social welfare (Germany), structure of, 22-24
Social welfare functions, evolution of (Germany), 17
Social welfare programs, averting unionization and, United States, 121
Social welfare secretaries. See Occupational social workers
Social welfare system, requirements of, Ireland, 66
Social work
  appropriateness of practice in workplace, 124-125
  Australia, challenge in health care, 7
  ecological base of, 106
  focus of, 125
  military, focus of, 146-147
  practice in South Africa compared with Israel, 106-107
  role in work-related problems, 108
  South Africa, focus of, 99, 104
  United States, professional education for, 134-135
Social Work degree (Germany)
  aim of, 35
  occupational social work orientation and, 35
Social work effort, evaluation of, program development and, 111
Social work fraternity, labor movement and, South Africa, 101-102
Social work function. See also Occupational social work function
  commitment to, 111
  costs of, 111
  non-support by management and, 111
Social work influence (Australia), 13-14
Social work interventions
  "community at work" and, 11
  focus of, 61-62
  in United States, 61-62

predominant social policy model,
    61-62
Social work landscape (Australia),
    changing, 3
Social work methods (Germany), adapted
    from United States, 20
Social work models, inappropriate to
    South Africa, 99-100
Social work posts, organizations that
    created, South Africa, 98
Social work practice
  availability of employers and, 45
  flexibility needed in, 14
  globalization and, 61
  military, United States, 145-147
  nature of determined by
      organization's management,
      55
  program development, factors
      impacting in South Africa,
      109-114
  scope of, 64
Social work practice in business
  goals of, 67-68
  United States, review of, 67-68
Social work profession
  Australia, future and challenges,
      13-15
  knowledge and skills available to,
      13
Social worker consultants, roles of
    (Australia), 9
Social workers
  as human resource managers, 59
  Australia
    philosophical differences
        between public and private, 3
    progressive thinking of, 2-3
  avoiding conflict with colleagues,
      108
  core competency of, 117
  Germany
    confidentiality of, 28
    freelance, 25
  in-depth interviews of, South
      Africa work settings, 97

India
  diversity of functions of, 45
  history of, 45
  objectives of, 45
  roles of, 45
Ireland
  administrative practices, 74-75
  defining what they do, 74
Israel, employed in different
    sectors, 81
public service, working alongside
    private practitioner
    (Australia), 2
role of, 69-70
service development approach, 74
South Africa
  changing practice priorities, 103
  employment of black, 98
  structure of practice, 104
  time spent, personal counseling and
      casework, 104
  views of, 100-101
Sociopolitical change, social workers
    and cross-cultural awareness,
    South Africa, 102
Sociopolitical imperatives, program
    development, South Africa,
    109,111-114,112-114
South African Council for Social
    Work, training and, 115-116
South African Iron and Steel
    Corporation (ISCOR), social
    workers in, 98
South African National Council for
    Alcohol and Drug Abuse
    (SANCA), work done by, 101
South African National Defence
    Force, social workers in,
    102-103
South African Police Force, social
    workers in, 103
South African Synthetic Oils Limited
    (SASOL), social work posts
    in, 98
South African workplace, major trends
    in, 112

Southern Gauteng EAP Workshop, support group for social workers, South Africa, 116
Soziale Betriebsarbeit. *See* Factory nurses
Specialist Dislocation Services, emerging area of clinical work (Australia), 9
Sri Ram Centre for Industrial Relations
  industrial social welfare and, 43
  recommendations of, 52-53
Staff reorganization, occupational social workers' role in, 4-5
Stanford Research Institute, alcoholism research and, 30-31
State-run railway services (South Africa), social work posts in, 98
Steel Workers, programs developed under, 133
Studies
  health promotion and, 138
  of occupational social work, 128-129
    South Africa, 108, 111
  of social work, United States, 121-122
Stuttgart
  exemplary model of occupational social work in public sector, 29-30
  substance abuse prevention and support program, 29-30
Substance abuse
  education and training courses on, 147-148
  problem identification and, South Africa, 114
  Temporary Aid to Needy Families (TANF) and, 152
  underidentification of women abusers, 152
Survival skills, training
  change management and, 9-10
  techniques (Australia), 14

Telecom (Telstra) Australia, social worker employment by, 4
Telecom Eireann, welfare services established by, 69
Temporary Aid to Needy Families (TANF). *See also* Welfare-to-work
  emphasis of, 150-151
  expectations of work under, 151
  plan for funds, 151
  problems encountered after entering workplace, 152
Third Reich, union activity after fall of, 19-20
Trade union movement
  Germany, social security law reforms and, 18
  history, 47
Trade union network, source of hiring and benefits, United States, 135
Trade unions
  activities, Histadrut focus on, 84
  Histadrut (Israel), influence of, 83-84
  services offered to members, United States, 135
Training. *See also* Education and training
  provided by occupational social workers, 129
  sensitizing managers in workplace, United States, 132
Training institutes, professional social work, views of, 54
Training programs
  Australia
    contract practitioners and, 12
    range of new techniques, 14
  duty of occupational social worker, 27

U.S. Army Public Affairs Division, modern industrial social work and, 123
Unemployment, social problems of, 66

Unemployment benefits, contributions toward, Ireland, 66
Unemployment insurance, Germany
  elements of, 22-23
  funding of, 22-23
  guarantees of, 24
  social system element, 22-23
  trade union movement and
    blue collar workers, 18
    white collar workers, 18
Union and employee consultative councils (Australia), contract workers and, 13-14
Union demands, South Africa, 101
Union-sponsored assistance programs, staffing of, United States, 134
Unionization, averting by social welfare programs, United States, 121
Unions
  activity after fall of Third Reich, 19-20
  Australia
    industrial, management and, 3
    public sector, management and, 3
  Germany, relations with employers strained, 22
  India, social workers and, 62-63
  South Africa
    conditions of service, 114
    living wage issue, 114
    workers' rights and, 113
  United States, social workers in, 133-135
United Auto Workers, programs developed under, 133

Violence, domestic and workplace, United States, 132
Volkspflege. *See* Factory nurses
Voluntary Services Organizations (VSOs), services provided by, Israel, 84-85

Wage accords (Australia), employer/employee disputes and, 3-4
Welfare amenities (India)
  lack of for agricultural workers, 44
  lack of for rural labor, 44
Welfare capitalism
  ideology behind, Ireland, 66-67
  occupational welfare services and, 69
  roots of occupational social work and, 70-71
Welfare functions, balancing with managerial functions, 60-61
Welfare Movement (Ireland), history of, 66-67
Welfare officers. *See also* Labor welfare officers; Social workers
  attitude toward, 68
  Central Employer's Organizations views on, 51-52
  duties under Model Rules, 49-50
  functions of, 55
  India, role of, 48-49
  Indian state government views of, 51-52
  Ireland, Miss Violet Sargent, 67
  job satisfaction for, 54-55
  part of Personnel Department, 59
  personnel department and, 51
  role of, 50
    differing views of, 53-54
    Ireland, 68
Welfare officers' association, India, views of, 54-55
Welfare practice, British industry, paternalistic nature of, 67
Welfare programs
  demise in Irish industry, 68
  issues of, 68
  paternalistic attitude of some, 68
  social work in India and, 45
  studies of, 68
Welfare recipients, high-risk population due to legislation, United States, 130

Welfare reform. *See also* Temporary Aid to Needy Families (TANF); Welfare-to-work
   welfare-to-work initiative, 153
Welfare services in industry, Irish compared with British, 67
Welfare state
   Australia, occupational social work defined in, 2
   South Africa, rejection of notion of, 99
Welfare system
   characterization of, Israel, 82
   inequity being addressed, South Africa, 99
Welfare system workers, social work profession and, 2
Welfare work
   as enabling function, 54
   material deficits and, 20
Welfare worker, as socializing influence, 121
Welfare-to-work (United States)
   barriers to work for population, 151-152
   high-risk populations and, 130
   implications for occupational social workers, 153-154
   population profile, 151-152
   results of initiative, 153
Western countries
   for-profit organizations and, 84-85
   trend toward privatization in, 84-85
Western Electric Company, employee productivity and, 68-69
White cultural heritage, emphasis of, 99
White domination, legacy, program development and, 109
Widow, Sickness, and Unemployment pensions (Australia), 2
Wives and daughters of industrialists, welfare of company's employees, motivation for assuring, 18-19
Women, unskilled in the workforce (Australia), 6

Work
   changes to, occupational social workers and, 150
   social context of, 68-69
Work environment
   importance of, 14
   India, social work professionals and, 62
Work organizations, problems created by, 68
Work-based case management services, former welfare recipients and, 154-156
Work-linked problems, occupational social work, approaches advocated by, 14-15
Worker grievances, employer-sponsored programs not trusted, 3
Worker protection laws (India), industrialization and, 43
Workers community of occupational social work, task of, 36-37
Workers' organizations, views on welfare officers, 52
Workers' rights, South Africa, 113
Workforce, women entering, 2-3
Working Group Addictions
   addiction support program, 34
   occupational social work's role in program, 34
Working poor, increase in, welfare-to-work initiative and, 153
Workmen's Compensation Act, 47
Workplace
   appropriateness of social work practice in, 124-125
   change in, occupational social workers' roles in, 119-120
   sensitizing to issues of violence, occupational social workers' role in, 129
   transformation, South Africa, 112-113
   transformation in, South Africa, 117

trends of change in, South Africa,
    112-114
Workplace contracts, complexity of
    (Australia), 6
Workplace hazards
    impact of occupational social
        workers, examples in United
        States, 140-142
    working with victims of, United
        States, 140

World Health Organization, health
    promotion and, 25
World of Work, social work field
    established, United States,
    134-135

YMCA, social work services provided
    by, 145
Youth, unemployed (Australia), 6

AN EXCELLENT RESOURCE BOOK!

It's easy to spout slogans like "Safety First," but what can really be done to increase safe behaviors?

WORKPLACE SAFETY
Individual Differences in Behavior

NEW!

Edited by
Alice F. Stuhlmacher, PhD
Department of Psychology, DePaul University, Chicago, Illinois

Douglas F. Cellar, PhD
Department of Psychology, DePaul University, Chicago, Illinois

Workplace Safety: Individual Differences in Behavior examines safety behavior and outlines practical interventions to help increase safety awareness. Individual differences are relevant to a variety of settings including the workplace, public spaces, and motor vehicles. This book takes a look at ways of defining and measuring safety as well as a variety of individual differences like gender, job knowledge, conscientiousness, self-efficacy, risk avoidance, and stress tolerance that are important in creating safety interventions and improving the selection and training of employees. Workplace Safety takes an incisive look at these issues with a unique focus on the way individual differences in people impact safety behavior in the real world.

Contents
- The Role of Individual Differences in Understanding and Predicting Workplace Safety
- A Comprehensive Method for the Assessment of Industrial Injury Events
- Gender Issues in the Measurement of Physical and Psychological Safety
- Predicting Motor Vehicle Crash Involvement from a Personality Measure and a Driving Knowledge Test
- The Five-Factor Model and Safety in the Workplace: Investigating the Relationship Between Personality and Accident Involvement
- Creating a Safer Working Environment Through Psychological Assessment: A Review of a Measure of Safety Consciousness
- Slips and Falls in Stores and Malls: Implications for Community-Based Injury Prevention
- Individual Differences in Safe Behavior: A Safety Practitioner's Viewpoint
- Index
- Reference Notes Included

(A monograph published simultaneously as the Journal of Prevention & Intervention in the Community, Vol. 22, No. 1.)
2001. Available now. 87 pp. with Index.

AMEX, DINERS CLUB, DISCOVER, EUROCARD, JCB, MASTERCARD & VISA WELCOME!

CALL OUR TOLL-FREE NUMBER: 1-800-429-6784
US & Canada only / 8am–5pm ET; Monday–Friday
Outside US/Canada: + 607-722-5857

FAX YOUR ORDER TO US: 1-800-895-0582
Outside US/Canada: + 607-771-0012

E-MAIL YOUR ORDER TO US:
getinfo@haworthpressinc.com

VISIT OUR WEB SITE AT:
http://www.HaworthPress.com

FACULTY: ORDER YOUR NO-RISK EXAM COPY TODAY! Send us your examination copy order on your stationery; indicate course title, enrollment, and course start date. We will ship and bill on a 60-day examination basis, and cancel your invoice if you decide to adopt! We will always bill at the lowest available price, such as our special "5+ text price." Please remember to order softcover where available. (We cannot provide examination copies of books not published by The Haworth Press, Inc., or its imprints.) (Outside US/Canada, a proforma invoice will be sent upon receipt of your request and must be paid in advance of shipping. A full refund will be issued with proof of adoption.)

The Haworth Press, Inc.
10 Alice Street, Binghamton, New York 13904-1580 USA

BIC01

TO ORDER: CALL: 1-800-429-6784 / FAX: 1-800-895-0582 (outside US/Canada: + 607-771-0012) / **E-MAIL: getinfo@haworthpressinc.com**

Please complete the information below or tape your business card in this area.

☐ YES, please send me **WorkPlace Saftey**
— in hard at $39.95 ISBN: 0-7890-1355-X.
— in soft at $19.95 ISBN: 0-7890-1356-8.

- Individual orders outside US, Canada, and Mexico must be prepaid by check or credit card.
- Discounts are not available on 5+ text prices and not available in conjunction with any other discount. • Discount not applicable on books priced under $15.00. 5+ text prices are not available for jobbers and wholesalers.
- Postage & handling: In US: $4.00 for first book; $1.50 for each additional book. Outside US: $5.00 for first book; $2.00 for each additional book.
- NY, MN, and OH residents: please add appropriate sales tax after postage & handling. Canadian residents: please add 7% GST after postage & handling. Canadian residents of Newfoundland, Nova Scotia, and New Brunswick, also add 8% for province tax. • Payment in UNESCO coupons welcome.
- If paying in Canadian dollars, use current exchange rate to convert to US dollars. Please allow 3-4 weeks for delivery after publication.
- Prices and discounts subject to change without notice.

Signature _____

☐ **BILL ME LATER** ($5 service charge will be added).
(Not available for individuals outside US/Canada/Mexico. Service charge is waived for jobbers/wholesalers/booksellers.)
☐ Check here if billing address is different from shipping address and attach purchase order and billing address information.

☐ **PAYMENT ENCLOSED $** _____
(Payment must be in US or Canadian dollars by check or money order drawn on a US or Canadian bank.)

☐ **PLEASE BILL MY CREDIT CARD:**
☐ AmEx ☐ Diners Club ☐ Discover ☐ Eurocard ☐ JCB ☐ Master Card ☐ Visa

Account Number _____

Expiration Date _____

Signature _____
May we open a confidential credit card account for you for possible future purchases? ( ) Yes ( ) No

NAME _____
INSTITUTION _____
ADDRESS _____

CITY _____
STATE _____ ZIP _____
COUNTY (NY residents only) _____
COUNTRY _____
E-MAIL _____

[type or print clearly]

May we use your e-mail address for confirmations and other types of information?
( ) Yes ( ) No We appreciate receiving your e-mail address and fax number. Haworth would like to e-mail or fax special discount offers to you, as a preferred customer. We will never **share, rent, or exchange** your e-mail address or fax number. We regard such actions as an invasion of your privacy.

☐ YES, please send me **WorkPlace Safety (ISBN: 0-7890-1356-8)** to consider on a 60-day no risk examination basis. I understand that I will receive an invoice payable within 60 days, or that **if I decide to adopt the book, my invoice will be cancelled.** I understand that I will be billed at the lowest price. (60-day offer available only to teaching faculty in US, Canada, and Mexico / Outside US/Canada, a proforma invoice will be sent upon receipt of your request and must be paid in advance of shipping. A full refund will be issued with proof of adoption.)

Signature _____

Course Title(s) _____
Current Text(s) _____
Enrollment _____
Semester _____ Decision Date _____
Office Tel _____ Hours _____

This information is needed to process your examination copy order.

(14) (16) (33) 08/01 BIC01

THE HAWORTH PRESS, INC., 10 Alice Street, Binghamton, NY 13904-1580 USA